STRIPPED NAKED

STRIPPED NAKED

Lauren Stratford

PELICAN PUBLISHING COMPANY
Gretna 1993

*To my support team
who continue to take the walk with me.
Your loyalty is unparalleled.*
Thank you!

---

*The word "Pelican" and the depiction of a pelican are
trademarks of Pelican Publishing Company, Inc., and are
registered in the U.S. Patent and Trademark Office.*

Library of Congress Cataloging-in-Publication Data

Stratford, Lauren.
    Stripped naked / Lauren Stratford.
       p.   cm.
    ISBN 0-88289-967-8
    1. Stratford, Lauren—Mental health.   2. Ritual abuse victims—
United States—Biography.   3. Multiple personality disorder—
Patients—United States—Biography.   I. Title
RC569.5.R59S77   1993
616.85'236'0092—dc20
   [B]   93-16878
                                              CIP

Except where otherwise indicated, all Scripture quotations in this book are taken from *The Living Bible*, Copyright © 1971 by Tyndale House Publishers, Wheaton, Illinois. Used by permission.

The main characters in this book are New Lady and Dr. Lady. They are therapists. Their names have been changed, obviously—not only for the reason of keeping their identities anonymous, but because Baby, a four-year-old alter personality, has renamed them. To her, Dr. Lady and New Lady are their real names.

The names of survivors and others have been changed when requested.

Manufactured in the United States of America
Published by Pelican Publishing Company, Inc.
1101 Monroe Street, Gretna, Louisiana 70053

CONTENTS

PREFACE

Into the Fire

**"This is a Hell
which is not easily understood
by those who have not dwelt in it."**[1]

To you who have read my first book, *Satan's Underground*, thank you for continuing with me as I share this next part of my story as it unfolds. To those who have not, I welcome you to hear this part of the story of my life, a life which like yours, is a work in progress. For all of you, let me share with you this short expression of why I felt compelled to write this book, *Stripped Naked*.

In *Satan's Underground* I shared my journey of escape and healing from ritual abuse at the hands of Satanists. After additional years in therapy and in interaction with my "support team," a group of professionals who help me in my life and work, I have found that I was not as healed as I first had thought. Little did I know when I finished that first book that my journey to recovery had only just begun. Victims and survivors alike will understand and perhaps identify with me as I write about the difficulties that I have encountered, the pains I've endured, and the fears I've had to work through. I have had to fight hard to continue to walk toward a healing that at times seemed unattainable.

There are victims who have yet to be freed and survivors who have yet to heal with whom I am most committed to share my life. Not just the victories, but also the apparent defeats, and the agonizingly slow and painful periods when nothing seemed to be getting better.

The title *Stripped Naked* only too accurately describes not only my feelings, but those of countless survivors after leaving a therapy session which has been particularly painful. Our memories are difficult, even horrific. Working through memories is like walking back *into the fire*!

To you who have been spared the agonies of abuse, whether physical or sexual or ritual in nature, I want to share what one person has gone through in going public with her story. I want people to understand why it is so difficult for victims to speak out, to be heard, and to be believed. I want to show why it is often not only terrifying, but potentially devastating if victims lack a support system to sustain them through the lengthy process of healing.

The determination and perseverance of survivors are not enough to get them through to their ultimate goal of healing. If a survivor is met with disbelief, denial, demands for proof, or even demands for a quick recovery, then the journey to recovery is impaired significantly. It takes so much more than the well-intended, but destructive, "Put the past behind you. Just trust in God and move on." It just doesn't work that way.

Even the most experienced professionals are quick to say that prolonged abuse requires a long season of work before healing can be accomplished. Healing of victims of abuse is a slow and painstaking process in the best of circumstances.

There are victims trying to get out of Satanism, the occult, and various mind control cult systems. There are victims in desperate need of healing who have been confused, frightened, and intimidated by not just the "bad guys" who wish them ill, but also by some who claim to be "good guys." I have certainly been victimized by my share of chameleons pretending to care for me and the welfare of all survivors while trying evidently to address their own agendas and prove that deliberate evil seldom, if ever, happens.

Most of all, victims need to be shown that healing is possible with courage, determination, and the sustained guidance of mental health professionals who are committed to their clients over the long haul. Especially for those of us who have been ritually abused, the journey to healing can be wild and tempestuous. There are many temptations to quit. That has certainly been true for me.

There are some who have suggested that perhaps I wrote the first part of my story too soon; that perhaps I should have waited until *all* the pieces in my life had come together and I was completely healed. Such criticism has been anticipated and understood. Healing evolves over a period of time. Memories return gradually, step by step, piece by piece, layer upon layer. I know this is difficult to appreciate and understand.

It has been very tempting for me to lay down my pen and say, "I've had enough! I don't need to hear any more from the critics and the naysayers." I answer that temptation with a resounding, "No! I will go on!" This is not the time for me to be deterred by the piranha journalists who try to re-define truth so as to leave us survivors outside of it. I have made and continue to make great progress in my healing. This is not the time to be deterred from carrying a message of hope to the many others who need to hear it.

There have been times in these past several years that I wished I had never spoken publicly about the atrocities that none of us want to believe are happening in our country. The tendency to find an easy escape into denial does not eradicate the fact that sexual abuse, incest, ritual abuse, and ritual murders do occur. If no one dares to speak out, then history will continue to repeat itself!

There *must* be a starting point for each survivor. If survivors have to be silent until all the puzzle pieces of their lives fit seamlessly together with no inconsistencies, no time gaps, and no errors, there will be no voices to stand up and warn us of the dangers to the next generation of children.

I continue in my profound commitment to communicate the truth about abuse and to forge ahead toward my own healing. For those whom I have reached and encouraged by telling my story, I am grateful. It has been an encouragement of no small measure to learn of countless others who are finding their own strength and courage to stand up and be counted. No longer do I stand alone!

PART ONE

1

Branded

**"I fear being a clown
in a world that is not a circus."[1]**

Such was one of the first communications ever of a fifteen-year-old autistic child trying to build a bridge between the world within and the world around her. And such is the fear of we who find ourselves branded as "victims" and "survivors." Will we ever be able to make sense of the world we find inside us? And will we ever be able to build bridges from our world within to the world around us? When we do find words to begin speaking, will anyone *want* to listen? Will anyone *be able* to listen? Or will they turn away because our words carry too much pain? I want to shout, "Please don't shut us out! Please hear us. Please don't make a world for us in which we don't fit and one in which we are not accepted."

No Longer Hidden

Mary Fisher, prominent conservative Republican and mother of two, courageously stepped to the podium at the 1992 Republican National Convention and declared, *"We have not entered some alien state of being. We're human beings."*[2] Mary Fisher is HIV positive, a "victim" of the AIDS virus. A virus with an image problem. Mary and countless others trying to live with AIDS have experienced the rejection, the denial, and the disbelief of being a victim.

We are not clowns, she might say with me, and not aliens. We are human beings who simply still need to be connected with the rest of the world in every possible way in order to survive. Don't ask us to hide. We need every bridge to the world around us.

If we look at ourselves as victims, must we cease to view ourselves as "normal"? Can we still enjoy the sunset and the taste of an ice cream cone—or is it forever different for us because we carry a label? Does it forever change how *you* will see us? How we see *ourselves*? And if our identity is in a label, do we enter into a world of our own and put out signs proclaiming, "No Trespassing"? How tempting it is to isolate ourselves. We, too, fear we will appear to others as clowns in a world that is not a circus. *We are not clowns!* We simply carry labels that seem uncomfortable to you—and often to us as well. And what about the label of Multiple Personality Disorder? Does that label brand us and force us into a world where we are seen as clowns?

Hidden in Plain View

America was shocked when the fifty-five-year-old and still strikingly beautiful Marilyn Van Derbur looked into the TV camera and declared for all the world to hear, "I am a victim of incest." How can this be? We knew Marilyn as Miss America of 1958 and a television personality. Marilyn's father was a millionaire socialite, a pillar of the community; their family, the American dream come true. And yet, between the ages of five and eighteen, Marilyn endured nightly sexual assaults by her father. How could Marilyn have that beautiful smile? How could she possibly have the poise and the confidence to be Miss America—"our ideal"? How could she even be around her father for all those happy publicity shots?

In Marilyn's own words, "In order to survive, I split into a day child who giggled and smiled, and a night child, who lay awake in a fetal position, only to be pried apart by my father. Until I was twenty four, the day child had no conscious knowledge of the night child."[3] During the day she really did not know what had happened at night. She was a victim who managed to hide from herself, too afraid and ashamed even to consciously know what had happened at night. That's how she could survive and still be our Miss America. But who would she be when she let herself know all that had happened? And who would she be if she told all of us? And who will *I* be if I try again to tell the stories of *my* past?

The nation was shocked again by reports of the long hidden crimes of Fr. James Porter who had molested literally hundreds of children as he was moved from parish to parish. *Hundreds* of children? How could that be hidden? Frank Fitzpatrick explained that he had totally repressed the memories of being sodomized by Father Porter for seventeen years. "Well, my memories started to come back . . . in September of '89, and what happened was I started to feel—to realize I had no reason to be feeling mental pain. Everything was going right in my life. . . . I just started to allow myself to feel this pain and then start to feel where it came from. . . . Gradually, I remembered the incident."

On the "Larry King Live" show, Larry asked Frank, "You had put it away somewhere?"

"I had put it away somewhere in my mind," Frank responded. "It was still there, but it was *just a lump of pain in my head*."[4]

Because of Frank's courage in confronting those memories and in speaking out, scores of people have come forward with their own stories of the crimes of Father Porter. Frank was a victim before he consciously remembered Father Porter's assaults. So were the others who subsequently came forward. The trauma profoundly affected each and every life in a different way. And what courage it took for each of them to allow those memories to come forth, to remember and then to proclaim the pain they had endured.

Standing in Plain View

Each of these people dared to speak out. Each of them felt personal pain. Sharing that pain was a risk, and yet sharing with others validated their experiences. Unspoken trauma runs wild. It is as if the wind catches it, blowing it hither and yon. Emotions remain unchecked. Putting words to trauma experience puts boundaries around the pain. Victims *must* speak to someone. Unspoken trauma becomes like a spreading poison, affecting the physical as well as the emotional health of the victim. Sharing begins the healing process.

Speaking out publicly is yet another step. Speaking out as these people did encouraged others to believe that it might be safe for them to open their closet of secrets, too. Someone has to be the first. And after that first person has spoken, one thing is certain—others will be sure to follow. Others follow, not because they are attention seekers, but because it becomes just a little bit less dangerous to look inward, to speak, and then to stand in plain view.

And Who Am I?

I first talked to a trained therapist at the suggestion of my physician. I was very ill physically with an irreversible blood clotting disorder that still endangers my life today. I was in and out of the hospital during the two years that I saw her. The original goal was to work on the issues of coping with my life-threatening illness, but as the therapy progressed, my therapist and I certainly travelled to other places together! It was with her help that I first began to recognize and speak about the abuses which I have shared in *Satan's Underground*. I first recognized myself as a "victim." Although I had no idea what words like "repression" and "dissociation" meant at that time, she saw these defense mechanisms at work in me.

I recall how during my first year of therapy I would sometimes become quiet and feel myself drifting off to another place or time to an event I had either repressed or dissociated. Then, I would hear her calling my name and my mind would return to the "here and now" of my therapy session.

In talking about this situation recently with her, I asked if, in retrospect, she thought I might have been showing any symptoms of Multiple Personality Disorder. She answered yes and described times when I sounded like a four-year-old child who needed to be nurtured. She said, "If only I knew then what I know now about MPD."

A Survivor and an Author

I really felt that I was pretty well healed until I began writing *Satan's Underground*. I had not been in therapy for quite some time. But as I got into writing about my past, I began to feel more pain, and I realized that there were many issues that had yet to be dealt with. I tried to avoid these issues. I had written the book and shared my story as best I could. It was all behind me now, wasn't it? No matter how hard I tried, I could not just brush aside all that was past.

When other survivors began to read *Satan's Underground* and see me on television talk shows, many of them assumed that I was completely healed. But that assumption raised hard questions for them. I began to get letters from survivors asking how I had managed to be so healed when they were still struggling. Some survivors expressed their frustration, others their sense of guilt, for not getting well faster as they (and I) thought I had.

In the meantime I put myself back into therapy to find out why I was still struggling. That's when I discovered that not only was I not completely healed, but that I still had a long way to go in my own journey to wholeness. And so in writing my second book, *I Know You're Hurting*, I shared some of the next steps as I understood them. I tried to share with a broader audience what I had learned about the healing process, that it took time and patience with one's self and, for me, the love of a compassionate and faithful God. I was farther along in my healing, but I had not arrived (will I ever?) at the end of that journey. I had a responsibility to be honest, but writing my books had thrust me into the role of a public figure. And there were surprises ahead.

The Nerve of That Man!

I will never forget the first time someone suggested to me that I had multiple personalities. I had just spoken to a group in Salt Lake City. I thought my talk had gone rather well, but as I was walking back to my seat, a gentleman who was on the panel of mental health professionals asked me rather loudly, "Ms. Stratford, do you have MPD?"

Here I was, standing up for all the world to see, doing my best just to tell my story as I understood it, a story in which I was a survivor with much of my healing behind me and suddenly I was being questioned! I could feel my face turning beet red. "No, I don't," I answered as politely and calmly as I could, and hurried to my seat. Again the gentleman spoke to me and the audience. "In listening to your talk, I think you showed signs of multiplicity." I was embarrassed and angry and confused. I didn't even know what "multiplicity" was, but I figured it had something to do with MPD, and I *knew* I didn't have that!

I rode to the airport with my friend Dr. Catherine Gould, a clinical psychologist who had also spoken at the seminar. "Catherine," I asked, "did you hear what that man said to me last night?"

Catherine nodded and said, "Yes, dear."

"But Catherine," I sputtered, "did you hear him say that he thought I showed 'signs of multiplicity,' whatever *that* is?"

Catherine nodded again and smiled.

"The nerve of that man! How dare he even *suggest* that I have MPD. He doesn't even know me." Boy, was I steamed!

I thought that if I were multiple I would certainly know it. I would know, wouldn't I, if there were other parts of me, other "people" living inside me? Surely my first therapist would have told me, and she had not said anything about anyone else . . . at least not until my most recent talk with her . . .

The Big Bang . . .

. . . came when I chose to return to therapy. I knew that therapy was hard work and I wasn't looking forward to more of the same. It boiled down to a simple question. Did I want to settle for the stalemate of my present place of healing, or did I want to move on and work towards the goal of complete healing? I dreaded the work and the memories and the new information that it might bring. With much apprehension, I chose to move on.

I began to work in therapy sessions with my new therapist. It wasn't many months later, in the safety of her office, that "Baby" made herself known. The same four-year-old who had tried to make herself known to my first therapist of several years ago, but who had quickly retreated when she had repeatedly called my name, evidently felt safe enough to try again to make herself known. I really don't know what Baby said to her when she first came out, if anything, except that her name was Baby, and that she was four years old. (Much more about the very special and amazing "Baby" later . . .)

When my new therapist first communicated to me

that I was also multiple, I came unglued. I was angry—
furious! I was not a multiple! And I wasn't about to become a multiple! No way! No how! *Absolutely not!*

I argued! I paced! I protested! I threw pillows! I denied it! If I denied it strongly enough, maybe it would
just go away! That's what I wanted! I wanted it to all go
away! Hadn't I already gone far enough by publicly ad-
mitting that I was a survivor of ritual abuse?

I had been a victim and I had recognized that fact. I
had even written and spoken about it. I had become a
survivor, a trailblazer for others. Survivor. That meant it
was in the past, didn't it? And now **THIS**?

In my ignorance about what it meant to be a multiple,
I was really frightened and confused. What did "multiplicity" mean? What did it mean to me—to Lauren
Stratford—who was the only person that I was aware?
Was I no longer in control of myself? Would other "personalities" take over and make me look peculiar? I had
never read or seen the movie *Sybil*, but I had certainly
heard a few things. Was I going to be shifting unpredict-
ably and flamboyantly from one person to another?
Would this body that I thought I was in charge of suddenly begin to do things that I didn't approve of? I had
already declared to anyone who had asked me that I was
not multiple. Would they think I had been lying? Would
anyone believe that it was possible for me to have been a
multiple all my life without knowing it? I was having a
very tough time with that one myself. Surely *someone*
would have noticed.

And at the time there were a lot of talk shows featur-
ing multiples and the main focus ever since the film *The
Three Faces of Eve* had seemed to be on *how many*? How
many personalities were living inside me? A trio? A
dozen? A hundred?

How long would it take me to discover all of "them"?
Would they all be friendly, or would some be my ene-
mies, making my life even more difficult than it already

was? I think my biggest fear was, could I keep them under wraps, or would they come out and take over without my permission? I was really overwhelmed with fear of the unknowns that being a multiple might bring into my life.

Crashing Inside the Dallas Airport!

I don't remember between which gates it happened, but I crashed on the American Airlines concourse. Me personally. No planes involved. And when I say "crashed," I do mean "*crashed*"!

There is a large poster hanging on the wall of the concourse just before passengers make a ninety-degree turn to get on the moving sidewalk. This particular poster has always been a landmark for me. When I get to where I can see it, I know I'm about halfway to my next plane.

The poster reads, "Is this the way you look when you hear the words, MENTAL ILLNESS?" On the poster is an enlarged face of a woman. Her expression is one of sheer terror. She is holding her hands to her head. That poster amused me every time I saw it. I'd smile and keep on moving. Planes don't wait for people who are gawking at posters!

The first trip I took through the Dallas Airport after learning that I was a multiple, I was again hurrying down the never-ending concourse. I almost zipped right past the poster, but I caught a glimpse of it out of the corner of my eye. My body stopped abruptly. Thud. My briefcase and suitcase dropped out of my hands. I felt as if my body, mind, and soul had crashed into the poster. My eyes were riveted on the face of the woman and her look of horror. Slowly, I walked closer to the poster.

Something was different about it. Was it the same poster or had it been changed? I looked closer. No, it was the same poster, but something was different. Those two words, "MENTAL ILLNESS," loomed larger than life.

They almost jumped off the poster. I felt as if they were reaching out to grab me. Then I realized that my mind was equating the words "MENTAL ILLNESS" with my recent diagnosis: "MULTIPLE PERSONALITY DISORDER."

I wondered as I looked at the astonished, "freaked out" look on the woman's face, Is *this* the way people will look at me when they learn that I have MULTIPLE PERSONALITY DISORDER? I cringed. I glanced to see if anyone was looking at me. Could they see? . . . Could they tell? . . . Did they know that I have . . . you know?

The announcement that my plane was beginning to board passengers abruptly brought my attention back to reality. Leaning over, I picked up my bags and slowly began to back away from the poster. Only God knows how, but I found the gate to my plane.

Settling into my seat, I closed my eyes to calm myself. I could still see the poster. It was as if the look on that woman's face had been indelibly etched on my mind. I felt especially vulnerable, as though everyone else in the airplane was looking at me, looking for signs of MPD.

I tried the professional look. I took out a folder filled with papers and notes for my talk and pretended to be looking at them. But I knew that I probably looked as silly as those TV news anchors who mindlessly shuffle a set of papers for those few moments before the cameras cut away for the commercial break.

My mind drifted from the plane to a radio program I had heard just the day before. A woman had called the radio therapy guru to say that her long-standing friend had just been diagnosed as having MPD. The talk show host asked her, "Have you seen her looking 'odd' lately?" Now I can laugh, but I remember that as I was listening, I felt my face begin to flush and get hot. Odd? Is that how people with MPD look? Did I look "odd" to these weary plane travelers? Were the initials *M P D* flashing in neon lights across my forehead like a modern-day scarlet letter?

In researching material for this chapter recently, I came across a quote that I just had to chuckle over, because I knew how I would have reacted to it if I had read the quote at *that* therapy session when my therapist first broke "the news." Dr. Richard Kluft, a world-renowned expert on MPD, said, "Only when the patient appreciates his situation can the true treatment of multiple personality disorder begin."[5] Appreciates? Right! There was not going to be any "appreciating" of my multiple personality status! Not by me anyway!

To any of you who might be tempted to believe that any of us survivors want to subscribe to a "fake" diagnosis of MPD, let me assure you that I, for one, was not happily embracing this diagnosis.

I wondered over and over—
- Have I been branded now?
- Weren't the other labels enough?
- Is this diagnosis one that must only be whispered about?
- Why do I feel so ashamed and embarrassed?
- Should I feel guilty?
- Will people know by looking at me?
- Will people keep away from me?
- Will they be afraid of me?
- Is it safe to tell others?
- Is it safe to tell *anyone*?
- Will others think I'm just "crazy" now?
- Am I?!

2

Hiding Inside the Mind

"I think of dissociation as the cryonics of trauma, designed to put parts of the trauma into deep freeze until a 'cure' can be discovered." [1]

If This Isn't Crazy, Then What Is?

Oprah Winfrey, herself a victim of sexual abuse as a child, continues to educate all of us with her daily television shows and her special reports. She and her staff won an Emmy for one such program about Truddi Chase, author of the remarkable autobiography *When Rabbit Howls*. [2] Truddi has many personalities within her whom she affectionately refers to as "The Troops." Her multiplicity is a result of severe abuse beginning when she was a very young child.

Truddi's stepfather was unspeakably cruel. Truddi was brutally raped by him beginning at the age of two. He would assault her sexually. He had sex with farm animals in the barn and then forced Truddi to have sex with the animals, too. She continued to be severely abused until she ran away at the age of sixteen. She dealt with her pain in the only way she could. Unable to escape physically, Truddi escaped into her own mind by splitting into many different personalities. As with Marilyn Van Derbur's "day" child and "night" child, Truddi's mind began to create different people within her. That way, if "one person" was being abused, the "others" could hide in apparent safety while allowing only the one who was out to feel the pain. Truddi eventually split into ninety-two different personalities in order to endure those years in hell.

On one occasion Truddi's father threw her into a pit, collected a basket of snakes, and threw them in on top of her. Oprah said, "He threw the snakes on top of you to make sure that you didn't tell anyone."

"Right," Truddi responded, "because if you *did* tell, there would be something *worse*. I didn't know what it was going to be, but what could be worse than that?"[3]

Dr. Robert Phillips, Jr. was Truddi's therapist for several years. Oprah asked him if child abuse could do so much damage that a child might split into ninety-two personalities to endure it. Dr. Phillips answered, "It can do this much damage and more. . . . the aftermath is just horrendous . . ."[4] Oprah responded with insight when she said that the splitting and forming of other personalities seemed to her like the grace of God to save a person from the horrors. Dr. Phillips went on to say, " . . . I really don't like calling it [MPD] a dysfunction, because it is a most functional way to help a child survive."[5]

"Well, this is what I want to know," asked Oprah in her inimitable style, "and, this is with all due respect, *if this isn't crazy, then what is?*" Dr. Phillips answered simply, "Well, it's functional. This helps someone survive, and the fact is that probably all of us know people who are multiple, and we don't know that they're multiple. They function."[6]

So If I Am Not Crazy, Then What Am I?

I was still struggling with Oprah's question. Was being multiple *really* the same as being crazy? I needed to get a handle on that. Even as my therapy proceeded, and it became more apparent that there were many more voices inside clamoring to be heard, I needed to understand. I was fighting the idea of becoming some strange and weird person to whom other people would not be able to relate at all. I was afraid I really knew nothing about myself.

And did it mean somehow that I had failed? After all those years of fighting against what it was that the cult and others who had hurt me wanted, had "they" won the war? Or was my multiplicity, as my therapist and others were telling me, a sane response to the insane cruelty of those around me?

Were the other people inside me that I had yet to meet really there to keep me sane, to preserve the good and gentle and loving part of me, to allow me to live in the midst of a hell I could not physically escape?

Tuning Out

One of the things I learned early on was that all of us do things sometimes without being totally conscious. As I type the words of this book, my fingers have been trained to find the way with relative accuracy without my having to consciously remember the location of every key. When I drive, certain actions have become more or less automatic, and I do not have to pay as much attention to them as when I first began driving. It really isn't that unusual for people to do things without seeming to be paying much attention to them. Doing things "automatically" frees up a part of the mind to consider other things.

If I had to concentrate about where to put my fingers next, it would be hard for me to put any mental energy into forming my next thought. If I could only pay attention to the details of making the car do what I wanted it to, I wouldn't have much space left for thinking about where I was headed or what my plans for the day were.

Sometimes when I drive down the freeway, like you, I miss my exit ramp because my mind is mulling over some decision or something I have just heard on the radio. At some point I sort of wake up and look around and say, "Where am I? I've missed my exit. What was I doing?" That's a form of dissociation—my mind drifting off in more than one direction at once.

Sometimes, I can be sitting in a boring church service (sorry, pastors). I don't really want to get up and walk out, but my mind has a different point of view. My mind leaves the church and starts wandering around the beach a few hours earlier than I had planned, or maybe it retreats back to the movie I saw just last night. My body stays in church, but my mind heads for greener pastures. That can be a plus and, in everyday life, it is an experience common to everyone. But what happens in *extraordinary* circumstances?

Ice Cream on The French Riviera

Sitting in one of Saddam Hussein's cells while Baghdad was under siege is not an everyday experience. CBS network correspondent Bob Simon was not prepared for being captured and taken prisoner during the Desert Storm War. He did not have the option to leave when his suffering came. He was beaten, tortured, and thrown in a cell separate from other prisoners. As part of the suffering intended for him, he was forced to listen to the same hell being inflicted upon his friends and fellow prisoners. He heard their screams and cries, and he cringed. It was unbearable. It was beyond what he could endure.

What he discovered was what many sufferers of trauma before him have discovered. With his body held in prison and his senses painfully assaulted, his mind took flight. He dissociated. He tuned out the input from his senses. He tuned in to the memory images in his mind. He pictured himself walking down a street on the French Riviera on a sunny day enjoying an ice cream cone. He allowed that image to fill his mind and drown out the excruciating sounds of brutal torture. While imagining the taste of his ice cream cone, he had flashes of relief. While still in prison, he had moments of peace, brief moments of respite that allowed him to survive. When he was released, for the most part, he remembered all that he had been through and even the technique he had stumbled upon for surviving the pain.

After hearing this reporter describe his dissociation on American TV after his release, someone said to me, "He should feel very guilty about that." I stood in amazement for a second. Then I sighed and thought to myself, Here's a person who has never experienced real trauma. They just don't have a clue!

Pastor Richard Wurmbrand was held prisoner by the Communists in Romania for many years in the most ghastly conditions. In his many books, Wurmbrand reports the "divided soul" and "split personalities" of his fellow prisoners. They had learned to survive in a Romanian prison by finding the same kind of respite Bob Simon found while shackled in Baghdad. "Although in prison I composed more than 300 poems, totaling 100,000 words, [memorized them,] and wrote them all down on my release, I could make my mind a blank during interrogation."[7] He could disconnect his mind when his safety and the safety of others was at stake. When he was safe, he could reconnect and remember and report what had happened to him.

Margaret Atwood, in an Amnesty International booklet on torture, tells the story of an old man whose job it is to clean the torture room each morning. He is not a prisoner. He lives outside the prison with his family and this is, for him, just a job. "The man who works here," she writes, "is losing his sense of smell. He isn't a torturer. He only cleans the floor; every morning the same vomit, the same shed teeth, the same piss and liquid shit. . . . As he sweeps, he tries not to listen; he tries to make himself into a wall, a thick wall. . . . He thinks of nothing but the walk back to his house, of the door opening and his children . . . running to meet him."[8]

Robert Jay Lifton in *The Nazi Doctors* coined the phrase "doubling" to explain the phenomenon of well-trained German physicians learning how to split into an "Auschwitz self" who tortured and murdered Jews and still retained the form of their everyday self who went home at the end of the day to have dinner with the family and read bedtime stories to their children.[9]

Dissociation Is a Talent

Dissociation is a talent? Wonderful! Maybe I should audition for "Star Search"! At first, that sort of sounded like learning to "appreciate" being a multiple, but my therapist helped me to understand. Everyone is born with a certain ability to dissociate just as everyone is born with certain talents, like athletic or musical talents. Some of the ability is natural. Some of it depends on practice. Some people dissociate readily in the face of relatively little trauma. Almost anyone can dissociate to some extent given enough trauma. People who are faced with repeated trauma can learn with practice to dissociate more and more effectively.

Children generally are better at dissociating than adults. When very young children (those under the age of five) are repeatedly put into traumatic situations from which there is no escape, the dissociation may take the form of developing a variety of personalities (or alters) to cope with different aspects of the trauma. If you are a child being held down and assaulted, the only escape is within. The development of different personalities to cope with different traumas, or different aspects of trauma, is a common response. Dissociation and the development of multiple personalities become a sane response to a brutal, vicious, and insane world.

Dr. Roland Summit, the brilliant child psychiatrist and

expert in abuse and trauma in young children, has put it this way.

> "A perpetrator who has learned to manipulate dissociation knows that the most outrageous invasions will be the most immune from detection! A dissociating child as young as three or four can sustain incredible abuse without apparent pain, cross the threshold from the scene of abuse to the outer world as if nothing had happened and return later to the abusive setting with no anticipation of harm. Such mind control is a blessing to victims, a boon to predators, and a curse on any traditional efforts toward risk assessment and victim protection."[10]

That's how Marilyn Van Derbur was able to feel safe with her father during the day. She had learned how not to remember so that she could survive. That's how Truddi Chase stayed alive from day to day, fragmenting memories among different parts inside her. And that was what was happening to me. Little by little I was being able to allow memories of overwhelming painful experiences to continue to surface, some of which had been experienced and remembered in pieces by different people inside me.

Dr. Virginia Klein, a psychotherapist, incest victim, and co-director of the International Network Against Incest and Child Sexual Abuse Cases, says, "In cult abuse, we become completely unconscious about it, because very often we are made to do things to other people. We are told, 'See what you did? You are very bad. You are evil'. So we dissociate or multiple personalities are developed."[11]

What human being, young or old, could survive such horror without disconnecting their mind from the trauma? They may need to disconnect to such a degree that it becomes necessary for them to develop new personalities to hold the overwhelming experience of the trauma.

One of my current therapists gave me this example. She said, "If we were both raped, I (my therapist) would probably *repress* it, because I haven't experienced the many episodes of trauma that you have. Therefore, I have not developed the dissociative capacities you have. I would remember the rape, but if it became too much for me to handle at that time, I would store it away in my unconscious mind as a whole memory. If and when that memory came back at a later time, I would remember it as a whole memory. I could tell you fairly exactly what happened.

"But, if *you* were in the act of being raped, you would more than likely *dissociate* the rape as it was happening. You would have only partial awareness, or perhaps no awareness at all, that you were being raped. Your trauma would be stored away, not as a whole memory, but as fragmented pieces, different pieces perhaps remembered by different personalities inside.

"When the dissociated fragments of that unprocessed memory came back, they would make little sense to you at first. Unfortunately, to be healed of those flashbacks that would usually be frightening and threatening to you, you would have to process and integrate into conscious awareness each aspect of the rape experience. Then the pieces could be put together for the first time, and the memory could be experienced as a whole."

This concept is hard to grasp, I know. Even though I am apparently experienced at doing it, it's complicated to explain. Ask my therapist how many times she had to go over this with me until I began to understand it!

What was beginning to be clear to me was that MPD was completely different from "crazy." MPD is in fact a *sane* response to an *insane* situation. It is the only way a little girl like me could find to survive while fear and pain were tearing me apart. I could not protect my body from the assaults and the pain. I could not protect my mind from the terror except by leaving "someone else" behind who could handle the pain—or at least a part of it—until yet another brave little someone took over for a while.

Another Brave Little Someone

I spent a day with a mother, her young child, and the child's grandmother. The child, who was about three years old, had been ritually abused by a practicing Satanist—her father. The little girl was precious. Golden locks of hair fell down the back of her head. I needed only to give her a stuffed animal, and we became instant friends.

Later that same day, we all went to a Marie Callendar's Restaurant for lunch. This little girl (we'll call her Maria) had been happily playing with her new stuffed animal and giggling with delight. As we entered a small separate dining room that we had reserved in advance, Maria's personality changed instantaneously. I watched in amazement as she went from a happy little girl to a very distraught and frightened little girl. It happened in the twinkling of an eye.

Maria's attention was abruptly diverted to the wooden-beamed ceiling of the dining room. She pointed to the ceiling and began to cry. "No pictures, Mommy. No hurt. No pictures, Mommy. No hurt me." Then what appeared to be an almost automatic reaction, Maria pulled two dining chairs together, climbed up on them, lay down, and went to sleep. She remained asleep even after we had finished our lunch. Her mother had to pick her up and carry her out to the car. Only when she was put into the car did Maria awaken.

Little Maria had no memory of the incident in the restaurant. Because she had already learned to dissociate during the times that she was being sexually and ritually abused, she dissociated the moment she saw the wooden beams of the ceiling in the dining room.

During our lunch, Maria's mother had explained that Maria had repeatedly talked about being taken to a barn where "bad things" happen. Ever since then, when Maria saw anything in a room that reminded her of that barn, she automatically dissociated so she wouldn't have to relive in her consciousness the bad things that had happened to her in the barn. As a special little someone, dissociation served Maria well.

Dissociation Is a Gift

I have begun to learn an alternative way of looking at "multiple personality disorder." Now that I am accepting and somewhat comfortable with my multiplicity, I do not look on it as a disorder. The word "disorder" means "an abnormal physical or mental condition." It implies some kind of chaos.

A couple of years ago, I was writing some notes for a talk I was going to give. When I got to the section on MPD, I began to write "multiple personality disorder." When I got to the word "disorder," I began to write "dis . . ." That's as far as I got. I just couldn't finish the word. I was rebelling against calling my diagnosis of multiplicity a "disorder."

Then all the positive things I had read about MPD and all the positive things that my support team had been telling me began to click into place. Suddenly I exclaimed out loud, "I don't have a *disorder*. I have a *gift*!" The Lord Who created me, created me in His image. He created me to be a creative person. He enabled me to create the people and the hiding places inside in order to survive many traumas. I began to thank God and commend myself for this gift. A *disorder* sounded like just the result of trauma. A *gift* was a way out, a way to survive!

Wow! I sat back in my chair and smiled. I was very pleased with myself. I imagined for a moment that I felt something like Albert Einstein must have felt in his brilliance, the difference being that he had years of brilliant moments and I was only experiencing one fleeting moment!

I picked up my pen and crossed out the three letters of the word I had already written down and I wrote the word, "GIFT. M.P.G. Multiple Personality Gift." Putting my pen down, I leaned back and closed my eyes. That's it, I thought. I don't suffer from a mental illness. I am a survivor of hideous trauma because I am blessed with a most exceptional gift.

I began to spread my profound discovery with anyone who would listen. There wasn't a therapist or a survivor with whom I spoke who didn't latch onto the words "multiple personality gift." Some months ago, I received a letter from a survivor who was a multiple and had heard that MPD had been changed to MPG. She signed her letter, "M.S.W., MOM, MPG." Master's Degree in Social Work. Mother. And the recipient of a Multiple Personality Gift! Impeccable credentials, wouldn't you say?

Who Is It? *What* Is It? . . . *Who* Am I? *What* Am I?

A dear friend gave me a stuffed bear in the shape of a person. It's about six inches tall. There are no identifying features on it, front or back. It is neither male or female. There are no eyes, no ears, and no mouth. As I began to look at it closer, I realized that I wasn't even sure it was a bear. It was just an "it," no more and no less. The thought came to me that this is what persons with MPG often feel like. "Who am I . . . really?" "Have I lost my real self?" "Am I a nobody or am I a lot of somebodys?"

The nameless, faceless bear sits on my writing desk as

a reminder that, unlike him (or her) *I am an individual*, and all of the ones inside the system are personalities in their own right. *All of me* is really very special and an object of beauty in the making, and I know that in the healing process, we who are survivors will begin to find ourselves, our *real* selves. We will come to know ourselves as the wonderful, creative, and courageous persons that we are.

With a hug . . . with a hand . . .
  with a little guidance . . .
    and a sprinkling of love . . .
      we will heal.
The pieces will come together,
  naturally, in their own time.
We are just like you.
  We come in all sizes and shapes.
    We have families and friends.
We fit all job descriptions.
  We get colds and the flu.
    We go to the doctor.
      We also go to a therapist,
        just like some of you.
We may not yet know all the people inside us.
  We may not know how to cope with those we do know.
    We may just be learning to talk with them.
We get confused sometimes about who we are.
  We get confused about how to be who we are.
    Come to think of it,
      don't you ever feel like that?

"I always wanted to be *somebody*.
I see now that I should have been more specific!"
—Lily Tomlin

PART TWO

3

The Birthing of Baby

**"It is time . . . to introduce you to my child.
There was a child went forth.
He'd hidden in the basement all these years.
The war's over and my child has come up from the
basement to blink in the sunlight. To play."[1]**

Baby is the first person inside me to speak up and
make herself known to people I had learned to trust.
She says she's four years old. Although she talks and acts
a bit younger than that, she thinks of herself as being
four. That means that I was four years old or younger
when Baby came into being. And even though *I* have
aged through the years, Baby continues to act like, talk
like, laugh like, and generally feels like a four-year-old.

At some point during my childhood, the trauma became too great for me to endure. The details of that
trauma I choose not to write about. Suffice it to say that
my suffering was severe enough that I could not bear it
alone. Baby came on the scene when I was about four
years old, splitting off from the trapped and frightened
little girl that I was in order to experience and remember the trauma that I could not handle. Somehow she
was born in my mind so that, while my body was held
captive, I could escape and, perhaps, survive.

When I, as a young child, was put into certain traumatic situations that were too much for me to bear, that
trauma was experienced by Baby. The rest of me could
hide away and not experience the terror that Baby did.

The rest of me didn't experience the trauma, and so I had no memory of it. Baby had the memory, but I didn't. And I didn't even know that Baby existed, much less all that she had endured.

The presence of Baby allowed me to act normally and even feel safe and happy at times. Like Marilyn Van Derbur's "night child," Baby took responsibility for experiencing and remembering many of the early painful events in my life. I could continue to function in the routine of daily life with no knowledge of the trauma, just as Marilyn did.

Baby was not alone for long. The trauma of my childhood continued, and another alter personality came into being who began to act as Baby's partner. Baby was not allowed to cry during the terror of the trauma. So Little Girl came into being to take the job of crying silently to protect Baby from further pain. Baby and Little Girl are very close companions and are quite protective of each other. When Baby retreats to a quiet place somewhere inside of me, she always takes Little Girl by the hand and leads her along.

All the members of my support team have met Baby and love her. They tell me that she is delightful, bright, and very protective of me. Baby has her own name for my therapists. She calls them Dr. Lady and New Lady. I've taken to calling them by Baby's names for them.

If one of my therapists tells Baby that she will hold Baby in her lap and rock her, Baby often adds, "Me bring Little Girl, too, OK? She sit with me. She get rocked, too." Together they envision a quiet and safe room, with a warm, comforting fire in the fireplace and a rocking chair with New Lady or Dr. Lady holding a contented Baby and Little Girl very snugly. No matter how distraught I may be feeling at the time, knowing that Baby and Little Girl feel safe, secure, and loved, makes me feel more at peace. I am learning that we are connected, and I am learning to care very deeply about their well-being.

I was not happy at all when I first heard about Baby making her appearances. It perplexed me to think that there was another "someone" inside me taking over my mind, dictating my speech and my actions. I desperately tried to deny Baby's existence.

I hadn't perceived the presence of anyone called Baby inside me. And I surely hadn't heard a voice internally talking to me, much less talking baby talk! I remembered well (how could I forget?) that my therapists had suggested that I was a multiple. That was hard enough to swallow. But a baby? No way!

Looking back, now, I feel bad, because I can guess that Baby was listening to my every word of protest about her existence. She was aware of me although I was not aware of her. She felt rejected and unwanted and, after all, why shouldn't she? She had taken the pain of my abuse so I wouldn't have to feel it. She stuck with me in the roughest of times. She thought it was her job to be my eyes and ears sometimes and to protect me from so much pain. In short, she loved me, and now it seemed that I was rejecting her.

Baby was deeply hurt. More than once, she said to members of my support team, "Lauren no love me. She no want me. Why?" I'm not sure how they responded to that question, but I'm sure that no amount of reassuring was enough to soothe Baby's deep disappointment to my reaction. When I was able to reach out to her, her love for me was intact, but her trust of me was not won back quickly. I still feel guilty about how bad I must have made her feel.

Baby, The Blabbermouth

My therapists have to keep reminding me that Baby has had to remain silent for a very long time, and now that she feels safe in talking to a group of people with whom she finds security, she needs to be allowed to take full advantage of her newfound freedom. When Baby is around the members of my support team, she comes out to chat at the drop of a hat. She loves to report anything and everything to Dr. Lady and New Lady. (My support team has told me to be sure to let you know that Baby often talks with great excitement and speaks very, very loudly.) If anyone on the support team wants to find out what's happening at the ol' homestead, all they have to do is ask Baby.

To Baby, the telephone is the greatest invention since peanut butter and crackers! She is very quick to call one of my therapists when she perceives any danger to me. In those circumstances I am not aware that Baby has taken over until I find myself holding the receiver up to my ear. Sort of like the hero in "Quantum Leap" who finds himself in some unforeseeable predicament each week. I've learned that usually Baby has been using my phone (to say nothing of my finger, my voice, my mind . . .) in order to call for help. When Baby is done talking, she quickly retreats inside, leaving me holding the receiver, not knowing exactly who is on the other end of the line.

Finally getting up the nerve to say a hesitant hello, I know what's probably coming next. "Hi, Lauren. It's Dr. Lady. Baby just called to tell me that you weren't safe last night. Can you tell me what happened?" Or, Dr. Lady might say, "Baby says that you're very sad. She's worried about you, and she asked me to talk to you." And more than once, she'd say, "Baby tells me she's very hungry. Have you been eating well these last few days?"

I used to get angry at Baby. I'd think, What gives *her* the right to report on *me*? Does she have to tell *everything*? Baby, the blabbermouth. I know I must have hurt Baby by calling her names, and I feel sorry for saying unkind things about her. But until then, I had thought I lived very much alone in this world. I'm not used to "someone else" being around to report on me. It felt like having a nosy little kid roommate who was a snitch, a tattletale. I've since come to see that Baby's phone calls always serve a good purpose. She works so hard to keep me safe. I have ceased rejecting her and her actions. She does so much to keep me safe!

I had been programmed by the cult to commit suicide in any one of several ways. (We will talk about cult programming in chapters seven and eight.) One method I had been taught was to put a needle into a vein in my arm and inject air into it. The result, I had been trained to believe, would be instant death. Because of an anti-clotting drug I must take regularly, I always have a supply of needles and syringes on hand.

More than once I had found myself holding the phone receiver to my ear, but at certain times there was something different. "Hello." The voice on the other end was more serious and urgent than usual. It was often nearly midnight. I would never call anyone that late, and no one calls me that late. Only Baby would call at that time, and even then, only if it was of the utmost importance.

On those late-night calls, any one of my support team might be on the other end of the phone. "Lauren, Baby called me because you were not safe. You had a needle in your arm and she was scared." I'd quickly look down, and sure enough, there would be a syringe laying beside me. I knew that I had Baby to thank for being my lifesaver.

Baby Wants Out of Her Job!

Baby has been alive almost as long as I have. She has worked long and hard, taking years of painful memories and trying hard to keep me safe. Now that I have been in therapy for several years, Baby can see that I (we) have allies in trying to keep me (us) safe. She has said that she thinks it's time for me to take some of the burden she's been carrying. "Me tired. Me no want work no more. Tell Lauren she do now," she exclaims emphatically. She has made that fact known more than once.

From time to time, both of my therapists ask her, "Do you think it's time for Lauren to remember some of the memories you've had to keep all to yourself?" Baby is only too eager to respond with, "Yeah, Lauren can do now." But if she is asked, "Do you think Lauren can take it if she remembers everything?", then there is always a long pause. Baby is recalling some of the things she has gone through for me. Finally, she answers, "Me no know." (That translates into, "I don't know.") Baby vacillates between wanting not to have to do her job any longer and a genuine concern for me if I were to try to take over for her. There is still a part of Baby that remains my protector, and quite frankly, at times I am only too willing and grateful for Baby to keep her job!

I care about that part of me that is Baby. I don't want Baby to have to take any more pain for me. To relieve her, though, I would have to face bringing into my conscious memory all the pain that Baby has endured. It is a central dilemma of anyone with MPD. It is a process in progress as I write this book. For now, Baby continues to express her love and concern for me and continues to be my protector, but her expressions of wanting to be relieved of her job are becoming more frequent. Hang in there, Baby. I'm so grateful that you're here. I'm trying to listen to all you have to say and let you rest and be healed, too.

What a Baby!

I've known for many years that there was an inner child in me who was hurting. I just didn't know that she was a very real person with a name. I've often heard therapists talk about "caring for the child within you." That expression would make me feel very agitated. I couldn't bear to think about a child within me.

I knew that any inner child in me was hurting so badly that I would be afraid to recognize her. If I recognized her existence as someone who held my hurts, how in the world could I make her feel any better? How could I make that hurt "go all gone" as Baby so eloquently expresses it?

I still had a picture in my mind of that little child sitting on the floor, huddled in a corner crying. I thought that if I even tried to pick her up, my heart would break. Besides, I didn't think that my holding her would make her feel any better. We were *both* hurting too much.

So I left her on the floor, huddled in a corner for many, many years. Even though I tried my best not to think about her, every now and then the picture of her would flash in front of me, and I would feel very sad. I knew that some day I'd have to deal with that sad and hurting child, but not now. The "not nows" accumulated into many lost years. When I went back into therapy, that child did not have to remain unattended to any longer. In the safe environment of my therapist's office, she began to come out.

My therapists wisely gave recognition to this inner child, allowing her the opportunity to begin unburdening her little heart. Baby expressed her extreme loyalty to me. She began to relate the times of abuse when she took the pain and the memories for me. As she put it, "Lauren no take it. Me take it." Baby was given as much time as she wanted during each session. As my therapists would tell me how loyal and devoted she is to me, my fear of her slowly began to decrease. As Baby was allowed to express herself, she began to reveal a remarkable resilience that my entire support team found delightful.

Baby loves to giggle. She finds all kinds of things to laugh at and enjoy. Simple things. Things a deprived four-year-old would find exciting. One day I was visiting with Lyn, one of the members of my support team. She was making a batch of chocolate chip cookies. Baby suddenly became aware of something that smelled *so good.* Lyn showed her the chocolate chip cookies baking in the oven. "Baby, you want a cookie when they're done?" she asked. Baby hesitated for a moment. She seemed uncertain about just what chocolate chip cookies were, but they smelled too good to be dangerous.

"Me get cookie? Just for me?" she asked excitedly.

"Sure," my friend answered. "You can have as many as you want." That was probably not the wisest answer, for as soon as the cookies were taken out of the oven to cool, a very excited Baby could hardly wait to get her hands on one. Lyn quickly explained to her that the cookies were still much too hot to touch. Baby kept vigil over the cookies as they cooled. Finally, it was time for Baby to taste her first chocolate chip cookie. Lyn put a cookie in her hand. She took just a tiny bite eyeing the cookie suspiciously. (Baby had been tricked with foods before.)

One small bite was enough to let Baby decide that these cookies were *good.* She wolfed one down, getting the still partly melted chocolate chips all over her face (and my face). After that first cookie, Baby clapped her hands in glee and giggled.

I asked, as I always question everything my support team tells me about what my alters do or say, "How do you know it wasn't just *me* who was clapping?" Lyn is a behavioral pediatrician with much experience in how children act at different ages. "Baby clapped her hands like a little girl," she answered. "Her fingers were pointing straight up, and curved out so that only the palms of her hands struck one another. That's a very childlike way to clap. If that's just you doing an acting job, you should be in contention for an Oscar!"

Baby was determined to devour the entire batch of cookies. So my friend got out a sandwich-size plastic bag and put a few cookies in it. "Here, Baby. This is for you. Your very own cookies!"

"For me?" Baby asked. "All mine? Oh goodie, goodie!" She clutched the bag of cookies as if she was afraid someone might take them from her. She found what she felt was a safe place in the living room, sat down on the floor, and began to eat them as fast as she could get them into her mouth.

One thing that we all have noticed about Baby is that she is terrified of making a mess. She has told my therapists some stories of "big time trouble" inflicted on her that certainly would explain this fear. If Baby gets even a small spot on her clothes, she gets not only upset, but frightened. As Baby stuffed the cookies into her mouth, she said, "Uh oh. Me dirty. Me sorry. No get mad. No get mad me. Me clean up." No matter how much reassurance from whoever is with her that it's all right and no one is mad at her, Baby is not satisfied until she has done all she can to make herself clean again.

It's funny how being a multiple seems to work. I still find it amazing that many of my alters, especially Baby, have the same fears and quirks that I have. The little things that bother Baby are things that bother me. Things that frighten and worry Baby are things that frighten and worry me. And conversely, even the little things that make Baby happy are things that make me happy, too. When I am working on a subject that is very important to me, Baby says that she tries very hard "to help Lauren so she can help the children." Baby wants to help me to sound the alarm and protect other children from experiencing the pain that she has experienced. I can almost hear her exclaiming, "Me, too! Me, too!"

In not only discovering that reality, but in accepting such similarities, I am getting more in touch with Baby and am beginning to feel more connected to her. I am gaining at least the beginnings of "co-consciousness" with her. Co-consciousness is the technical term that means I am more able to be aware of her feelings and thoughts as she is aware of mine. I am excited about that development, because my therapists say that it is a sign of healing. But I am still frightened to embrace Baby, that little child who is huddled in a corner, scared and hurting.

I Didn't Mean to Hurt You

I was looking for a birthday card for a friend of mine. In scanning the cards, my eyes were drawn to a particular card. On the front was a precious drawing of a little blond-haired girl. She was holding a kitten partially wrapped in a baby blanket. As I continued to look at the card, I had a feeling that I was looking at Baby. I was mesmerized, and for several minutes I just stood and stared. My eyes filled with tears.

I want to give this to Baby, I thought. But then I felt silly. Baby doesn't need a card, I told myself. She wouldn't even know it if I did get a card for her. But my heart overrode the protests of my mind. I reached for the card, took it to the checkout counter, and paid for it.

On the way home, I kept asking myself, *Now* what are you going to do? How do you propose to give this card to Baby? I had no answers. Maybe the card would just sit on my desk forever, but I knew in my heart that I had done the right thing. When I finally arrived home, I put the card down. I didn't even take it out of the sack. There it remained, untouched. Every time I walked by, I would glance at it, but I really didn't know what to do with it. Finally, I took it out of the sack, sat down at the table, and picked up a pen. I took a deep breath and

began to write my first message to Baby. The words did
not come easily. I could only try.

Dear Baby,
 I don't know what to say to you.
 I know you are there.
 I know you have helped me for a long time.
 I want to help you now,
  but I don't know how.
 I hurt for you too much to pick you up.
 My therapists tell me that you are pals
  with Little Girl.
 I am glad, because I know you're not alone.
 Maybe one day I won't hurt as much.
 Then I can hold you in my arms
  and give you a great big hug.
 I *can* tell you that I love you.
 Tears run down my face when
  I think of how much you have taken for me.
 I know that Dr. Lady and New Lady
  are taking good care of you until I am better.
 Thank you for being there for me.
 I hope I can be there for you one day.
 Please be happy.
                                     From Lauren

 I felt drained and exhausted as I printed the words,
"For Baby," on the envelope. I hastily stuck the card in
my purse and left for my therapy session. What am I do-
ing? Why did I put the card in my purse? I wondered. If
I give it to New Lady, what is *she* going to do with it? I
began to feel relief when I decided that that was *her*
problem, not *mine*!
 "Here," I announced to New Lady, handing her the
card. "This is for Baby!"
 "What do you want me to do with it?" she asked.
 I thought for a moment and replied, "I don't know.
That's *your* problem."
 She opened the card. Seeing that I had written a

message to Baby, she asked, "Could I read this to Baby?" I shrugged my shoulders. "I guess. I don't know how this works. You're the therapist." That was my standard answer at the time for anything asked of me that had anything even remotely to do with my multiplicity.

After reading the card to herself, New Lady looked at me. Knowing that I was none too happy with the whole idea, she said, "I really do think this would make Baby happy." Resting my chin on my hands, I consented to what I considered to be the inevitable. "Okay. If you think it would help her."

And so, with New Lady sitting on the sofa next to me, she asked for Baby. At this point in my trying to retell the following events, I go blank. *I* did not go through the next few minutes. Baby did. I can tell you about what happened only as New Lady reported it to me. "Look, Baby. This is for you. Lauren wrote a card just for you."

Baby was excited. "What it say?" she asked impatiently. "Read me." New Lady read the card slowly so Baby would hear every word. When she was finished, Baby was silent. Finally, she said sadly, "Lauren no love me. She say no hold me." Out of all the sentences I had written, Baby remembered the one sentence that read, "I hurt for you too much to pick you up." And that was the one thing Baby seemed to want more than anything else.

New Lady tried to reassure her that one day I would be able to hold her. "Lauren is hurting too badly to hold you right now, but one day she'll be able to pick you up and hold you just like you want her to." From the look of disappointment on her face, it was obvious that Baby didn't seem all that reassured. "But look, Baby," New Lady hastened to add, "Lauren says that she loves you."

Baby remained silent. I can only imagine her thoughts. I'm sure she was hurt by my writing that I couldn't pick her up. I suppose she interpreted it to mean that I didn't *want* to hold her. New Lady told me that Baby's final remark was that the words were "too big" for her to understand. It was probably easier for Baby to think that she was unable to comprehend than to think that I really was unable to hold her.

Baby's heart was broken. My heart was broken.

4

To Baby, with Love

Since I felt that I had failed in my first attempt to console the lonely and hurting Baby who lived inside me, I was tempted to give up. I thought I simply didn't have what it took to love and nurture that inner child. I felt resigned to the idea that she would be left in that corner forever, hunched in a tight little ball, crying, lonely, and frightened.

"But it isn't true," I said out loud as I drove home from New Lady's office. "I *do* love you, Baby. I *do* want to pick you up and hold you." No sooner had I spoken those words than a flood of feelings for this very lonely child poured from my heart in sobs. Oh, God, how I hurt for her! She wasn't just *any* child. She was *me*! I suddenly realized that my sobs were the sobs of a very young child. I began to listen to myself. I was "crying like a baby." No. Not crying *like* a baby, I *was* a baby, and that baby was crying her little heart out.

By the time I arrived home, I felt that I had made a vital connection with the very real person of Baby. "It's a start," I whispered. Parking my car in the garage, I turned off the ignition, laid my head on the steering wheel, and wept some more. As exhausted as I was, I felt a spark of hope. It was a good feeling. It was a very good feeling.

I thought and thought about what more I could do for this inner child called Baby. I wasn't ready yet to visualize picking her up and holding her. I felt that my heart would burst from the pain and hurt of that experience. I could see myself putting her back on the floor for fear of not being able to handle the feelings that were sure to overwhelm me. Neither Baby nor I would survive such a trauma! But the desire to do something for Baby grew and grew.

For some reason, I began to feel a yearning for the gigantic stuffed white bear with the fat belly that sat in the entry way of a friend's home. It was at least as tall as I am. Why, the bear was so huge, it would block the entry way to *my* house! Besides, I knew it must have cost a fortune! So why did this particular bear keep popping into my mind?

Suddenly, I had a scary thought. What if *Baby* wanted me to buy a bear like that for her? Was that where that yearning was coming from? Were *her* feelings beginning, just a little, to be *my* feelings? No way, Baby. I can't afford a bear like that, I thought to myself. I didn't know quite what to do—until I remembered one particular store that specialized in stuffed animals. I had visited there several times in the past few years. There I'd be, looking at all the stuffed bears and other animals. Each time I'd find myself stopping in front of these particular bears . . . Guess what they looked like? Uh-huh. They were all white and each one had a fat belly. There were big bears, little bears, and in-between bears. I can recall that I'd always be drawn to hold that one that had the fat belly. It felt so soft and comforting.

I began to realize just why I was drawn to the white bear with the fat belly. Perhaps it wasn't myself, Lauren, who found the bear so appealing. Just maybe it was Baby who, in her own silent way, was expressing her longing for this white bear with the fat belly. When I began to think about the possibility, I thought, Why don't I go to a toy store and look for a white bear with a fat belly? This is one thing I *can* do for Baby.

I drove to the nearest toy store I could find. I was so excited. I was finally going to make Baby happy. Parking my car, I turned off the ignition and put my hand on the door handle. Suddenly, I froze. I could not get out of the car. I had no idea what was going on, but there was a knot in my stomach. Tears filled my eyes and began to course down my cheeks.

"I can't go into the toy store, Baby. I just can't. I'm sorry," I said in a choked voice. I began to understand why I was unable to get out of my car and go into the toy store when I pictured myself in the stuffed animal section looking for "that" bear. What would happen if I *did* find it? I started to picture myself reaching for the bear, only to have Baby take over, sit down in the middle of the aisle, and begin to play with the bear. Just the thought of it mortified me.

What in the world would people think of a woman my age sitting on the floor of a toy store, giggling with delight, and talking to a stuffed animal? Then I thought, What in the world would *I* do, when Baby retreated back into her safe room and I became myself again? Would I find myself on the floor in the middle of an aisle holding a bear? I had no idea what I would do then. My best guess is that I would beg "Scotty" to "beam me up" right away!

Suffice it to say, I did not venture into the toy store that day, and Baby did not get her bear. I was saddened as I drove out of the parking lot. Once again, I felt that I had failed Baby. I wondered if she would ever understand. I wondered if I would ever be able to console her and hold her. I did love her, but I couldn't find the right way to show her. I felt that Baby was probably grieving over what she must have perceived as my not loving her. I grieved because Baby was and is a part of me. We were both hurting very, very much!

Baby Needs a Mommy

Dr. Lady told me that she was in her office recently when she heard the sounds of sobbing coming from her waiting room. She found me (or more aptly, she found Baby) huddled on the floor in a corner. Baby's head was buried in a tightly clutched "Bear." "Bear" was the name Baby had given to a stuffed animal that Dr. Lady had given her.

Dr. Lady knelt down on the floor in front of Baby. "Baby, why are you crying? What's the matter?"

"Me want a mommy," she answered in between wails that only a baby can make. "Me no mommy." Dr. Lady coaxed Baby to stand up, and walked Baby into her office. Baby kept up the crying and the broken record of "Me want a mommy."

"You hurt me?" Baby asked suddenly of Dr. Lady. "Oh, no. I never hurt babies. I love you." Baby's familiar grin appeared, but as quickly as it had appeared, it disappeared. Some stored memories were beginning to flood her little mind. What did Dr. Lady mean by, "I love you"?

Baby looked Dr. Lady in the eye and, in a deliberate tone of voice, asked, "You got thingy?" ("Thingy" was Baby's name for penis.) Baby never wanted anything to do with anyone who had a "thingy."

"No, Baby. I don't have a 'thingy,'" Dr. Lady reassured her. The grin quickly reappeared on Baby's face. Dr. Lady had just passed "The Mommy Test."

"You be mommy? Me have mommy now. Me have mommy."

Dr. Lady told me later that she wasn't quite sure how to respond to Baby. This didn't quite fit into anything that had been covered in her many years of training and experience! She realized that Baby had never known nurturing of any kind. Baby only knew pain and punishment. Now was not the time to disappoint Baby.

As Dr. Lady sat pensively, trying to sort out her reply, Baby continued, undaunted. "New Lady be mommy too? Me have *two* mommies!" Baby's eyes lit up! "No thingies. You love me!" Baby was ecstatic.

When Dr. Lady told me what had happened, I cringed at the thought of being found on the floor of her waiting room, crying and clinging to Bear. I cringed at the realization that if Baby was on the floor, I was on the floor, crying and clinging to Bear. Whatever Baby did, I did. My multiple personalities all share the same body. (If I've been reminded of that once by my therapists, I've been reminded a million times!) When I view my alters from that perspective, I'm not always so eager to be told what they've done and said. But for my little four-year-old alter, I was beginning to learn much patience and tolerance.

Dr. Lady and New Lady have become "mommies" for Baby. She is easily pleased. A simple hug brings squeals of joy and a little lullaby sends her into orbit. She has coined her own phrase for all this. She calls it being "mommied." If, during a session, Dr. Lady or New Lady neglects to spend a few moments with Baby "mommying" her, they are sure to hear about it later on their answering machines. "Mommy, dis Baby! Why you no mommy me? You no mommy me today. You mommy me next time?" And they do! They always do!

Baby Fights Back

Baby is a courageous and spunky alter. She had to be to survive so much trauma in protecting me. I have known about her for almost three years, and she still takes much of my pain. Dr. Lady has told me that Baby has a lot of energy and bounces back quickly after relating traumatic memories as part of our work in therapy.

Hugs and kisses have become an important part of Baby's life. She can be in the midst of crying "big time" on the phone with one of her mommies, but the moment one of them tells Baby to get ready for a hug and a kiss, she is consoled and waits excitedly. No sooner has Dr. Lady or New Lady sent a hug and a kiss to her over

the phone, than Baby is giggling with delight and bab-
bling on about her new mommies. Baby always seems to
see the sun shining through the clouds and the rainbow
at the end of every storm.

I marvel at Baby's ability to bounce back. I may never
understand her devotion to me. I still feel that I let her
down. I think I'm getting closer to the point when I
could give back to her some of the comfort and love she
needs, but I fear it may not happen for some time to
come. I can only hope and believe that Baby will hang in
there with me for a while longer.

Enough Already!

Several days ago, something triggered a flashback of a
sexual assault. I choose to omit the details. The scene re-
played over and over in my mind. I felt dirtier and more
ashamed each time I relived it. "God, please take this
memory away," I prayed. "I can't endure these feelings.
I can't stand to hear the sounds." I felt overwhelmed by
a sense that I was disgusting and dirty. I took so many
baths that day that my skin became wrinkled like a
prune. It is an understatement to say that Baby was not
happy about all the bathing.

Baby intervened and phoned Dr. Lady with the news.
"Lauren think she dirty. She no dirty. She clean," Baby
emphatically yelled. "Tell her no take bath no more. We
clean! We both clean! You tell her. Bye, bye."

Here I was again with the phone in my hand. "Hello?"

"Hi, Lauren. It's Dr. Lady."

"I didn't call you. Did you call me?"

"No, you didn't call me. Baby called me," she answered, with just a hint of humor in her voice. "Baby is
tired of taking baths. She says, 'enough already.' Can
you stop taking baths?"

"I don't know, Dr. Lady. I know in my head that I'm
clean, but I still feel dirty." I thought for a moment,

pondering Baby's understandable impatience at having to live in the bath tub. "All right, I'll try . . . but just for Baby's sake."

I did try. By the evening, I quit filling the tub with water, but I still felt dirty. It took a couple of days for the feeling of being dirty to wear off. At least now I know, if I just wait it out, the calm does return . . . eventually. However, it never comes fast enough for me!

Sing It To Yourself, Baby

"For Pete's sake, Baby, I can't stand to listen to the song one more time!" If I had played it once, I had played it a hundred times, and I was getting very sick of it. There was only one problem. Baby wasn't sick of it. In fact, the more she heard the song, the more she wanted me to play it again.

How do I know? I don't know. It's like when I knew I had to buy the birthday card for Baby. How can I explain to you what I can't explain to myself? I have to accept my therapist's word that co-consciousness with Baby is slowly developing. One of my deepest wishes is that I will get to know Baby better; her wishes, her needs, her fears, whatever. I want to be able to communicate with her without having to go through one of my therapists. And I rather think that Baby has the same wish. One day, I am confident, our wish will come true.

For now, I'm stuck trying to deal with this song. I have long been an admirer of the singer, Chris Christian. One of the songs on his recent CD that struck a chord in my heart was his rendition of the African-American spiritual, "He's Got the Whole World in His Hands."

On this song, Chris recorded the voice of Courtney, his three-or four-year-old daughter. As Chris sings about how God is holding the whole world in His hands, little Courtney begins to name everyone in her family. At the end of the song, she finally asks in just about the cutest little girl's voice you've ever heard, "Daddy, how many hands does God have?"

Courtney's voice melts my heart. I am drawn to her, and yet, my heart hurts for Baby as I listen to her. So I decided to skip that song until I was a little more healed myself. Guess how Baby reacted to my decision? I think that Baby and Courtney were becoming friends. Baby doesn't have any friends her own age, so it was perfectly natural for her to feel a bond with Courtney.

Although I didn't want to listen to one more rendition of "He's Got the Whole World in His Hands," I found myself playing it over and over too many times to count. The track would just end and another song was about to be played when I felt an overwhelming necessity to press the replay button. Baby just couldn't hear enough of Courtney's voice. I hate to admit it, but my guess is that Baby began to mimic Courtney's words. Once in a while, I would hear myself talking along with Courtney as the song was playing.

Come on, Lauren, I argued with myself. This is really crazy. I didn't know whether to be annoyed with myself or with Baby. In total frustration, I yelled, "Sing it to yourself, Baby! By now you know every word of the song by heart. Sing it to yourself!"

Someone Take Baby, Please!

It got to the point where, Lord help me, Baby was becoming more and more vocal. It seemed like it was always her turn to talk, and talk she did! As she became more active, I felt as if I needed a break. Baby wanted more and more love and attention, and those were the two things I still wasn't able to give her. Thank God for therapists who recognized and understood my predicament. They were simply wonderful. They were lifesavers . . . *my* lifesavers.

If Baby didn't get her chance to talk during one of my

therapy sessions (excuse me, during one of *our* therapy sessions), she would get on the phone when I got home and call the therapist. She let it be known that she had been overlooked. She usually interpreted it as "You no like me no more." Neglecting to care for the needs of Baby made for one unhappy Baby.

I tried my best to remember to bring a stuffed animal or a doll with me when I went to my therapy sessions. Sometimes I'd forget, and to be truthful, sometimes I just plain didn't want to be seen carrying a stuffed bear into an office building, up the elevator, and down a long hall before reaching my destination.

Creativity in meeting Baby's demands for attention seemed to be in order. In fact, I became quite creative in hiding Baby's "paraphernalia" as I journeyed to and from my therapy sessions. I did note, however, that I was going to have to get some kind of toy box to store all the toys that Baby and my other alters were accumulating.

When I just didn't feel like carrying one or two stuffed animals with me, I found that I would reach my therapist's office with a carry-all bag in my hand. Dr. Lady or New Lady would ask, "What's in the bag?" I would honestly have to answer that I didn't have the slightest clue. I'd empty the bag, only to find one of Baby's favorite stuffed animals or dolls. She had decided that if *I* wasn't going to bring her favorite animal or doll with me, *she* would have to do it for me. That, I could handle. At least it was tucked in a bag and hidden from the view and the opinions of those who passed by me.

At one session, Baby and one of my therapists were on the floor rolling a large spongy Nerf ball back and forth. The next time I went back to her, Baby remembered the ball. For Baby, there was no time for small talk. "Me play ball. You play me?" she asked the therapist. So we soon found ourselves sitting on the floor once again. Those few minutes spent with Baby made for a very contented Baby.

There was a time when I regarded such times spent with Baby as wasted time, but no more. I am finding that, as Baby is being nurtured with time, care, and love, so is the child within me. I never ever dared to hope that I would progress far enough for such healing to become a reality.

When Baby discovered marking pens (thanks to Dr. Lady), I was again ready to give Baby away to anyone who would take her. I am the kind of person who has very little tolerance for clothes that aren't clean, for clothes that are wrinkled, or for clothes that have marks on them.

Baby must have learned a long time ago about how upset I get if I spill even a drop of Pepsi on my blouse. So when Baby got her hands on the marking pens, I'm sure she tried not to be messy. But giving a four-year-old a set of coloring markers and a pad of paper for the first time, then expecting her to stay within the boundaries of that paper, is like putting a bear beside a tree and expecting him not to scratch his back! This was big-time fun for Baby.

Guess what color of pants I was wearing when Dr. Lady introduced marking pens to Baby? Yep. White! When Baby finished her drawing, I noticed slashes of vivid color out of the corner of my eye. Guess what color those same pants were when Baby's drawing time was over? White? Well, yes . . . and black . . . and red . . . and blue.

"How did *this* get on my pants?" I asked Dr. Lady. I had to ask, because I was not there when Baby was drawing, and Dr. Lady was good at putting away "the evidence" before I came back. This time, however, there was no hiding the evidence. My pants told the story.

Dr. Lady chuckled. "Baby didn't stay on the paper when she was drawing pictures." I wasn't as amused as Dr. Lady was. "Do these marking pens have washable ink or is the ink permanent?" I asked impatiently. "Well, they're supposed to be washable." The words "supposed to be" didn't exactly give me the reassurance for which I was looking.

I couldn't drive home fast enough. The first thing I did when I got in the apartment was to take my pants off and wash them. After scrubbing them vigorously, I rinsed them. I was afraid to look at them. I just knew they would still be white and red and black and blue. Taking a deep breath, I peeked. A sigh of relief. Dr. Lady was right. Every mark was gone. I left a message on Dr. Lady's answering machine and said simply, "You were right."

At my next session, the *small* drawing pad had been replaced with a *gigantic* drawing pad. Smart lady, I thought to myself.

A Secret of Horrors

I took for granted that Baby was having a ball coloring and drawing things that made her happy. After all, isn't that what *all* children do? I neglected to take into consideration that Baby wasn't just *any* child. She had been holding some very traumatic memories for a very long time. She had never been given the opportunity, nor had she felt safe enough to express them before now.

I have been told that Baby is irresistible—that she is very intelligent—that she has a million-dollar grin. But behind that charm is a sea of turmoil. I was heartbroken when I learned that Baby had no happy pictures to draw. I asked my therapist to show me some of the things she had drawn, but then, as she was bringing out the drawing pad that contained the pages of Baby's drawings, I became uneasy. I wasn't sure that I wanted to see what Baby had drawn. I had never before asked Dr. Lady to unlock the secrets revealed in the drawing pad.

"Wait," I said apprehensively. "I don't know if I'm ready for this."

"You don't have to look at it," she answered. I think even she was a little concerned about showing me the drawings.

My heart was saying, Good. Let's forget about it. But I knew that it was vital for me to learn about the memories that Baby had been holding to herself all these years, memories of things that, after all, had happened to me. "Yes, I do have to look," I replied with a fearful voice. "I think Baby wants me to know." Maybe she had drawn pictures of some of her memories, knowing that they would be shared with me. I wasn't sure that there would ever be a *right* time for me to see them.

I felt as if I was being drawn into a game of hide and seek in which I was the one who was hiding, and Baby was the one who was yelling, "Ready or not, here I come!"

Dr. Lady sat beside me. My eyes were riveted on the cover of the drawing pad. I felt threatened and frightened by its pages that had been safely kept from me. They loomed larger than life. I was ready to back out.

Some kind of co-consciousness with Baby struck a chord in my heart, and I knew it was time to begin sharing the memories with her. Taking the pad from Dr. Lady and placing it on my lap, I slowly opened the cover. I was not in any way prepared for what I saw.

The pages were filled with drawings that frightened me. On occasion, I had to ask Dr. Lady to interpret them for me. The pictures were all of bodies that had been hurt in one way or another. The majority of them depicted ugly scenes of sexual abuse.

The colors of the marking pens that Baby chose to draw with were blue, black, and red—and those colors only. I asked Dr. Lady what they meant. "Baby uses blue for herself, black for the bad guys, and red for anything having to do with sexual abuse and/or blood."

I could only bear to look at three or four pages of Baby's drawings. There were no happy faces. There were no drawings of flowers or of the sun or of trees or of any of the things most children draw. The only animals I saw were those of dogs, dogs with disproportionate and large sexual organs that came to a sharp point. In fact, all of the drawings of the perpetrators had large penises that were pointed at the ends. There were bodies with limbs cut off, bodies with blood dripping out, and faces with "poop" smeared on them. I'd had enough. I could not bear to look at any more of Baby's drawings.

I began to feel ill. Taking hold of the cover and slamming it closed, I pushed the pad back onto Dr. Lady's lap. I couldn't bear to venture any further into the painful life of Baby. For the first time, I think I knew a little of how Baby felt. For the first time, I realized the hell she had been withholding from me so I could survive and stay sane.

Dear God, Baby, how I wish your life held carefree memories of happiness, of sunshine, of playing and laughing. How I wish you could have drawn pictures of yourself skipping down the street, climbing jungle gyms, and digging your toes into the warm sand as you built sand castles by the seashore. I began to wonder if Baby had *any* happy memories. She certainly wasn't drawing any.

It was then that I realized that I was ready to write words to Baby that I had never been able to write before, and I knew, for the first time, that I would be able to keep my promises to her.

Again I picked out a card. The child on the card was similar to the child on the first card, but this time, she was sitting in her mother's lap. Painstakingly I wrote these words.

> Dear Baby,
>   This picture is for you. The baby is what I think you must look like. I think I looked something like that when I was your age. You are a pretty baby. You are a very good baby.

I hope you can think of me holding you in my lap. I want you to feel very safe. You can sit in my lap anytime you want.

I will always be here for you. When you are happy or when you are sad, I will put my arms around you and hold you. I hope you can feel my love.

Lauren

I wondered if Baby was watching as I wrote the card. I wondered if I had the nerve to ask New Lady to read it to her. I wondered what Baby's reaction would be. Would she be as disappointed as she was with the first card?

There was nothing nonchalant about my attitude as I handed this card to New Lady. This time, I was not in unchartered territory. I felt my heart pounding faster. I felt a lump in my throat. I was afraid. If I failed this time, I wondered if Baby would continue to be my outspoken advocate or would she retreat forever, never to be heard from again? As often as I had referred to her as "Baby, the blabbermouth," I knew that I needed her. Now, I was even beginning to want her.

As New Lady began to read the card to Baby, my heartfelt expression kept running over and over in my mind. "Baby, I don't want to lose you."

Perhaps it sounds silly for an adult to be so dependent on an inner child who is only four years old, but as I have been writing about her for several months now, I have developed a relationship with her that I not only thought would never exist, but that I had actually feared. In the course of my penning these words about Baby, she has become the single most important person in my life.

She is not only a "personality" or an "alter" to me, she is a very real person. She is becoming a living, breathing, and feeling person in her own right. (My therapists have told me that this is normal when a survivor is developing co-consciousness with one of their alters.) I long to reach out and hold her tightly, for in holding her and loving her, I will be holding and loving myself.

At the end of the therapy session, I asked New Lady if Baby liked the card. "Baby *really* liked *this* card," she replied. "Baby did want to make sure though that you would really hold her this time." New Lady paused for a moment and then added, "I do think it would be good for both of you if you at least tried."

"I will try. I'm not sure how to do it, but I'll try." I have kept that promise. With each day that passes, I try to allow myself the permission to grow closer to Baby and for her to grow closer to me. The pain of trying to console a little four-year-old who has been with me as protector, advocate, and defender for so many years is still overwhelming to me. But I am dedicated to giving back to Baby all of the things she has given to me—and then some.

I realized how strongly I was committed to that goal when I picked up a three-by-five note card a few days ago that was sitting on the table. It simply read, "A full tummy and a mommy's love." I do not remember writing it, but I accept the possibility that perhaps Baby was expressing her wishes through me. If all it takes to make Baby contented is a full tummy and a mommy's love, then she has it!

Postscript

A few days ago, New Lady shared a recent phone conversation she had had with Baby. New Lady was expressing her concerns about my safety. "Me been around the longest," Baby said proudly. "Don't worry, New Lady. Me take care of Lauren."

I owe you one, Baby!

5

The Menagerie

Carrying the stuffed animal out of my therapist's office, I was embarrassed. I put it under my arm to hide it, but it was too big. Its head and legs stuck out, visible to anyone who walked by. I tried to hide it behind my purse, but it was longer than my purse. So I put it back under my arm and hurriedly walked to my car, trying to look as if I didn't know it was there. I hoped that people would think I was taking it to a child.

"Bear" was mentioned briefly in the previous chapter. He was a birthday present from Dr. Lady. I found out this year that when it is *my* birthday, it is also *everyone else's* birthday. And if everyone else wasn't recognized on my birthday, especially Baby, there would be trouble in the camp! Either Dr. Lady or New Lady would be sure to hear about it.

Dr. Lady must have known that, because in the birthday card she gave me, the text had originally read, "Happy Birthday to a very special someone." Dr. Lady had wisely crossed out the word, "a," and added the letter "s" to the word "someone." After her revisions, the card read, "Happy Birthday to very special someones." She signed it, "Love, Doctor Lady."

I don't usually keep cards, but this was one I couldn't put in the wastebasket. The card now sits on my writing desk. Everyone, especially Baby, seems contented that the card is still there. I can't explain it, but when I look at the card, I sense that the other alters are proud of it too, that it is not only *my* card, but it is *their* card as well.

Getting back to Bear. At home I put him with the other stuffed animals that sit on shelves in my dining area. Baby obviously wasn't pleased to find Bear sitting with the other bears. One morning I found Bear sitting quite prominently in the center of the coffee table in front of the sofa. It wasn't possible to overlook Bear when he had become the centerpiece of the entire room! Everything that had been lying in a clutter on the table top was strewn all over the floor; *my* papers, magazines, pens, remote controls, etc. Now there was only one thing on the table—that very important person Bear.

There has been an on-going tug-of-war of sorts since that morning. I don't want Bear sitting on the coffee table. I really need my clutter of papers, pens, etc. I am lost without them. So I am repeatedly picking Bear up and putting him back on the shelf. Baby is repeatedly retrieving Bear and sitting him in the center of the coffee table. I'm not sure if either of us will ever win. We are *both* stubborn!

Bear originally had come with a bib and a baby bottle. There is a small hole in his mouth to accommodate the bottle. I did not want to put up with the potential mess that a baby bottle could make, especially in the hands of Baby, so I hid the bottle in a kitchen drawer. I found out not any too soon that Baby had been watching just where the bottle had been hidden.

Baby loves to eat anything she can get her hands on. I've often awakened to the crunchy feel of cracker crumbs in my bed. I can only assume that Baby either sneaks crackers under my pillow before I go to bed or that she gets up in the middle of the night and gets a handful of crackers from the kitchen and brings them back to bed with her.

Here's the problem. Baby wants to share her food with Bear. From time to time, New Lady brings peanut butter and crackers to our therapy session for Baby. And I, dutifully, if reluctantly, take the peanut butter and crackers home with me. I usually put them on the kitchen counter. On those nights, I inevitably wake up to find not only cracker crumbs in bed with me, but sticky peanut butter on my pillow cases and sheets. That may make *Baby* happy, but it does not make *me* happy!

A few mornings ago, I awakened to find not only peanut butter and cracker crumbs in bed but, after rolling over and feeling something bumpy underneath me, I pulled out guess who? Yep. There was Bear, complete with sticky peanut butter all over his bib and face. Baby had been thoughtful enough to share her favorite bedtime snack with Bear. I didn't exactly rejoice with Baby or with Bear! Poor Bear! He got the scrubbing of his life just to make himself presentable again.

I took Bear to my therapy session the next day and declared that Baby needed more therapy than I did! I explained to Dr. Lady why Bear was minus his bib. My tone of voice was not too accommodating as I related Baby's antics. Dr. Lady chuckled and said, "Have patience with Baby. She was only sharing."

It was at that moment that I had a brilliant idea. It would solve everything. "Why not have Dr. Lady take both Baby and Bear home with her? Then Baby could share with Bear in Dr. Lady's bed and she'd see how difficult it was to have patience with Baby and her night surprises."

I looked at Dr. Lady and told her that I was trying to be patient with Baby. The combination of Baby and Bear together did put a strain on my "mommying," but I had to admit that they make quite a challenging team.

Little Ted

Little Ted is another member of my menagerie. He is very, very special to Baby and to Little Girl. Little Ted is a stuffed animal just like Bear, but Little Ted plays a totally different role in the lives of Baby and Little Girl.

Little Ted used to live in the closet of Button Lady's office. (Button Lady is Baby's name for Barbara. She was my therapist until she became ill and had to curtail her practice.) When I would go to my therapy sessions with Button Lady, she would get Little Ted from a shelf in the closet and bring him into her office. Baby took to Little Ted like a duck takes to water. I wish I had a photo of Baby's face when she first saw him in the arms of Button Lady.

Little Ted wears a one-piece set of overalls that is sewn onto his body. The first thing Baby noticed when Button Lady handed him to her was that Little Ted's bottoms can't be pulled down. That observation was the single most important thing about Little Ted, for that meant that he had never been molested. With every therapy session that followed, Baby always checked to make sure that Little Ted's overalls fit him securely and that there was no hole in the bottoms between his legs.

"Little Ted, hero," Baby would exclaim excitedly. "Bottoms no come down. He always be safe." But then a problem arose. A safety problem, no less! Baby wanted to check out where Little Ted lived between office visits. "Where you keep Little Ted when me no here?" Baby asked Button Lady.

"Come with me. I'll show you," she responded. "Here," she said as she handed Little Ted to Baby. "You can put him on the shelf." Button Lady led Baby to a storage closet. When she began to open the door, Baby noticed right away that it was very, very dark in there. "Little Ted no see in here. He scared."

As if that weren't bad enough, when Button Lady showed Baby the vacant space on one of the shelves where Little Ted lived between Baby's visits, Baby became even more agitated.

"Little Ted no room. He no play here." It took a fair amount of convincing from Button Lady for Baby to put Little Ted on the shelf. She had bought a small blanket to wrap Little Ted in. Before Baby would leave him on the shelf, she made sure that Little Ted was wrapped "just so" as assurance that he would keep warm.

As Button Lady began to close the door to the closet, another problem arose. "Little Ted no want door close," Baby protested. "It too dark. He no get out." Baby was not a happy baby when she was walked back to Button Lady's office. Baby said a quick, "Bye-bye," and retreated.

After I became Lauren again, Button Lady explained what had taken place with Baby. When she told me about Baby not wanting her to close the closet door, I felt as if she was talking about me. It's always amazing to me when I discover another fear that I and my alters share.

When I enter small waiting rooms, I'm always careful to leave the door open about six inches. If the door is closed, I begin to feel very uncomfortable. I first realized that I had a fear of small or cramped places once when I got down on the floor and slid about two feet under my bed to retrieve a small ball that my cat had been playing with. I suddenly panicked—big time! Had I been able to maintain even a modicum of control, I would have been able to easily slide out from under the bed, but I "lost it." The more I panicked, the harder it became to free myself. By the time my face had cleared the mattress, I had scratches on my arms, and the back of my blouse was torn.

Recalling that panic as I listened to Button Lady telling me about Baby's fear, I knew only too well from where her fear had come. My fear of closed in and cramped spaces was Baby's fear. And Baby transferred her fear to Little Ted, thinking that he would feel the same way. To Baby, Little Ted was not an inanimate object. Little Ted was a living, breathing, and feeling person, and Baby was very protective of him.

Not only had Baby become protective of Little Ted, but she had become very attached to him. That attachment became a "numero uno" big problem when Button Lady became ill and had to stop seeing me. That meant, of course, that if Button Lady couldn't see me, she couldn't see Baby. And if Baby couldn't come to Button Lady's office any more, what would happen to Little Ted?

Baby cried and cried and cried. Little Ted was her hero, and now he was being taken away from her. Baby didn't think of Little Ted as someone she visited once or twice a week. Little Ted was hers. Period! Baby thought that she was keeping Little Ted safe and happy, but in reality, Little Ted was helping Baby to survive the frightening journey to healing.

What Baby didn't know is that Little Ted was special to other clients of Button Lady. That's why Baby had to always leave him at Button Lady's office after each visit. Baby never liked to say "goodbye" to Little Ted, but managed to do so because she knew that she would be seeing him again in just a few days.

Now we were down to the nitty-gritty. Baby was *never* going to see Little Ted again. Baby wailed. Baby needed tissues to blow her nose. Baby could not be persuaded by any reasoning. Neither promises of another teddy bear or of visits to check on Little Ted budged Baby from her repeated insistence that, "Little Ted *mine!*"

I even went to several toy stores to see if I could find a duplicate of Little Ted for Baby. I did find other "Little Teds," but their outfits had different patterns, and I knew that Baby would notice the difference.

Does this sound as crazy to you as it does to me? I wish that I could write about this differently, but I can't. This is the way it really happened. This is what MPG is all about. I am not trying to sensationalize this subject, and I am not trying to see how "way out" I can make it sound. Quite the opposite. If I were to have tried to write about my multiple personalities even six months ago, I couldn't have done it. It has taken many months of getting to know the "others" sufficiently well to become comfortable enough to share them with you. It has been a slow process just to accept them, let alone to "appreciate" them.

I'm more comfortable in sharing Baby with you, because she has been with me the longest and has been my strongest defender and advocate through the years. Without Baby, I may not have survived. So even when she becomes a little obnoxious, I'm learning to overlook it. God knows (and Baby sure knows), that *I've* been obnoxious at times! Certainly Baby deserves the right to speak her mind and to become demanding and throw a temper tantrum now and then. A little four-year-old who has taken the pain of my life has surely earned the right to be heard. And hear Baby we did!

Baby was not going to part with Little Ted. No way! Come hell or high water, Baby had made up her mind that the two of them belonged together, not just in Button Lady's office, but wherever Baby was. That meant only one thing. Button Lady was going to have to give Little Ted to Baby.

I thought, Fat chance of that happening. Little Ted probably means as much to another client as he means to Baby. I felt like we were in a "rob Peter to pay Paul" situation, and someone was going to have to suffer the loss of Little Ted. I was thankful that I wasn't in Button Lady's shoes. True, I had to put up with Baby's protests and wailing, but I didn't have to be the bad guy.

I was not looking forward to our next therapy session. I knew that we were headed for another free-for-all with Baby. When Baby cried, I cried. Her tears were my tears. When Baby's heart was sad, my heart was sad. Her heart was my heart.

Therapy day was fast approaching. Maybe I can keep from switching to Baby, I thought, trying desperately to convince myself. Maybe Baby won't come out today. But in my heart I knew that that was not likely. Reality sank in on my way to Button Lady's office. "Who are you trying to kid?," I yelled out loud. I didn't know why I was yelling. No one else was in the car . . . except for Baby. Perhaps I was hoping that Baby was listening. Perhaps I was trying to convince Baby of the improbability of her getting Little Ted. I'm not sure. I only know that I wasn't looking forward to this session.

I was going through my own trauma of losing Button Lady as my therapist. I had shed enough tears myself for the loss that I was feeling. After all, Button Lady meant at least as much to me as Little Ted meant to Baby. I didn't want to part with Button Lady, but I knew I had to. Somehow, Baby was going to have to accept the fact that she, too, was going to have to part with Little Ted.

I have since talked to Button Lady about how she gave Little Ted to Baby. It was like a scene right out of the movies. The birth mother gives the baby she cannot keep to the adoptive mother who cannot have children. The long-awaited moment has finally arrived. The birth mother puts her baby into the outstretched arms of the adoptive mother. The new mother draws the infant close to herself. Tears fill her eyes as she tries to thank the birth mother, but she chokes with emotion.

As Button Lady held Little Ted, she looked into the sad eyes of a crushed Baby. "Here, Baby. Little Ted is yours now. He can go home with you." Baby's tear-filled eyes grew wide. She clutched Little Ted and her arms held him tightly.

"For me?" Baby asked Button Lady. "Little Ted for me?"

"Yes, he's all yours," she answered. "I know you'll take good care of him."

Baby giggled with delight. Suddenly, Baby's giggles stopped. "Me no take pants off," Baby announced seriously. "He stay safe with me. Me make him happy." And thus, Little Ted became a permanent member of our home.

I really don't know what Baby does with him. I have found Little Ted in bed with me on several occasions, and I'm as sure as I can be that Baby checks on him to make sure that his bottoms haven't been taken off.

On one visit to Button Lady several weeks later, I dutifully brought Little Ted along. When Baby came out in Button Lady's office, she proudly showed him to her. "Button Lady, see?" Baby said proudly. "Bottoms stay on. Little Ted no get hurt."

I suppose that Little Ted will forever be Baby's hero. Baby has needed a hero for a long time. I took a snapshot of Little Ted sitting on a wooden rocking horse that is in my living room and put it in a frame for Baby. I wasn't sure if Baby was aware of the picture until I began to find the framed photo in different places. One day it would be on top of the television. Another day it would be on my bed stand.

Every time I find Little Ted's picture in a new place, I envision Baby looking at it and saying, "Little Ted me hero! You mine. Me keep you safe."

Little Ted has become a hero to me, too. He has done something that I haven't been able to do yet. He has put some happiness into an otherwise very sad little four-year-old's world.

Sunshine

Bottoms that stay on. That continues to be the single most important issue for Baby to check out—whether it be a stuffed animal or a dolly. "Sunshine" is a doll that was recently given to Baby by New Lady. She is dressed in a bright yellow dress. Baby gave her the name "Sunshine" because the color reminded her of the sun.

You can guess what the first thing Baby did when New Lady handed the dolly to her. Up went the dress. Sunshine was wearing white pantaloons. Upon checking them out, Baby was concerned that the "bottoms" as she calls them, could be taken off. New Lady had to reassure her that Sunshine's bottoms were on snugly, that they had never been taken off, and that Sunshine had never been molested. That reassurance seemed to satisfy Baby.

All was well with Sunshine and Baby until New Lady informed me that Baby, during one of our therapy sessions, had shown her that Sunshine's pantaloons wouldn't stay on. Baby was very upset. I can only guess that Baby had probably checked Sunshine's bottoms one time too many, and in doing so, the elastic that held the pantaloons up began to stretch.

Baby was so concerned about Sunshine's safety that New Lady and I decided that something had to be done about Sunshine's pantaloons. I looked at New Lady, and New Lady looked at me. I didn't know about her, but I sure knew about me. I am not a seamstress! For me, it is a major project to sew a button on, much less tightening the waist of some pantaloons.

New Lady didn't say anything. I kept waiting for her to volunteer and say, "That's no problem. I'll take Sunshine home and get those pantaloons fixed in a jiffy." She didn't say a word. So I agreed to fix Sunshine's pantaloons. On the drive home, I said, "Baby, you're going to be sorry that I'm taking on this project in place of New Lady. You picked the wrong mommy for this one."

I arrived home. Out came the white thread. Out came the sewing needle. I guessed that was all I needed for this project, but I was wrong. You see, there's this teensy-weensy hole in the needle where the thread is supposed to go. It wouldn't. "Dumb needle," I whispered impatiently. "I bet a man invented the sewing needle."

I found out that I need a new eyeglass prescription. Surely my eyes weren't getting worse. It's just that my glasses don't work as well as they used to! I took the needle and the thread onto my patio where the sun was shining brightly. Holding the needle at just the right angle, I took one more stab at the teensy-weensy hole. Ah! Success! That's more like it.

I looked at Sunshine's pantaloons with needle and thread ready and waiting. Nothing happened. "Yo, Baby, if there was ever a time I needed you, it's now." Still nothing happened. "Where are you when I need you, Baby? You know I'm doing this for you." Still nothing.

I waited . . . and waited . . . and waited. Suddenly, a streak of genius flashed through my mind. Why not sew the pantaloons directly onto the body of Sunshine? They would *never* come down then. With my needle in one hand and Sunshine and her pantaloons in the other, I proceeded to do just that. When I was finished, I looked at my creation. Marvelous! The new "industrial strength" Sunshine and her pantaloons could survive even a Timex commercial. Sunshine's pantaloons were tug-proof, drop-proof, and even, peekaboo-proof! I was certain that Baby was very, very proud of me. *I* sure was!

I took Sunshine to my next therapy session. Showing my brilliant job to New Lady, I waited for some eloquent words of praise and adulation for my handiwork. "Oh, yes," she said in a monotone voice. "They'll never come off, will they?" I thought, That's it? They'll never come off? I reminded myself of how proud Baby was of me. She was there when I sewed Sunshine's pantaloons on. She saw how hard I had worked. I have since passed down a new edict to my therapists. No one is to get Baby anything with pants that can come off!

You know what? Sunshine also had two pigtails of braided hair. Guess what happened to one of them? Uh huh. Did I try to braid it? Nope. Not me. Not this time. Those honors went to New Lady this time around.

Me-Baby

An entire chapter wouldn't give Me-Baby the honor she deserves. If I awakened to a raging fire in my apartment, I just know that neither Baby nor I would get out without first finding Me-Baby. And if Baby and I were about to die from smoke inhalation, guess who would get the oxygen first? Yep. I can hear it now. "Fireman, Me-Baby deaded? Put air on her. She no breathe." Believe me, Me-Baby is that important to Baby.

Me-Baby came as a Christmas present from Dr. Lady. She is a Cabbage Patch Preemie with the bluest eyes and the happiest smile ever. When I first saw her, I was tempted to ask Baby if she would share her with me.

Uh oh! I peeked under Me-Baby's pants. There were *real* diapers on her bottom with just stick-on tape holding them in place. I had a vision of me re-diapering Me-Baby about twenty times a day—maybe more. "Dr. Lady, this is definitely not going to work."

Baby took Me-Baby and tried to look between her legs. Me-Baby was wearing an infant sack that newborns come home from the hospital in. Baby's face lit up. This was even better than pants. No one could ever get to Me-Baby's bottom. Me-Baby was most definitely the safest baby in the whole wide world.

The bonding between Baby and Me-Baby was instantaneous. My therapists have told me it was a joy to behold. I often wish that I could be there at the same time Baby is so I could see and hear the sights and sounds of Baby tending to Me-Baby.

I have to admit that I, also, have bonded to Me-Baby. I've often held her, patting her on her back, and rocking her. Baby has asked Dr. Lady on more than one occasion to talk to me about Me-Baby. "Lauren hold Me-Baby. She cry on Me-Baby head and make Me-Baby all wet. You tell Lauren no cry on Me-baby head." But I have learned that in caring for Me-Baby, I am also caring for the child in me. So, from time to time, I allow myself to hold Me-Baby and let the tears come.

I find Me-Baby in the strangest of places. I'm writing this book in the fall, in the winter, in the spring, in the summer—have I left out any of the seasons? It's been forever, I think. But now it is summer, and it is hot. I've been walking a couple of miles a day around the park to get the cobwebs out of my brain. In the course of my walking, I've been getting quite a suntan. I think this may be my first one. The lines of demarcation are like the difference between night and day. I've been showing off my suntan to my therapists. Perhaps Baby has been listening to me talking about my suntan. It just makes sense; she listens to everything else I say. I think she thinks that everyone should have a suntan, not excluding Me-Baby.

Dr. Lady had purchased a sunsuit for Me-Baby. Baby had been complaining that it was too hot out for Me-Baby's infant sack. Besides, I had put Me-Baby's other outfits in a safe place; so safe, in fact, that even I couldn't find them after searching for them exhaustively. Hence, the purchase of the new outfit. Get this. The sunsuit is backless! Perfect for a suntan, wouldn't you say?

A few days ago, I couldn't find Me-Baby. In the evening, I opened the french door that opens onto the patio to enjoy the cooler air. There was Me-Baby, lying face down on the top of the table. At first, I was irritated. After all, I liked Me-Baby, too. I didn't want her to get baked from the sun. Then the thought came to me that perhaps Baby had put Me-Baby face down so she could get a suntan on her back. Baby is no dummy! If she had heard me bragging about my suntan, I bet she thought it would be good for Me-Baby, too.

I checked out my thoughts with Dr. Lady about why Baby had put Me-Baby on the table. Dr. Lady confirmed what I had thought. A couple of weeks ago, Baby had shown Dr. Lady how Me-Baby's back had no clothes on and remarked that she wanted her to get "brown" like Lauren.

Dr. Lady went on to say that at our last therapy session, Baby brought Me-Baby back. "Why Me-Baby no get brown like Lauren?" she asked. "Me put Me-Baby in sun. She still white. What me do wrong, Mommy?" Dr. Lady suggested to her that it would be better if Me-Baby stayed inside where she wouldn't get so hot. So far, I haven't found Me-Baby on the patio, but I do check to see if she's there when the sun begins to bake everything in sight.

Fluffy

I went to the mall at Easter time to run an errand. I usually go into Pier One Imports. Their stores are always so colorful, and I enjoy just browsing around. I've always felt that Pier One Imports was a "safe" store, because I've never seen any stuffed animals in it.

It was a Saturday when I walked in, fully expecting to enjoy looking at all of their unique wares when *Bam*! I was greeted by a whole row of stuffed animals—all of them white, fluffy Easter bunnies. Whoa! This is definitely not the best idea! I thought. Stuffed animals are not the thing Baby needs to see. I started to turn around, but these bunnies were the cutest I had ever seen.

Oh, how I wanted to pick one up! They had long, long ears and the undersides of their ears were as pink as their noses. Their feet were pointing up in a sitting position. They were absolutely irresistible, but I knew that I could not, I must not, I dared not give in. I knew that Baby would want one, and I definitely could not afford a bunny that cost sixteen dollars and ninety-five cents. I promptly turned around and exited the store.

It was too late. Apparently I hadn't exited fast enough. At my next therapy session, Baby went to work right away. She doesn't mess around when she wants something! Baby had some very important information to tell Dr. Lady. "Mommy," Baby yelled, "me want bunny me see store. Lauren no get bunny. She say she no money. You get me bunny?"

When Dr. Lady got Baby calmed down and told her that she would talk to Lauren to find out about the bunny, Baby was happy. At the end of the session, Dr. Lady asked me about a bunny that Baby had seen. My only thought at that moment was that it wasn't safe to go *anywhere* anymore. I explained my experience at Pier One Imports. Dr. Lady responded by saying that she would see what she could do.

From then on, Baby was constantly phoning Dr. Lady to ask if she had gotten the bunny yet. Each time, Dr. Lady answered, "Not yet, but I will." Baby didn't like that answer. She gave strict instructions to her. "Better hurry. They be all gone." As softhearted as Dr. Lady is, she went to Pier One Imports and bought a bunny just in time for Easter.

The day arrived for Baby to get her bunny. Dr. Lady had set the bunny on the floor of her waiting room. I opened the door. Evidently, the first thing Baby and I saw was the cutest bunny we ever had seen. Dr. Lady told me later that simultaneously she heard a thump (Baby landing on the floor) and a squeal of delight.

Dr. Lady opened the door. "Me get bunny. Me get bunny," Baby repeated over and over. "Dis bunny me see store. See, Mommy, he have pink ears and pink nose. See? See?" Dr. Lady admitted to me that this bunny was the cutest one she had ever seen, too.

"However, don't ever get me into Pier One Imports again," she warned.

"Why?" I asked.

"Because I wasn't content to just get the bunny for Baby. I couldn't get out of the store without buying an outfit for myself!" I laughed and said, "Look at it this way. You made two people happy by going into the store, Baby and yourself."

Baby promptly named the bunny "Fluffy." Fluffy has his own place of prominence on a green canvas-back director's chair. Just a few days ago, Baby informed Dr. Lady that she feeds Fluffy that "orange stuff" that Lauren eats. "Lauren say it good for bunnies," explained Baby. Dr. Lady thought for a few seconds. "Oh, you mean carrots?"

"Yeah, me feed Fluffy carrots."

What can I say? Fluffy probably eats better than Baby and I!

My menagerie continues to grow as I continue to heal. At first, I viewed my growing menagerie with a feeling of, "Oh, God. Not another alter," but given time, I have grown to cherish my menagerie. Each member of my menagerie marks another step forward in my journey to healing.

6

The Wit and Wisdom
of Baby

Baby is a stand-up comedian. One cannot listen to her for very long without at least chuckling. I had no idea how funny she was until the select few persons Baby has felt free to share with began to tell me about Baby's wit and wisdom.

At last, here's something to smile about in my writing! I hope you enjoy these anecdotes about Baby as much as I have learned to enjoy them.

On the Subject of Trees

I was again visiting my friend Lyn. We were chatting about any number of inconsequential subjects when suddenly Baby came out—for no apparent reason. Lyn noticed that the look on my face had suddenly changed. She had talked with Baby enough to recognize that Baby had come out and that she was looking at something she had spotted through the sliding glass patio doors.

"What are you frightened of?" Lyn asked, noticing the fear reflected on Baby's face. Baby answered by getting up and walking to the glass doors. Lyn opened them. Baby walked out and pointed to a metal stake that was about three feet long. She pointed at the sharp end.

"What that?" she asked fearfully. "For hurt babies?"

"Oh no," Lyn quickly replied, realizing that Baby must be thinking that it was some sort of torture device. "I don't ever hurt babies. This is a tree feeder."

Baby looked puzzled. "A what?"

"Look, Baby. This end has a sharp point on it so it can be put into the dirt next to a tree. See the holes? Water comes out of the holes in the ground so the roots of the tree can drink water."

Baby began to laugh. Lyn's explanation must have sounded a bit preposterous to Baby. "Trees no can drink water," she announced, giggling.

"Oh yes they do," Lyn answered, trying to be serious. "Look here at the other end." On the other end was a small plastic container. "And this is where I put the food for the tree."

That was going too far for Baby. Baby wasn't *that* dumb! She thought my friend was trying to put one over on her. Baby put her head back and giggled and giggled.

Exhibiting her amazing wit and wisdom, Baby pointed to one of the trees in my friend's back yard and said, in a scholarly tone, "Trees no drink water. Trees no eat food. Trees don't got no mouths!"

What can I say? Baby will be Baby!

On the Subject of Earthquakes

Some time ago, the Southern California area was rocked by a six-point-plus earthquake. I live in an apartment complex several floors above the ground. For several seconds, I and everything in my apartment shook violently.

Most of us who live in California are used to earthquakes and take them as something that comes with the territory. Unless they're of a high magnitude, we just ride them out and then go about our business as usual. Not Baby.

Shortly after the earthquake, I received a phone call. "Hi Lauren. This is Dr. Lady. I need to talk to Baby."

"Why?" I asked. "What did she do *this* time?"

Dr. Lady gave her usual chuckle. "Well, Baby just called and left a message on my answering machine. She said that the earthquake frightened her. She wanted to inform me that the bad guys are after you. She said the bad guys made your building shake to scare you."

What can I say? Baby will be Baby!

On the Subject of Big Words

Integrity

Lyn was talking to Baby. She used the word "integrity" in a sentence. On second thought, she decided that it might be wise to ask Baby if she knew what the word "integrity" meant. "Do you know what the word 'integrity' means or is that too big a word for you?"

Baby was silent for a moment. She didn't like not knowing anything! She was always quick to point out that she was a very smart baby. "Yeah, me am smart," she would always say.

It took only a few seconds for the look on Baby's face to change from one of deep thought to the "I know" look. "Yeah! Like shampoo?" she asked. My friend had to think about that one for a minute trying to figure out what shampoo and the word "integrity" had in common. When she finally got it, she began to laugh. She realized that Baby was referring to the TV commercial that advertised the shampoo, Tegrin.

What can I say? Baby will be Baby!

Pathetic

Lyn was again explaining something to Baby and in one of her sentences, she used the word "pathetic." Again she thought that she was speaking over a four-year-old's understanding, and again came the question, "Baby, do you know what the word 'pathetic' means?"

Baby didn't have to think about this one. She knew right off the bat.

"Me know. Like noodles," she announced proudly.

Lyn really had to think about this one. After all, the words "integrity" and "Tegrin" at least sounded something alike. But "pathetic" and "noodles"? No way! This time, it was my friend who had to take time out to think.

Baby crossed her arms and smiled smugly. She thought it was funny that she had stumped Lyn. I imagine Baby was thinking that my friend was pretty dumb.

"You no get it?" Baby asked. "You know. Like noodles," she said just a little louder and a little slower than the first time. I think Baby thought that if she said it a second time my friend would be sure to get it. But alas, my friend continued to remain silent. "Ah!" She finally figured it out. "You mean like pasta, pasta noodles?"

"You right! Pasta noodles," Baby exclaimed. "See, me know." Lyn answered that she was right. She wouldn't think of bursting Baby's balloon. Well, at least pasta was closer to the word "pathetic" than noodles were.

What can I say? Baby will be Baby!

On the Subject of Doggies

As I was driving down a busy street several weeks ago, I noticed a large dog. However, this dog was standing upright on two feet waving at all the passing cars, trying to entice drivers to stop at a car dealership!

The doggy costume the man was wearing was darling. It was made of two shades of brown. The head had big eyes and long floppy ears.

All of the new cars on the lot had brightly colored balloons tied to them. By now, I knew enough about Baby to know that she found things like balloons and stuffed animals irresistible. A frightening feeling began to overwhelm me as I wondered how Baby would react if she noticed the man in the doggie costume. Gripping the steering wheel tighter, I quickly turned my head away from the man and glued my eyes on the road. Too late! Baby seldom missed a thing. A very tall doggie standing on two feet waving at her with multiple brightly colored balloons wafting in the air was impossible for her not to see.

Several days later, at the end of my next therapy session, I found myself holding a silver foil balloon on a stick. It was yellow with red hearts making a circle around the words, "I LOVE YOU." Dr. Lady had added the words "BABY XOXOX."

As on so many occasions before, I had to ask Dr. Lady why I was holding a balloon. Dr. Lady confirmed my worst fear. Baby had not only noticed the doggie and the balloons at the car dealership the other day, but she had phoned Dr. Lady when I got home to inform her that I refused to stop and get her one of the balloons. To appease Baby's great distress, Dr. Lady had bought her a balloon and had given it to her during the therapy session.

I sighed to myself and thought, Oh great. What's going to come next? And just as I had thought about Bear, I wondered how I would get to my car holding a balloon on a stick without becoming totally embarrassed.

It was on a Monday that Baby had been given the balloon. As the days of the week passed, I soon had not only forgotten about the balloon, but I had somehow managed to put the man in the doggie costume out of my mind. That is, until Saturday rolled around again and I was driving down the same street. There was the man in the doggie costume again. I wondered if I should speed up, make a U-turn in the middle of the block or dare to continue driving and hazard the slight possibility that Baby wouldn't notice the doggie this time.

Suddenly, I thought that if I quickly waved at the man he would most likely wave back, making Baby a very happy baby. I didn't slow down as I waved to him. In fact, I speeded up. Nevertheless, the man did notice me waving. He stooped over and waved back. If only you knew who you are *really* waving at, I thought to myself.

I was pretty proud of myself. After all, I had finally made an effort to tend to the needs of Baby. I heaved a sigh of relief. Now, I don't have to worry about driving by the car dealership on weekends any longer, I silently said to myself.

This past weekend, I had no qualms about driving by the costumed man. If he was still there waving to passersby, it would be no sweat. After all, I had taken care of Baby. She wouldn't ask for more . . . would she?

As I neared the car dealership once again, I realized that I was putting on the brakes. My car came to a stop beside the curb . . . right in front of the car dealership . . . and right in front of the "doggie"!

I would have to wait until my next therapy session to find out what happened between my car stopping *at* the curb and my driving *away from* the curb, except for the fact that a brightly colored helium-filled balloon was now floating in the car as I drove away. I just kept repeating the words, "Oh no! Oh no! Oh no!"

Therapy day finally came. I told Dr. Lady my story about Baby and the doggie. "Please, Dr. Lady, find out what happened between Baby and the man in the costume." I knew that only Dr. Lady could get Baby to fill in the loss of time for me. The following is Baby's recounting of her visit with the doggie.

"Doggie came to car. Me ask for balloon. He give me one. Me tell him me know he doggie. He tell me he man. But me smart! Me know he doggie. Then me say, 'Bye, bye,' and Lauren drive car away."

After hearing what Baby had to say, I thought, Oh God, no! I'm never again going to drive on that street on a weekend. I was sharing this adventure with a friend today. She gave me some wonderful advice on a tactic I should follow if, perchance, I forgot about not driving on, you know, "that" street on a weekend. "It's really simple, Lauren," she said with a twinkle in her voice. "Just say, 'Yo, Baby. Sit tight. I'll get a balloon for you. *Just don't talk to the doggie'!*"

What can I say? Baby will be Baby!

On the Subject of Candy

Lyn and I discovered together what Baby's favorite edible item is, with the exception of chocolate chip cookies. Thank God I didn't know what was going on at the time. At the time this happened, which was in the beginning of my learning that I have multiple personalities, I wasn't all that sure if I ever wanted to develop co-consciousness with Baby. Baby is so much more brave and fearless than the other alters. I wasn't used to not being *there* or *here* or *wherever* I go when Baby comes out. (Not, I remind you, that I'm comfortable with it now.) However, I think a therapy session with Baby on the subject of discretion would be in order. Do you think a four-year-old would understand what the word "discretion" is?

Anyway, Lyn and I were at the Price Club. The Price Club is a huge discount warehouse, a warehouse full of food items. Baby might add, "and candy. Lots of candy. Whole bunches of candy." I can just imagine that Baby felt as if she was in Fantasyland.

As soon as we entered the warehouse, we were met with the sight of mountains and piles of cans and bags and cartons and everything else a gigantic food warehouse has. Baby's eyes focused on the food right away. My friend later told me what followed.

She was getting groceries for her family. I was just along for the ride. I've never seen so many aisles with so much food in my life. In the Price Club, one doesn't buy a *can* of something. One buys a *case* of something. We finally reached the candy section. There were bins and boxes and stacks of candy. "Me like candy!" Baby announced, picking up a bag of M & Ms. "Me have dis?"

"Sure, Baby. Just put it in the cart for now and I'll get it for you." Baby was a little hesitant to surrender her prize possession, but she finally dropped the bag into the cart.

Lyn tried to go about her chore of walking down what seemed to be miles of aisles. But after several moments, she looked behind her. I was nowhere to be found. Up and down the aisles . . . there I was. No, that's not correct. There *Baby* was, half the store away, loading her arms with all kinds of candy. Lyn watched as Baby came chugging towards her trying to make it to her grocery cart before any of the candy dropped. "Me have dis too?"

"Well, Baby," she said as she eyed the bounty, "that's a lot of candy. That's enough for now. You stay with me now so you don't get lost."

It took no longer than a few minutes more for Lyn to notice that I had deserted her again. She took one look in the direction of the candy section. There was Baby, staring at the candy. Before we had a repeat of the last incident, my friend turned her cart around and headed for the candy section full steam ahead. She was ready for the same question from Baby. Before Baby could ask the question, my friend answered her. "We can't get everything." That wasn't what Baby wanted to hear. "Me give you some. Me give Lauren some."

"Okay, One more bag. What do you want?" Baby chose another bag of M & Ms. It amazed my friend when Baby held up her hands and said, "See. Dis candy no stick hands." Proof positive that television commercials influence children!

What can I say? Baby will be Baby!

On the Subject of Parks

Evidently, Baby had been noticing other children playing in parks we drove by from time to time. She began to hound New Lady about taking her to the park. She wanted to play with the other kids. When New Lady approached me on the subject, I didn't have to even think. You see, to anyone who would be looking on, *Baby* wouldn't be in the park playing with three- and four-year-olds. *I* would be in the park playing with three- and four-year-olds. "No way, Jose," I emphatically declared. "I'll stay right here in your office, and you can take Baby to the park!"

After much persuasion and talks on how important it was for me to let Baby experience new things, I finally gave in, but I was none too thrilled. I told New Lady that everyone would think that I was retarded. She said, "That's all right."

"That's easy for you to say," I commented. "You're not the middle-aged woman who will be acting like a four-year-old sitting in a sandbox!"

The big day came. Park day! What can I say? Baby was ecstatic. I was scared half to death! We arrived at the park. "Oh, goodie," I said out loud in the privacy of my car. "Just what I need." The park was full of kids. I mean *full* of kids!

"We" got out of the car. I went away, and Baby took over. New Lady said that Baby had the time of her life. New Lady taught her how to swing. Baby wanted to play on the teeter-totter, but she was afraid of it. So New Lady nixed that. She moved on to a moving bridge. The child climbs up some big steps and stands on these boards that move. I presume it is sort of like the foot bridges you see in movies that span rivers. New Lady said that Baby hung on the ropes on either side of the bridge and Baby did her thing. She giggled and kept saying. "Mommy, look. Me can do it. Me do good! Me have fun!" Then New Lady bought Baby an ice cream bar. Baby kept scrunching up her face and saying, "Ooh, it cold!"

I was relieved when New Lady informed me that Baby talked in a softer voice at the park. She said that it was as if Baby sensed that she shouldn't yell quite as loudly as she usually does when she talks. "Thank God for small favors," I whispered under my breath.

I felt bad when New Lady said that Baby was hurt because she couldn't play with the other kids. Baby wants playmates so badly. When it came time to leave, guess who didn't want to go? "When we go again?" Baby asked. "Soon. After Lauren finishes writing her new book." When New Lady shared that piece of information with me, I decided that it might just take another ten years for me to finish this book!

Baby couldn't wait to talk to her other mommy. When we got to her office, the first thing Baby did was to show Dr. Lady how well she did on the bridge that moved. She showed her how she bent her knees to make the bridge move. In her own irresistible way, Baby declared excitedly, "Mommy, I did so good. I did it 'badder and badder'!"

Dr. Lady joined in Baby's enthusiasm. I guess Baby took her enthusiasm as a signal that maybe *she* would like to take her to the park, too. Dr. Lady told me about the conversation. She is not a "taking Baby to the park" kind of person. My therapists compliment each other beautifully. The park was most definitely for New Lady. The park was most definitely *not* for Dr. Lady, but Baby really pushed, and Dr. Lady gave in. When she told me that she had reluctantly agreed to take Baby to the park the next time, I suggested that perhaps we could go at 3:00 AM when it would be deserted. Dr. Lady took to that idea. It was probably the best idea I had come up with all year.

"Oh, by the way, you'll love this one," she said as she laughed.

"Love what one?"

"After I told Baby that I would take her to the park, she said, 'I'll hold you to it'!"

What can I say? Baby will be Baby!

On the Subject of Her New Friend, Scott

I never had realized just how much Baby pays attention to everything. Everything I say and do and who I'm with and everything else about my life. Scott and his family have been good friends to me. Apparently Baby was aware of their kindness to me.

Scott and his family live in another state so I try to limit my calls to once a month or so. Scott's phone number is programmed into the last button. Evidently, Baby had learned in watching over a period of the last year, that if the last button was pushed, Scott would answer the phone.

About a month ago, I got a call from Scott rather late in the evening. "I hear you went for a drive today," he remarked. "How did you know?" He began to laugh. "Baby called me tonight." I couldn't believe it. Scott and his wife have a speakerphone attached to their telephone. They also have a boy and a girl just a little younger than Baby. Scott said that his children never pay attention to the phone calls, but when they heard Baby's voice over the speakerphone, they came running into the room and attentively listened to every word. He said that they were both engrossed with Baby's voice.

"Lauren, Baby is a real four-year-old. I felt as if I were talking to a four-year-old child."

"You were, Scott," I reminded him although I was still getting used to the idea myself.

"Lauren, Baby laughs just like my son Timothy laughs. Both Timothy and Amanda laughed with Baby. Lauren, you were a real four-year-old. Children respond to children, and my children were right there with you, or Baby, I mean."

"Scott, how in the world did Baby know you?" I asked. He said that Baby kept saying, "Me know you long, long time." The next morning Scott's wife asked little Amanda if the person she had listened to on the phone the night before was a big person or a little person. She said that Amanda laughed like that was a stupid question. "Baby's a little person like me!" She also said that Amanda is waiting for Baby to call again.

Back to the end of the phone call that night. I asked Scott how the conversation ended. Scott said, "Baby is sure in tune with you. She said, 'Me hang up now. Lauren be mad if me talk too long.'"

What can I say? Baby will be Baby!

On the Subject of Santa Claus

It was Christmas time. I wanted to let Baby experience her first Christmas. So I went to the mall to see Santa Claus. No, don't worry. I didn't sit on his lap. Rather, I sat on a bench and watched as the little children climbed onto Santa's lap. I whispered, "Baby, this one's for you." It was hard for me. I kept brushing tears from my face. I'm sure that Baby was longing to sit on Santa's lap like the other children. I began to question if this had been such a good idea after all. I didn't want to show Baby a new experience and then have her not be able to do what the other children were doing. So I got up and drove back home.

At my next therapy session, Dr. Lady get an earful about Santa. She wisely got out a piece of paper and wrote down everything that Baby wanted from Santa. The list basically boiled down to that white bear with the fat belly. I think Baby had everyone she knew combing the toy stores for this bear. She had even torn a page out of a magazine that had an ad for a white bear on it and gave it to Dr. Lady. When Dr. Lady showed it to me, I wondered where *we* got the magazine from and if *we* had paid for it.

That reminds me. Lyn heard me use the "we" word

for the first time. "Are you referring to yourself as 'we' now?" I guess that was the first sign of my accepting myself as a multiple.

Back to Santa Claus. With Santa and Christmas presents on Baby's mind, I imagine she didn't miss much. There were Christmas trees, Christmas ornaments, Christmas music, and Christmas lights. Christmas was everywhere.

I couldn't resist going into a little shop in the mall that specialized in hand-painted anything you wanted on a variety of ornaments. I looked and looked. I wanted to get a very special ornament for Baby. The minute my eyes rested on one particular ornament, I knew that it was the one that I would give to Baby. It was a green wreath with two red hearts. A teddy bear with a bright red bow around his neck was holding onto the wreath. A cream-colored scroll crossed the bottom of the wreath. I picked it up and held it to my heart. Baby, this is for you, I thought to myself.

I stood in line, waiting for the lady who was doing the hand painting on the customer's ornaments. I looked at the ornament and wondered what I should have the lady print on it. Two hearts. Baby has two mommies. Suddenly, before I had it all thought out, I heard the lady asking me, "Yes? You're next. What do you want me to print on your ornament?" I laid the ornament on the table. The words just blurted out. "I want the word 'Mommy' on each heart. On the scroll at the bottom I want '1991 — To Baby.'"

I couldn't wait to get home to pick a special place to hang Baby's ornament. I found it. I hung it on a wall where Baby could look at it every day of the year. The thought hadn't occurred to me that my cat Maxwell might think the ornament was for him. He kept stretching his long legs out to paw it. So I picked him up, put him in my lap, and told him about Baby. Yep. I really did that. I took him to the ornament and told him that this was especially for Baby. Then I showed him all the toys that were scattered on the floor—of which he has plenty. Miracle of miracles. Maxwell hasn't touched the ornament since. Every once in awhile, I look at Baby's first Christmas ornament. In my heart, I hope that Baby is looking at it, too.

Back to Santa. Dr. Lady received another of her famous collection of messages from Baby on her answering machine. This time the message said, "Mommy. Dis Baby! You no can go place me see Santa. He no there now. He on street. He wave me when Lauren go by in car. Me wave Santa, too. If you want see him, you have go street. No go other place. He move."

What can I say? Baby will be Baby!

And the Clincher of Them All

About a week after the embarrassing doggie incident, I again was driving down that street on a Saturday. Yes, right by "you know who." I was careful to stay on the inside lane, and I allowed a couple of cars to drive beside me on the outside lane. I had hoped they would block Baby's view of the man in the doggie costume. Apparently not!

When I arrived at the mall, I found out that no less than a million other people had arrived before me! It took me at least fifteen minutes to find a parking space. I have a handicapped person's placard, but even the blue handicapped spaces were taken. Unfortunately, I forgot to make a mental note of where I finally found an empty parking space. (More about that later!)

As I began to meander around the mall, a little bit of magic sparked in my heart. The spirit of Christmas was everywhere. People were bustling about. Some were laden down with boxes and sacks. Children were ecstatic. Many of them were tugging at their mommy's or their daddy's leg pleading, "Take me in here. Buy me a toy."

Usually I'd hear the bedraggled parent answer, "Honey, we've bought enough toys. It's time to go home now." Then I'd hear a whimper of protest from a very tired little boy or girl who was being firmly towed along by a hand that was holding onto the child.

I didn't even think of Baby. *I should have!* She was apparently noticing all the brightly wrapped presents that others were carrying. I came to one of those "we have everything you'd ever want to buy for Christmas" stores and stopped to look at the window display. **Big mistake!** The last thing I recall is seeing an enormously large white stuffed bear . . .

The next thing I remember was hearing a loud siren wailing nonstop. A security guard was by my side in not more than a few seconds. I looked around to see what all the commotion was about. Evidently the trouble was *me* for the guard had me by the arm and was escorting me to the store's office.

Once inside, the guard asked me why I had not paid for the stuffed animal. Boy, was I angry! *"What dog?"* I asked indignantly. "The dog you have under your arm. What do you think, I'm dumb?" he asked. I glanced under my left arm, and there it was—a small brown dog with long floppy ears. I thought, Oh no! and I lost time again . . .

Then I remember the guard ushering me to the cashier and asking me to pay for the dog—$6.95 plus tax. As I walked out of the store with my head hung down, I knew, *I just knew* that Baby was at the bottom of this fiasco. I was so upset at her that as I walked to the parking lot, all I could see were acres and acres of nondescript automobiles. I had no idea where I had parked my car.

I was ready to give a piece of my mind to Baby right then and there. She had embarrassed and humiliated me, not to mention scaring me to death! And now, the one thing I wanted to do the most, to get to the safety of my home, I couldn't even do, because my car was lost somewhere in an incredibly immense maze of cars. It was not all that difficult to blame the whole thing on Baby.

I walked back to the Broadway Department Store. I just stood there. I must have had that "I'm lost, my car is lost, and I don't know in what direction I should point my feet" look.

A sales lady came up to me. Evidently I wasn't the first person she had ever seen with that "I'm lost" look, because she softly, almost pitifully asked, "Dear, are you having trouble finding your car?"

"Oh yes," I replied. At that moment, I felt that this lady was my last hope in retaining my sanity. "I don't even know if my car is at this end of the mall or at the other end where the May Company is."

"Well, honey, I think I can help you. I've helped a lot of people who don't remember where they parked their cars." I remember thinking that this lady was truly a saint sent from above! And she was, because she methodically named all the streets that surrounded the mall and she helped me figure out along which street side my car was parked. I could not have thanked her more, and I could not have been more relieved than when I settled into the driver's seat and slammed the door shut.

"Ah, peace at last," I sighed. But I was still plenty mad at Baby. I felt like taking the dog back to the store, but I didn't—for two reasons. I had no idea at what store the dog had been purchased, and I wasn't about to risk another Baby episode! So I drove home in total silence. I think Baby knew it was for her good, maybe even for her life, to keep quiet.

Once home, I finally looked at this stuffed animal that had almost gotten me arrested for shoplifting. I had to admit that it was cute. And I noticed that it looked a little like the doggie man who always waved at us as we drove by each Saturday.

When I looked at the price tag and saw that the dog had been marked down from $12.95 to the sale price of $6.95, I was very thankful that Baby hadn't wanted the enormously large dog I had seen in the store window. I was sure that the price tag on that dog must have been $150 or more! "At least you know a bargain when you see one, Baby," I said with relief.

My nerves began to calm down, and my anger began to subside. As I was setting the doggie on the sofa, Dr. Lady called to see how I was doing. I must have sounded frantic. "Dr. Lady, you've got to talk to Baby before we all go to jail one of these times."

"What happened?" she asked. I related my almost "too-terrible-to-tell" story. Dr. Lady laughed intermittently as I got to points in the story that I suppose would seem humorous to someone who had not just gone through my trauma. "It's not funny, Dr. Lady. This is serious!"

"I know, Lauren," she responded. "But I'm sure Baby wasn't trying to get you in trouble. Let me talk to Baby, and I'll find out what happened." The last thing I heard was Dr. Lady asking if she could talk to Baby . . .

It couldn't have been more than a few minutes when I heard Dr. Lady calling, "Lauren."

"Yeah, I'm here," I answered dryly. "What happened?"

"Well, it seems that Baby found a dog that looks like the man who waves at her. She picked it up and put it under your arm. You began to walk out of the store without paying for it."

"No, no, Dr. Lady. *I* did not walk out of the store without paying for it. *Baby* walked out of the store without paying for it."

"Well, anyway," Dr. Lady continued amusedly, "it was Baby who talked to the security guard in the store office."

Swell, I thought. I couldn't wait for Dr. Lady to continue. (If you believe that, then I have a piece of swampland to sell you!)

"The security guard asked you why you were trying to steal the stuffed animal and didn't you know the legal ramifications of shoplifting?" Of course, this poor man was expecting a woman to answer. Instead, he got a four-year-old. Lucky man!

Baby piped up excitedly, "Me want doggie like doggie wave me on street. Me take doggie home." As Dr. Lady paused for a moment, I began to remember bits and pieces of my being in that office.

I have no idea what the guard's response was, and I'm not sure I want to know. I am sure that if he had tried to take the doggie away from Baby, there would have been a tug-of-war and a very unhappy Baby sitting on the floor crying her heart out.

Somewhere between the office and the cashier, I came to the rescue. I vaguely remember the guard ushering me to the cashier, and I remember shelling out a ten-dollar bill and receiving some change back.

"I explained to Baby that she couldn't just take something she wanted without paying for it," Dr. Lady continued. "Baby protested that restriction. Baby said, 'Lauren no buy me what me want. She say she have no money.'" I thought to myself, You got that right, Baby!

Dr. Lady told Baby that the next time she saw something she wanted, to tell her and she would tell Lauren. Then Lauren could buy it for her. I thought, Oh great! Every week, Dr. Lady is going to be presented with a verbal list of toys that Baby wants. Then what am I going to do? It did seem that since this was Dr. Lady's idea, perhaps *she* could buy the toys!

With each passing day, the likelihood of my wearing a dog tag that says, "If I turn into a four-year-old, please call my therapist," looms larger. Dr. Lady has promised that she will come and rescue me if she is ever called, but

I have the feeling that she thinks I'm only kidding. *I'm not!*

Dr. Lady's last words to me were, "This one is for your book."

My last words were, "Yeah, and who would believe it?"

What can I say? Baby will be Baby!

On the Subject of Careers

"I want to grow up and help kids and grown-ups like Lauren do."

What can I say? Baby will be Baby, and I am deeply moved.

PART THREE

7

Mind Control

**". . . but these methods will never work
on people of education and intelligence."**[1]

Pastor Richard Wurmbrand locked in a Romanian
Communist prison. His only crime—refusing to deny
his beliefs. Fifty pounds of chains on his feet. Tortured
with red-hot pokers. Spoonfuls of salt forced down his
throat. Starved. Beaten on the soles of his feet continu-
ously with a rubber club. Beaten on the back until four
vertebrae were broken. Eighteen holes carved into his
body. Handcuffs with sharp prongs piercing his wrists.

Squeezed into a tight-fitting wooden box with nails
driven into every side. Any movement within the box
meant the nails would pierce him. Thrown into a "refrigerator cell," an ice box so cold that frost and ice covered the inside. Tied to a cross that laid on the floor
while hundreds of prisoners were forced to relieve their
bodily wastes on his face and body. And yet with all of
this torture, he could not be broken! He clung to his beliefs with remarkable tenacity. He survived the unmen-
tionable, the unthinkable, the unbearable until . . . until
the brainwashing process began.

The prisoners were ignorant about brainwashing.
There was an intuitive sense that brainwashing worked
only on the weak or the uneducated. Radu Ghinde, a
well-known Christian writer, expressed the sentiments
of many political prisoners at the time by saying, "If they

[the Communists] haven't changed me in fifteen years, how will they do so now?"[2]

"When theories about brainwashing were being discussed one evening, Ghinde scoffed. 'Rubbish! Pavlov played tricks with the behavior patterns of dogs, and the Communists in Korea adapted some of his ideas to make American prisoners change sides—but these methods won't work on people of education and intelligence. We're not G.I.'s!' 'Nor dogs', said Daianu, a prominent poet, professor of mystical theology, who was serving a twenty-five-year sentence."[3]

But Richard Wurmbrand, who had resisted severe physical pain and abuse, ultimately called brainwashing "the most horrible torture."[4]

The Poison That Kills

The brainwashing in that prison began innocently enough—or so it seemed. This man who had survived the most horrible tortures imaginable at first spoke of the brainwashing methods as absurd. Remember that word, *absurd*.

At first there were the endless simple-minded lectures that lasted for hours. The same points were driven home over and over again. Then, the lectures were replaced by even simpler repetitious sentences. At first this tactic seemed even more mindless and ineffective than the lectures. Over loudspeakers that were heard in every cell came the words:

"Communism is good."

The voice grew louder with each repetition:

"Communism is good.
Communism is good.
Communism is good."[5]

Wurmbrand later said that although he could not

avoid the sound of the sentence repeated all day and all night, he tuned it out and became only partially conscious of the words. Yet when the loudspeaker was turned off, the words continued to ring in his head. He realized that the words had penetrated his mind.

> "Communism is good.
> Communism is good.
> Communism is good."

The loudspeakers began to blare once again:

> "Christianity is stupid.
> Christianity is stupid.
> Christianity is stupid.
> Why not give it up?
> Why not give it up?
> Why not give it up?
> Christianity is stupid.
> Christianity is stupid.
> Christianity is stupid.
> Why not give it up? . . ."[6]

This phase of the brainwashing progressed day after day. With each new set of simple but carefully worded sentences, the words began to assault the minds of even the hardiest, the most stubborn and strong-willed resisters.

> "Nobody believes in Christ now.
> Nobody believes in Christ now.
> Nobody believes in Christ now.
> No one goes to church.
> No one goes to church.
> No one goes to church.
> Give it up.
> Give it up.
> Give it up.
> Nobody believes in Christ now . . ."[7]

Time began to lose meaning. Hours, days, weeks, and months became just one endless monstrous day. The brainwashing was continued and increased in intensity.

Wurmbrand describes it vividly. "I recall one day clearly. They had given us postcards to invite our families to come and bring parcels. On the day named, I was shaved and washed and given a clean shirt. Hours passed. I sat in the cell, staring at the glittering white tiles, but no one came . . . I was not to know then that my postcard had never been sent . . . "[8]

The final assault was put into motion. The succession of declarations on the loudspeaker were the cruelest of all . . . and the most effective:

> "Nobody loves you now.
> Nobody loves you now.
> Nobody loves you now.
> They don't want to know you any more.
> They don't want to know you any more.
> They don't want to know you any more . . ."[9]

He records that although he could not bear to hear those words, he could not shut them out. To reinforce his disappointment, one of the lecturers lied to him and told him that other wives had come—that he was the fool—that he had been abandoned—and that his child had become an atheist who had no desire to see his father. Each sentence hit him harder. It would have been more merciful to have received physical blows to the body. To his sorely grieving heart and mind, the initial sentences were directed again. Day after day the speakers blared:

> "Christ is dead.
> Christ is dead.
> Christ is dead."[10]

It was the final straw. This man of steel, Pastor Richard Wurmbrand, had survived fourteen years of imprisonment and torture, spent three years in solitary confinement seeing no one but his torturers, had survived the heinous acts recounted above. But he finally succumbed to what he refers to as ". . . the soul-killing poison of the last and worst stage of brainwashing."[11]

Richard Wurmbrand now lives in the United States and is among the most admired men of our time. His courage has been recognized by governments and private citizens alike. Yet he once penned these most painful of words: "And in time I came to believe what they had told us for all these months. Christianity was dead!"[12]

No torture of the body alone could accomplish the goal of his tormentors. Ultimately, in this atmosphere of confinement and oppression, it was the endless repetition of simple sentences that penetrated and poisoned his mind. In a matter of months, Wurmbrand moved from calling such ideologies and strategies *absurd*, to giving in and accepting as truth that Christianity was dead.[13]

If Richard Wurmbrand, a mature and seasoned man of God, likened by many to Paul the Apostle, could not withstand the poison of brainwashing, what would happen to children subjected to the same tactics? Thousands of Croatian children fleeing the current war in the former Yugoslavia have travelled with their parents to Austria and Hungary. A short calculated message on television instilled dread and fear into the minds and hearts of many little children. A short TV spot stated that the Serbians systematically cut off the fingers of any Croatians they could find. Many of the Croatian children kept their hands firmly and fearfully in their pockets after hearing that message. One can only imagine what additional terror came to dwell with them because of that simple isolated lie told in the midst of terror and turmoil.[14]

We read over and over again the accounts of the children of Hitler's Germany, of Stalin's Russia, of Mao's China, of the Ayatollah's Iran, and Saddam Hussein's Iraq, and on and on and on . . . The combination of fear and the repetition of *absurd* lies continues to be an effective way to produce children who are "loyal" and terrified enough to obey the whims of those who choose to control them.

Brainwashing for What?

"Brainwashing" is a term that is used loosely in our society to refer to everything from Madison Avenue to Hollywood. There is the hyperbole of suggesting that we buy soap or vote for president based on mysterious and insidious influences.

Techniques of persuasion abound, but that should not keep us from recognizing that true brainwashing is a very real phenomenon in which an extreme degree of coercion can be brought to bear to control the thoughts and behavior of another. Wurmbrand is a good example. He was able to withstand extreme physical torture and degradation and keep his beliefs until he was subjected to brainwashing.

Brainwashing is used to produce profound change in the victim's belief system and thought processes to conform to the mind-set the perpetrators want to induce. Although the brainwashing messages at first may seem irrational and absurd to the victim, the process of brainwashing forces the victim to appear to abandon beliefs voluntarily.

Through the use of brainwashing and mind control, the survivor's cognitive beliefs are changed. Survivors believe . . .

- There is no escape.
- The cult controls me.
- I have no power.

- I am incapable of protecting myself.
- It is dangerous to remember what has been done to me.
- It is even more dangerous to tell.
- My life will forever be hopeless.

The circle of such beliefs produced by systematic brainwashing is reinforced by further abuses. Then there is participation which is followed by overwhelming guilt. The survivor feels destroyed. As the cult begins to take control of the survivor, he or she is conditioned, not only to *expect* further victimizations, but to *accept* further victimizations. The circle goes round and round. Where it stops nobody knows . . . until there is intervention.

Brainwashing and mind control are closely intertwined. If a person has not undergone some degree of brainwashing, their thoughts and actions are much harder to control. Conversely, if the victim has undergone brainwashing, their thoughts and actions are more easily controlled. People who have been traumatized or abused prior to being put into a brainwashing experience are all the more vulnerable to succumbing to the impact of such trauma.

Brainwashing leaves no outward scars. It leaves no gaping wounds. It is simply the most effective and perhaps the most simple way of owning a person.

Mind Control and Ritual Abuse

So what do these stories have to do with the story of my life. Quite simply, they *are* the story of my life and of the life of all victims of ritual abuse. I have openly shared the fact that my life has been profoundly affected by the horrors of ritual abuse. And I have tried to sound the alarm about what is happening to others. Some of my experiences were recounted in my first book, *Satan's Underground*. The most important purpose of that book, as perhaps of this one, was to expose the reality of ritual abuse—and its goal—the subjugation of its victims to the will of others.

Ritual abuse is a sophisticated mind control program being applied to children and adults. The Los Angeles County Task Force on Ritual Abuse describes it this way:

> "Ritual abuse is a brutal form of abuse . . . consisting of physical, sexual, and psychological abuse, and involving the use of rituals. . . . Mind control is the cornerstone of ritual abuse, the key element in the subjugation and silencing of its victims. Victims of ritual abuse are subjected to a rigorously applied system of mind control designed to rob them of their sense of free will and to impose upon them the will of the cult and its leaders."[15]

Control, Not Pleasure

One of the reasons that there is so much denial concerning the subject of ritual abuse is that there is a basic lack of understanding about its purpose and goals. I have heard critics of the stories of ritual abuse who dismiss the accounts because of a fundamental misunderstanding of what ritual abuse is about.

Many law enforcement officials who are quite knowledgeable about the sexual exploitation of children and adults have been baffled when it comes to ritual abuse. And this is understandable. The strength of these astute investigators is their ability to find patterns of behavior in what might seem random or simply revolting patterns of criminal behavior. Some are expert, for example, in serial killers and are able to predict the behaviors of severely disturbed people by carefully understanding patterns that would be foreign to a healthy mind. Their effectiveness comes from their ability to understand these patterns.

What might handicap some of these investigators in looking at ritual abuse is that they are looking for the wrong motive. Pleasure is not the motive here. Simple access to children and adults is not the motive. That can be achieved too easily with much less rigamarole. The motive here is control. Control over the long term. Ritual abuse is not just some method for silencing the children and discrediting their claims of "real crimes" being committed against them. In ritual abuse, sexual abuse is one of the tools, not the goal. The goal is control.

Thus, the purpose of ritual abuse is not the pleasure of the perpetrator. It is done to break the will and control the mind of the victim. The child's mind is the ultimate goal, not access to the body. When the will is destroyed and the child feels cut off from basic securities, the perpetrators are in a position to truly own that child and control the child's behavior.

Let's keep this in perspective. I know that it can sound preposterous to suggest that a child's mind can be bent by trauma at such an early age. Let me remind you of an even simpler concept. How many of you have been laughed at, taunted, or told that your nose is too big or that you have too many freckles or that you're too fat or that you have skinny legs or that you're . . . whatever it was that your peers or the adults in your life came up with. All of us have some such story to tell.

More importantly, have you been able to forget those unkind and harsh words? Have you been able to lose the feelings of hurt that they conjure up? Or do they all stick with you? I will bet you still remember them as if they were spoken to you just yesterday. If your husband tells you that you don't look like the woman he married . . . or if your wife keeps calling you a couch potato who is definitely not the man she married . . . do those words run off you like water runs off a duck's feathers, or do they stick to you like glue? And is something else triggered sometimes that makes the pain even worse?

Brainwashing does not have to be highly sophisticated to leave its mark. We've probably all been recipients to some degree of brainwashing. We just don't call it that. Words can be just as effective a weapon against the human will as a gun can be against the human body.

Some trauma is designed to insure the silence of the victim. When perpetrators ritually abuse children in preschools or day care centers without the knowledge of the family, then keeping the child from telling the family is crucial to continuing the abuse. When perpetrators tell a child, "If you tell our secret, we'll kill your cat," do you think the child will be able to tell? Especially if the child has witnessed the brutal killing of other animals by these people. When perpetrators say, "If you tell, we'll do to your little sister and brother what we did to you," do you think that child will be inclined to run home and tell the secret? Or will that child's deep love for their family and desire to protect them become part of the conspiracy of silence woven by perpetrators?

You Went Where? You Did What?

"Plane rides to Hawaii?" "Plane rides to China?" "Boat rides to secret islands?" "You were hurt by *whom*?" Children who have been victimized by ritual abuse sometimes tell stories that are beyond the bounds of credibility, reporting impossible trips or the presence of TV or movie celebrities as abusers. Even some adult victims tell stories that are so implausible as to make their credibility take a drastic plunge. Ah, yes! Just what the cult wants! *No one* can be so naive as to believe such allegations. "My child was at the preschool for four hours and some bad people took him to Hawaii and brought him back during those four hours? That could not have happened!" Some therefore dismiss all the disclosures of abuse altogether. Just because it was not possible for a child to have experienced some of the things the child reports, like plane rides, does not mean that that was not what the child truly experienced as what happened.

Sophisticated technology has been put to good use by cult perpetrators. The words I'm looking for are "simulation," "look-alike," "feel-alike," and "see-alike" technology. A simulator which reproduces what seems like reality. A simulator that can reproduce phenomena that is seen, heard, and/or felt.

Children are easily tricked to think they have been somewhere they have not. We have the new world of fast-changing visuals to thank for this. Have you heard of "Virtual Reality"? Articles are abounding on the market about "VR." *Discover* magazine, *Newsweek*, a new book titled, *Virtual Reality*, and even a movie, *The Lawnmower Man*, have the new frontier of VR exploding on the scene. Sophisticated and expensive VR video games can be found at some video arcades.

The trick of VR is that you're not just playing the game, you're not just looking at a screen, but in wearing the HMD (Head Mounted Display) and putting on the sensor wired gloves, you are in the game. You are there, wherever "there" is. Let's try to bring virtual reality back down to earth for a minute.

Children who have been ritually abused have been telling, in their own language, about screens, computers, images, sensations, pain, torture—in short, being changed into something else or someone else—for quite some time now. No amount of reasoning by Mommy and Daddy or therapist has been able to sway the children's stories. They state what they know to be true, and that is that!

The child who went to Hawaii and back. Impossible? Not with virtual reality and other forms of trickery. Boat rides to secret islands. Impossible? Not with virtual reality. "You were hurt by *whom*?" Impossible? Not with virtual reality. Anything is possible with virtual reality. Way out stuff? No longer!

Sam Donaldson on "Prime Time Live" did a segment on VR. He stated that "VR lets you travel to places you've never been, and see things you've never seen and do things you've never done without ever leaving the room. The goal of VR is simple. It's total submersion. Complete detachment from reality. You can be any size, any place at any time. You literally become a part of whatever you are creating. The issue is total escapism."[16]

Many of the articles I have read on VR express concern about the possibility of VR being used for unethical purposes. I grimace and nod my head each time I read of another scientist expressing such concerns. I know these concerns to be all too appropriate!

Howard Rheingold in his book *Virtual Reality* states that ". . . as VR simulations grow more realistic, their potential for being dangerously misleading also increases."[17] "The danger of more and more realism is that if you don't have corresponding truthfulness, you teach people things that aren't so."[18] Well said, Mr. Rheingold.

Come On, You've Got to Be Kidding!

Kids are having a field day with the inventions our new technology is bringing to them. It is impossible to keep up with the newest game on the block. I heard an advertisement before Christmas that said, "Don't just *play* Nintendo. *Be* Nintendo." It advertised 3D, super graphics, the whole nine yards. I then saw an advertisement by Sega Genesis for "The Kid's Chameleon Game," otherwise known as "The Multiple Personality Game."

Then I saw an ad for "The Mind Trainer" that uses ear phones, blinders, and strobe lights. Another ad caught my attention. This was for the Saturday cartoon, "Yo, Yogi." It was advertising 3D glasses that would actually "trick the brain" via optical illusion. This particular segment on the cartoon would only last for a few minutes, because the brain would figure out how to cancel the trick.

I just stored the information away, and I wondered what next would be on the market. I wondered, Might it just be possible that we're getting close to putting videos on the shelves like the one that is temporarily only available from the underground market—the Jewish concentration camp videos that allows the player to torture and extinguish the lives of Jews any way he pleases? Please know that this is not some kind of suggestion. But I know that this kind of combination of evil and technology that has already happened in the market of video games will surely be applied to this newer, more technological approach.

And do not think that such technologies go unnoticed by cult perpetrators. Often, they have some access to them before the public does. Cult perpetration is becoming more and more sophisticated. Can it be made so sophisticated as to be virtually undetectable?

The Tragic End, Listen and Remember

I watched "Hate on Trial," a frightening program hosted by Bill Moyers on PBS. "Hate On Trial" consists of actual footage from the trial of Tom Metzger, the organizer and the leader of "The White Aryan Resistance." He was being sued for inciting the racist murder of a young Ethiopian student by a group of his followers. Metzger acted as his own defense counsel. The brilliant Morris Dees, executive director of the Southern Poverty Law Center, was the attorney for the victim's family.

I was so drawn into this drama that I felt as if I was sitting in the court room. I listened as attentively as if I was one of the jurors in the jury box. Not one sentence escaped my hearing.

Dave Mozella, a member of "The White Aryan Resistance" testified against his one-time mentor, Tom Metzger. He talked about the systematic training that led him to the point of being willing to kill for "the cause" and at the direction of Tom Metzger.

Morris Dee's closing remarks to the jury.

"We have a brainwashing system here.
Don't you understand?
Dave said that he would die for Tom.
He would forsake his parents to be with Tom.
The foot soldier did what the general
   told him to do."[19]

The only difference between Dave Mozella and a brainwashed victim of a cult is that they are foot soldiers in different armies. It's that simple . . . and it's that dangerous.

8

Cult Alters

"Fear—fear is better than violence.
Fear lives with you twenty-four hours a day."
Daniel Walker,
serial murderer

What Is a Cult Alter?

We have wandered around together quite a bit in these past few chapters. First, we looked at the relationship of severe childhood trauma to the creation of alters by survivors like me. We create alters in response to pain in order to protect ourselves. Our alters experience and bear the memories of pain, and thus keep the helpless child within safe from those memories. I have introduced you to Baby and a little girl who are part of a group of alters that live within me and act as protectors. I shared the struggle that I have had within myself to view the existence of these people within me as a sign of great health, creativity, and a will to survive.

Then, we seemingly shifted gears and looked at mind control and brainwashing as it is practiced by people who choose to use whatever cruel and inhuman tactics they deem necessary to exercise control over the lives of others. We looked at the reality of the fact that even mature and intelligent adults have a breaking point beyond which they begin to crumble internally, to respond automatically, and to be controlled by the will of those who have the power to inflict pain on them.

In this very difficult chapter I want to talk about how these concepts come together. What might happen if people who were experienced in brainwashing and mind control applied those techniques to young children to *intentionally* encourage the splitting that leads to multiple personalities? And what could happen if alters were created in response to these circumstances? What would happen if those alters were then repeatedly assaulted and traumatized? And if each of the alters that came into being, created by the victim in response to trauma, was subsequently systematically brainwashed and programmed individually to make them more vulnerable to the control of the cult, what might the result be? Children might automatically dissociate such horrendous cruelties. But what about the adult victims who find that they have newly formed cult alters who have been programmed to ambush them? Do they just as easily and automatically dissociate themselves from such cruelties?

How I wish that these were hypothetical and theoretical questions put forth as interesting, if abhorrent, intellectual possibilities. However, that is *not* the case! Believe me, these "possibilities" *are* the facts of the stories of victims of ritual abuse.

Again, I remind you that the central purpose of ritual abuse is the *control* of others. There are adult members of cults who, by experience and training, are skilled in the use of trauma. They know how to inflict pain in such a way as to cause dissociation, to recognize that process, and then to manipulate their victim during the creation of a new alter. There are those who know how to use pain and torture with individual alters to achieve control over them.

For generations, they have done this within families to their own children. In the past few decades they have begun to do this evil work in preschools, day care centers, and the like in order to have access to children of unsuspecting families. Cults also continue to access adult victims of ritual abuse to program new alters that have emerged as a result of trauma and torture inflicted on them by the cult.

Are the people who would do this crazy? Are they psychotic? Have they gone mad? Only if we change our definitions and label as "crazy" people who choose to control others at whatever cost. This is a moral dilemma, not a psychiatric one. Were the Nazi doctors crazy? Were Hitler and Stalin and Ceaucescu crazy? Were the political torturers of Argentina crazy?

Cult members who repeatedly torment young children to cause them to dissociate and create new alters are intelligent, deliberate, methodical, and precise. They know what they are doing, and they do it meticulously well. We cannot dismiss this as a form of madness. These are people who make evil choices in order to have control.

Setting the Scene

It's just two weeks before Christmas. The family is trimming the tree and singing carols. An inviting fire is snapping and crackling in the fireplace, bringing a welcoming warmth to the living room. The ambience is perfect, setting the scene for a cozy evening of love, warmth, and closeness.

Lea, an eight-year-old foster daughter, slowly comes down the stairs. Abruptly the atmosphere changes. A feeling of coldness fills the room. Lea stops halfway down and stares into the living room. The family's merriment dies to a chilling silence. They turn to look at Lea. She is drooling with saliva dripping off her chin.

"Why are you using balls to trim the tree?" Lea asks in a guttural voice. "I want it trimmed with body parts."

The family is stunned. Time stands still. Ornaments drop from their hands. Lea is a victim of ritual abuse who has multiple personalities. Her foster mother loves her and has her trust. She has been helping Lea to process the ugly memories of her previous family life that have begun to surface. But this voice is not a voice that she recognizes. This voice has an almost ghoulish sound to it.

She is the only family member who can get any words out. "Who is this?" she asks, trying to show concern without revealing her fear. "I haven't heard from you before. Are you someone new?"

Lea takes a few more steps, stopping at the bottom of the stairs. In the same deliberate tone of voice, Lea slowly speaks. "My name is Killer." That is enough to frighten everyone.

The voice continues, sometimes making growling sounds. "I'm hungry. I want some body parts to eat. I want to drink some blood."

Only Lea's foster mother remains as "Killer" approaches. She tries to remain calm, but it is difficult to do because she does not know this "Killer," and she has no idea what to expect next from this alter. "Killer" had been formed early on in Lea's childhood as the result of her family's cult practices, but he has remained silent until now. Just what job "Killer" has been programmed to do was unknown until he announces in a ghoulish tone of voice, "I like to kill babies."

Trying her best to talk in a normal voice, Lea's foster mother says, "I bet you don't really *want* to kill a baby. You just feel like it's *your job* to kill a baby, don't you?"

"I said I like to kill babies. I like to drink blood, and I like to eat body parts. And I'm going to kill you too. I'm going to stab you and push you down the stairs." There is no missing his message!

Lea's foster mother has experienced this kind of thing before with Lea. She realizes from previous experience that Killer is an alter that Lea has probably created in response to monstrous abuse, and has been programmed to believe that his only reason for existence is this awful job.

Killer is only aware of one identity and one job. He knows only that the consequences of not doing his job will be more pain and abuse like that which was inflicted on him after he was created. If Lea's foster mother had expressed anger or threatened discipline or punishment, Killer would not be surprised, and would conclude only that she was no different from those torturers who inflicted pain so freely in their attempts to control him.

Killer also reveals that Lea has a stuffed animal that watches her moves and can hear every word she speaks. If Lea revealed her hidden secrets about any of her abusive experiences at the hands of her family who had ritually abused her, the stuffed animal would tell them. Then everyone would be in danger, including Killer, Lea's other cult alters, and Lea herself.

How Do Cults Cause the Creation of Alters?

Let's say that Lea (or a child like her) began to be abused as an infant by her family. *Her family?* Yes, in cult families especially, children are abused and trained to dissociate at the earliest possible age. Remember, that dissociation is a talent that can be developed by practice. Cult members begin to encourage and develop this "talent" in their children at the earliest possible age. This sets the stage for the development of behaviors and alters that can be controlled by the cult.

Let's imagine a very simple, if chilling, example. Suppose that as an infant Lea is repeatedly subjected to pain, perhaps the pain of a candle flame or the lighted end of a cigarette on her palm. If Lea reacts either by crying out or trying to withdraw from the pain, she is punished with an even more painful stimulus like electrical shock. She is thus trained to endure the pain of the flame silently and without moving. The only way a child could do so is somehow to discover the way to dissociate the pain of the flame.

Bob Simon, you will recall, stumbled upon this method during his imprisonment in Iraq. The ability to dissociate becomes more highly developed as time goes on and the torture continues. Lea becomes more proficient at dissociating in order to protect her body and her mind. As we have seen before, dissociation is a perfectly sane and reasonable response to pain that cannot be avoided. If her body cannot escape the pain, she teaches her mind how to escape instead. This example is extremely basic.

Liken the structuring of Lea's cult alters to that of a high-rise office building. Constructing a sound and sturdy foundation, upon which all the floors are built, is absolutely mandatory. If floor number one were constructed without a foundation, it would collapse. The foundation has to begin deep in the ground. It may not be visible to the human eye, but it is there, nevertheless.

The blueprint for the foundation was drawn by an architect who has studied for his job through years of schooling. In making that blueprint, he uses all the intellectual tools of his training. The specs are meticulously figured and drawn into the plan. Each spec insures that the high-rise will last for years to come. There is even the possibility of new floors being added as the years come and go, because of the stability of the foundation.

Lea's foundation, upon which layer upon layer of dissociation can progressively be built, was meticulously designed and constructed from birth. Eventually, with repeated and systematic sessions involving pain and terror, Lea learns to dissociate automatically. At some point she uses her most creative response to this kind of pain and begins to create alters to protect herself. There come into being groups of infant alters in a victim too young to have any language. The groundwork has been laid for her to continue to dissociate automatically as she grows older. Lea is beginning to be what some professionals are calling a "*structured*" multiple.

As Lea grows from infancy into childhood and the abuse—what the cult would consider training—continues, she dissociates with increasing ease. Through dissociation, each and every episode of abuse is repressed and stored away in her mind. Here is the key: *If she had not been taught or conditioned to dissociate involuntarily and automatically before she was even able to speak, the abuse of the cult would be in danger of being exposed when Lea became four or five years old and could begin to speak.*

Instead, as Lea continues to develop, the secrets of the abuses she has endured, and subsequently the actions she was coerced to perform, are automatically and involuntarily dissociated, virtually insuring that the cult's activities remain hidden both from Lea herself and from those to whom she might otherwise turn for help. The cult wants to fragment Lea as much as possible in order to have independent control of as many alters of her personality as possible.

The cult cannot actually create alters within Lea. Only Lea has that capacity in response to the trauma she experiences. But with the use of brainwashing, programming, and other mind-control techniques, the cult can have drastic influence on the behavior of many of the alters that have been created. If the cult had its way, each alter would be programmed to be responsive to certain stimuli and do certain well-defined jobs. The "problem" for the perpetrators is that they can never really cause their victim to split off a part of themselves that doesn't in some way carry parts of the whole person.

Cult-trained alters are often subjected to repeated torture, brainwashing, and programming to try to make them feel that they are completely under the control of their programmers. They are repeatedly given the message that they are under the complete dominance of the cult. Many alters come to believe that they were even created by the cult and have nothing much to do at all with the victim from whom they originally were split. In some cases, alters are even trained to believe that they created the alters with characteristics like those of Killer through some process of free choice. This is to make them feel responsible for the jobs they are coerced into performing. The reality is that whatever painful training or programming or brainwashing is done to a particular alter, a significant part of the victim is at the root and still very much connected to each and every alter within.

But with the relentless efforts of the cult, attempting to divide and conquer an individual's mind and heart, there begins to exist within Lea a network of cult alters who feel more accountable to the cult than to Lea. Lea herself can be completely unaware of the existence of these alters. Cult perpetrators who understand this process know how to gain access to her alters very quickly, just as a skilled computer programmer and operator knows how to hide, and later find and use, a given file.

If the blueprint for Lea had been carefully followed, and not interrupted by foster care, her control by the cult by the time she reached adolescence and adulthood would have been extensive and yet would have remained completely outside her conscious awareness. The cult would have done its job well. Fortunately for Lea, her process of recovery is well underway in the safe haven of her foster parents' home and family.

Do I Have Cult-Trained Alters?

Yes, I do.

Can you put yourself in my shoes? Can you imagine what it felt like to me when I began to realize this fact? Can you understand how much it costs me to talk about it?

I have written about the pain of learning that I had multiple personalities and the profound fear that this difficult truth engendered in me. I have introduced you to Baby, and shared how she has been, and continues to be, a protector for me. I have expressed the transformation in my heart and understanding of the concept of Multiple Personality Disorder (MPD) to Multiple Personality Gift (MPG).

And now in order to be as complete as I can in this first-person account of my life, I must address the existence of alters who, although created by me to protect me from pain, were subsequently traumatized severely and systematically to cause them to respond to cult directives. The purpose of this activity was to control aspects of my behavior while keeping the cult activities out of my conscious awareness. Had they succeeded fully in their efforts of controlling the alters within me, I would clearly not be writing this book!

Ultimately, they did not and will not succeed. For that I thank God and those who have extended their love and support to me! But what a painful revelation it has been for me to discover that some of the alters in me have felt more accountable to the cult and its directives than to me. They are a part of me, and yet because of programming and brainwashing, they have acted in ways that were not in my best interests. For instance, they tried to interrupt my therapy. To be perfectly honest, some of them have attempted to act on their programming to end my life. That most certainly was not in keeping with my wishes!

My dilemma? How much detail about these cult alters *can* I share with you? How much *should* I share? And how much would it be *safe* to share? If I were to give you the specific details of cult-trained alters in me, it might be of some limited benefit to the average reader in understanding this subject. It might help some therapists who are faced with similar alters—and I am very tempted by that goal to do so. It might be of some help to other victims to know the details, as I have identified them so far, of cult alters within me in order to help them in their healing.

And yet if I were to be explicit and entirely forthcoming about cult alters within me, their specific histories and behaviors, would I not be endangering myself even more? Would I not be made more vulnerable to assaults by those who understand how cult alters work? And would I not be raising too many questions that I simply could not answer? This has been a real dilemma for me that I have discussed at great length with my therapists. My decision is simply to keep most of the *details* of cult alters within me *private*. My responsibilities for that area of my life lie with me and my therapists.

I realize from the response to my first book that there are many other victims struggling with the reality of cult alters in their lives. For that reason more than any other, I will share what I think it is safe for me to share. And I would urge those of you who are in my shoes, learning to work with cult alters within you, to be cautious and consider your own safety first before sharing personal details with anyone else. That is the same advice and counsel I would give to all survivors. If there is any doubt about safety, I feel it is wise that you confide only in those whom you completely trust. No "good intention" can justify actions which bring added risks to any of us in this difficult area.

In making this decision about privacy, I am acutely aware of the ordeal I have already suffered at the hands of "investigative journalists." They have somehow concluded that if I dare to share *any* details of the pain of my life, then I am fair game. I am then required to prove *all* the details of my life, or at the very least, to submit to their often ignorant and arbitrary "cross examination" about those details.

Speaking at all about the reality of cult alters in my life is very difficult. What I choose to keep private, I shall keep private. And I will not establish any different precedent or standard for other survivors of ritual abuse. I will share what I *safely* can for the sake of helping other victims and potential victims to come, but I will keep my-self safe. And I will keep safe those who have confided in me. If I don't make every effort to do that, then in the end we all will lose.

People of good heart will surely understand.

Cult-Trained Alters

Brainwashing and programming are inseparable in ritual abuse. Brainwashing is a means to an end. Programming is a means to an end. The goal of both is the control of a person. Control is the crux of ritual abuse. These three words—brainwashing, programming, and control—are the sum and substance of ritual abuse.

Programming is done *after* an alter has been created. Programming makes an alter vulnerable to being triggered to behave in certain pre-arranged ways. A certain program may remain dormant for a long time, only to be triggered years later. Programming is not unlike brainwashing in that a programmed alter has been severely hurt and permitted to learn only one way of thinking and acting.

Programming is a methodical, systematic, and repetitive process. Pain and fear are its main ingredients. If you were a child and I were to tell you that if you didn't kick your puppy you would get kicked, you would probably hesitate. You love your puppy. You don't want to hurt him. But . . . if I kicked *you* hard enough to cause severe pain and then said again, "Kick the puppy now!" you would as a child, more than likely, kick the puppy. It would cause you great pain, but you would obey. If I then said to you, "Now, kick the puppy even harder or I'll kick you so hard you'll never forget it," as much as you might not want to, you would kick the puppy enough to make him yelp and limp off to lick his wounds.

I would continue to terrorize you, instilling intense fear of escalating pain if you didn't obey more and more automatically. I would finally say, "It is your job to kick this puppy whenever I tell you to. If you do your job you won't get hurt, but if you don't do as I say, I'm going to kill you." As much as you disliked these orders, you would obey because self-preservation and the avoidance of pain are basic instincts. You would then become a captive of programming. (I am intentionally oversimplifying the programming of alters, but I think you're getting the general idea.)

Add to that the concept of first setting a child up to dissociate, and then applying this kind of technique to a single alter, an alter whose only experiences may be involved with this issue of hurting the puppy automatically in response to orders. If this alter is otherwise hidden inside, and "comes out" only to be faced with this same cruel message over and over again, this alter can perceive itself as having only one identity and one job. The alter becomes "single-minded" in response to programming.

Cruel? Absolutely. Insane? Most definitely. But cruelty with a purpose. Insanity with a goal. Any means justifies the end of control. *Nothing* is off limits—if it gets the job done!

Cruel Tricks

The cult will use any methods necessary to enforce their control over a survivor. They will even appeal to the nobility of some alters. The cult will sometimes make an alter feel responsible for the safety of another person. For Baby, whom I hope you've come to love by now, the phone appeal was, "If you stop helping Lauren, then we won't hurt the baby we have here." Baby was then subjected to the sounds of a screaming baby over the phone and told she was responsible for this pain because of helping Lauren too much. Or knocks would come on the front door. Baby would later explain to Dr. Lady,

"They say they have little baby. They show me baby. If I no open door, they make baby deaded. But I scared." Do you think Baby wants to be responsible for a baby getting "deaded?" No way!

Baby really believed that the bundle she saw was a little baby who would be killed, and that she would be responsible, if she did not open the door. She also knew that if she did open the door, she would be hurt and subjected to another round of painful programming to try to stop her from helping Lauren. Baby, like all alters, found herself in double-bind situations. If she opened the door, it would certainly not have been "voluntary" in any sense of the word.

Baby has learned, with the help of my therapists, how to handle these kinds of efforts by the cult. My therapists have taught her the meaning of the sentence, "They're playing a trick on you." She has come to understand that she can leave the door locked in the face of this kind of triggering and not be responsible for a baby being hurt. Thank God, Baby, you are very smart! We are learning fast!

Pain—and Lullabies

It is not my intention to make this a "how to" manual of programming. Any method of inflicting pain, whether physical or emotional or even spiritual, is a method adaptable to programming of human beings and alters. These methods have been enumerated in any number of books and publications dealing with brainwashing and torture, including many of the publications of *Amnesty International*. The methods, and even the ultimate purpose, are not really very different.

The Los Angeles Task Force on Ritual Abuse included an essay entitled "The Uses of Mind Control" in its report. You can refer to it in the Appendix of this book. The focus of that essay is on the methods used in children, especially in out-of-home settings. I will not repeat all of that in this chapter.

Let me add, though, that a very common way of programming and controlling alters that produces no pain whatsoever, yet is very effective, is through the use of subliminal tapes. A lullaby can be played to a person without anyone suspecting a problem. Behind a seemingly innocent lullaby can be a dangerous message of programming directed to an alter. These types of cult-created subliminal tapes are used in abusive preschools at nap time.

I used to occasionally watch a Sunday afternoon program on television that talked about the benefits of listening to tapes that had subliminal messages on them. I was concerned when, on a particular program, the spokesperson said, "Many of you have asked how subliminal taping is done. Subliminal taping is a highly technological process. We cannot reveal such information." Nor was it possible to listen to just the subliminal message alone to be sure it was a message one wanted to hear. My immediate reaction was to think, Why? If these subliminal tapes are so powerful and effective, why is the process kept so top secret? As for me, I will never knowingly listen to a tape with subliminal messages. Subliminal tapes can be used for any purpose. That is unsettling, to say the least.

Fear Is Better

Fear remains the single most effective way to try to keep an alter under the control of the cult. Consider Daniel Walker, a serial killer. He was interviewed on NBC's program "Unsolved Mysteries" on an episode entitled "Diabolical Minds."[1] Daniel Walker was included on this show in the same league with Adolf Hitler and Saddam Hussein. Two sentences of the interview with Walker struck me powerfully and stayed with me. I will probably never forget them.

Host Robert Stack asked Walker what the secret of his "success" was in being able to kill so many others. Mr. Walker looked straight into the camera and answered, "Fear—fear is better than violence. Fear lives with you twenty-four hours a day." I felt chills. I knew in every part of my being how true that statement was.

The single theme running through the lives of victims, survivors, cult-trained alters, and people with multiple personalities still being threatened and controlled, is fear—stark fear. Fear is the most powerful tool in the hands of an enemy, whoever it might be. Hitler used it. Stalin used it. Ceaucescu used it. Daniel Walker used it. Saddam Hussein continues to use it. And those who take pleasure in controlling cult-trained alters use fear as the single most effective element of their assaults.

Fear brings subjugation of the abused to a higher authority. It brings automatic obedience and submission. Until the circle of fear is broken, the one willing to show no mercy will continue to be in control.

How Are Alters Triggered?

The process of summoning an alter and reminding them of their duties is called "triggering." Since the process of programming essentially involves the repetition of certain stimuli in the context of pain, almost any stimulus can be set up as a trigger. Certain sounds, sights, smells, words, knocks, tonal patterns, whistles, songs. Really, anything that can be repeated over and over.

Triggering programs can be the sight of common objects like knives, flames from a candle or match or a cigarette lighter, photographs of seemingly harmless things—or of things I'd rather not describe. Some triggers are associated with certain times of day. Some alters respond only when the hands of the clock are in a certain position, such as both hands straight up. The darkness of evening hours, when the lights are turned off in the house and the survivor is trying to go to sleep—can also be used as a trigger.

What Are These Jobs?

First let's look in detail at how and why a cult-trained alter might operate within a survivor to do a particular job. Imagine a cult victim with cult alters whom we shall call Naomi. Naomi may "lose" a period of time. That is, there is a gap of minutes or hours that Naomi neither can remember nor account for. When she emerges from that period of lost time, she finds one of her arms bleeding from several cuts that have been made by a knife or a razor blade. In that interval of time a cult alter has emerged at the prompting of a cult program to perform the job it was painstakingly trained to do—to injure Naomi in this specific way.

At the time of carrying out this behavior, the cult-prompted alter perceives that it has hurt only Naomi. The alter does not believe it has done harm to *its own* body, only Naomi's.

Other programs or "jobs" include:

1. **Nightmares**
   Oh, the nightmares! I could not begin to even hazard a guess as to the number of times I've awakened myself in the middle of the night yelling, "No," or "Don't," or "Help." The terror is indescribable. Functioning well the next day is difficult. Some alters have explained to my therapists that giving me nightmares is what they have been trained to do. I am so truly thankful to them that most of my nightmares are diminishing in number and in intensity.

2. **Silencing**
   Some alters try to disrupt therapy and other supportive relationships by causing the survivor to

stop talking, stop going to therapy or to a group that is supportive. In effect, their job is to cut off all communications that are healthy and life-enhancing for the survivor.

3. **Suicide**
There are any number of alters and various suicide programs, some of which seem to be universal to survivors of ritual abuse, some of which are personally designed for the victim. These jobs are likely to be triggered when things are going well for the survivor and she is becoming too independent of cult-control efforts. Some young children who have been ritually abused in cult-related preschools have been found by therapists to have suicidal programs—for example, an urge to drink household products marked as poisons—that are also triggered by making certain kinds of disclosures.

4. **Memories**
All survivors, as they begin to regain memories of what has happened, experience flooding of memories. That is, the memories come so quickly that the survivor is overwhelmed and unable to function. Just as some alters contain memories for the protection of the survivor, those same alters can be trained to give the survivor more access to memories than she may want. Sometimes the survivor is overwhelmed and disabled by physical pain that comes from the memory of past trauma. Therapists refer to such pain as "abreactive pain." Alters can control the pace and severity of these memory experiences.

5. **Burning**
Some alters cause the survivor to burn herself or himself, usually on the fingers, hands, or arms.

Flames from a gas stove, hot coils on an electric stove, or a lighted cigarette are common methods.

6. **Isolation**

Any of these behaviors could cause people who are trying to be supportive of a survivor to back away. In addition, there are alters who will cause the survivor to withdraw from healthy relationships. Survivors need contact with the outside world. They, like all of us, need healthy and supportive relationships. Isolation and withdrawal from meaningful relationships can give the upper hand to the cult perpetrators. Isolation gives the survivor the feeling of powerlessness, helplessness, and hopelessness.

7. **Returning**

Some alters have a variety of jobs designed to make the victim feel a compulsion (not a desire) to return to the cult at certain times. This can be extremely difficult for the survivor and those who support her if it is not understood as the result of programming and not of some change of heart on the part of the survivor about wanting freely to return to the cult. Even desires to return are a result of the painful programming of alters done by the cult.

8. **Reporting**

Some alters have the job of communicating with the cult about what is happening in the victim's life. Reporter alters will tell the cult about the behavior of different alters, about the status of programming in certain alters, and will even, when required, report in detail to the cult about what is taking place in therapy. This makes it more difficult for the survivor to break away from the cult.

Let's use this last program of cult reporters as an illustration of how cult alters perform their jobs. I understand it this way: Reporters are often alters who are the most difficult for the therapist to reach. Expressly because their job is to inform the cult of the host personality's overall condition, they remain silent within the complicated network of the other alters.

Many cult alters, at least in the first months of the host personality's therapy, have no cognitive knowledge of the other alters. They remain in a sterile hiding place, untouched and uninfluenced. One could describe their existence by comparing their cognition to certain animals that have no peripheral vision. Such animals have eyes that can only see what is straight ahead. They see nothing that is on either side. Most cult alters have that kind of limitation. Their peripheral vision is so limited that they have no knowledge of the existence of other alters. They each exist in a world unto themselves.

Reporters are a different breed. They have a wide periphery of vision. Their hearing misses little, if anything. Often there is a battery of reporters who report to the main reporter. Often, information is gathered from the work of cult alters who have jobs other than that of reporting.

Reporters can be likened to the reporters for a large metropolitan TV network, such as in Los Angeles. Most of the reporters do the footwork. They are kept busy running hither and yon to on-site locations, getting the latest scoops on breaking news stories. There's a bad car accident of the San Diego Freeway. There's a fast-moving fire in a high-rise office building in Century City. There's a bank holdup in Beverly Hills with hostages being held by the robbery suspect. The police fear the worst for a child who has disappeared while walking home from school in a middle-class neighborhood. All are headline stories, and the network is anxious to be the first to air them or, perchance, be lucky enough to get an exclusive interview.

Once these stories are shot and are stored safely away in video cams, these on-location reporters bring the videos back to the station where they are viewed and edited. Who sits behind the news desk for the six o'clock prime-time broadcast? Is it the on-site reporter who brought the story back to the network? No. It is the *anchorperson*. He is the one whose job it is to get the news to the public. We will call him the number one, "numero uno" reporter.

The reporter who is seen as the number one, "numero uno" reporter in the structured hierarchical system of the cult alters becomes the *anchorperson* of the reporting network. He gathers the information from the other cult-programmed alters and reports it just as the news anchorperson reports all pertinent and important news on the prime-time broadcast. Only the cult alter who is the number one reporter has the important job of relaying *his* information to the cult. This is normally done via the telephone, and, more than likely, it is the cult who phones the host personality, in this instance, Naomi, and triggers the reporter to come out. Most often, the host personality switches to the cult-programmed reporter so fast that he or she has no cognitive awareness that the switching has taken place.

It would not be unusual then, when asked by Naomi's therapist if she is still having contact with the cult, for her to, in all truthfulness, answer no. Hopefully, after an extensive time in therapy, the survivor's therapist will gain the trust of one of her cult-programmed reporters. The alter might then feel safe enough to identify himself as an alter who does indeed report back to the cult.

The therapist could quite possibly find herself in a double-bind situation. The question comes into play, Should I tell Naomi that one of her cult alters has an ongoing connection to the cult when she has been so proud of her conviction that she has no connection to or communication with those who have ritually abused her? Depending on the informal agreement or written contract between Naomi and her therapist, the decision will have to be made as to whether or not she is told.

Naomi might either go into a state of denial or she understandably might become guilt-ridden, ashamed, and depressed. She might even consider quitting therapy. Such information could be devastating to her internal system. She might verbally express feelings of, Why go on? I'm not making any progress. I thought that I was getting better, but I guess I'm not.

Just because a survivor learns that there is an alter who is reporting back to the cult does not mean that she is not trying hard enough or that she really doesn't want to get better. I must reiterate to those who assign the diagnosis of "Munchausen" to survivors who are in therapy for the long haul, that it should be obvious by now that that just isn't true. The ups and downs, the difficulty of therapy, the torrents of tears, the pain of each new fragmented memory, and the learning that some of their alters still are hanging on to their old jobs in fear of reprisals does not make for a Munchausen! Therapy is hard work. Therapy is exhausting. And progress is made only with gutsy determination!

I Know. I Understand.

I watch as a young woman is taken away on a gurney by a policeman and ambulance attendants. She has been secured physically by a straitjacket. A cult-trained alter has slashed her arms with a razor blade.

Tears fill my eyes as they are drawn to the blank look on her face. I think I know what she is feeling. She is frozen with numbness and fear as thoughts race around in circles too fast to slow them down. Not again! Not again! Why did I do this again? Why couldn't I stop myself? Why? Why? She feels helpless and hopeless, that she has lost all control not only of herself, but of her entire life. What point is there to try to continue? There is no reason to go on. She'd rather be dead than go through this experience even one more time.

I know. I have been there, too! She and I and most survivors have felt like islands unto ourselves—islands of isolation until skilled professionals help us to begin to build some bridges—to make some sense out of all the craziness—to help us understand the whys of crisis after crisis and what can be done to end them.

For now she may only hear accusations. "You just want sympathy. That's why you slashed yourself. Quit feeling sorry for yourself. That's not going to help!"

For now she may only feel guilt and remorse. She doesn't know why she did this. She doesn't even really seem to think that *she* actually did it. She can't remember what happened. For now she is left in the hands of those who may not understand either.

As the attendants take her around the corner and out of my view, I feel sick. I want to run after her and cradle her head in my hands. I want to say to her, "*I know. I understand. I've done this, too. I didn't know why. I only knew that I was bleeding and I couldn't quite explain why. I have heard the accusations you will hear. All I can say is that I understand.*"

Something bad happens. The survivor feels as much a victim in a moment like this as if she had been mugged. And yet when she looks, she sees that she has the blade in her own hand. I know the feelings—crazy, guilty, ashamed, embarrassed, hopeless, and most terrifying, a growing conviction that death seems the most sane alternative of all!

Nice to Meet You . . . Not!

The most common reaction of those who are meeting a cult alter for the first time is to shy away. It's sort of the,

"If I just kept quiet, maybe he or she will disappear" approach. The first time I heard a cult alter in another survivor speak, I was ready to jump over a row of chairs and bolt for the door! Believe me, it's no fun when you don't know what or who you're dealing with.

It is important to remember the history of a cult-programmed alter. They have been created and have learned how to survive in a world that is as evil as evil can get. When they make themselves known, they don't exactly cuddle in one's lap and begin to purr!

They have known one world only—a world of pain, of fear, of hideousness, and of the macabre. The way they present themselves is absolutely appropriate for what they know and understand the world to be. In the beginning it's a little like dealing with cross cultural differences, trying to understand the world view of an alter who has known only abuse and pain. Cult alters don't scare too easily! They have been forced to live in a world where their relationships are based on power, a "one-up-manship," so to speak. They are taught not only to keep one jump ahead of therapists who might come into the picture, but also to learn to go any competitor one better.

Thus, they remain, each in their own solitary world, fiercely determined not to give ground to anyone else. Not safe. Not safe at all. And yet—we must not forget—most of these alters are also at their roots little children, split off from a victim at a very young age. And they act like that—like little kids raised by the cult to act tough and stand up to anyone.

At their foundation, cult alters are scared little children trying to survive by obeying impossible commands. Does that help? Cult alters can seem very scary and can indeed do a great deal of harm to a survivor. But in order to work with them, in order to help the survivor to be able to make free choices, it is important to remember that cult alters are survivors of a different world, in touch with a very different way of thinking. Those who are working with survivors must be prepared to put out the welcome mat for cult alters and, as they are ready to do so, allow them to communicate and tell their stories. They are inevitably a confusing and contradictory lot. They are courageous and afraid, weak and strong, naive children and adults with experiences beyond anything we would want to know. They act like bad guys because they are afraid of what will happen if they try to be good guys. It is important to come to know each of them: how they were created, how they are programmed, and how they are controlled.

The Great Debate

Theologian I am not. I know just enough not to attempt to address issues about which I am not knowledgeable. However, the issue of demons and demonization in connection with MPD and cult alters has been a growing concern to pastors, to mental health professionals, and to survivors alike.

For instance, if an alter says that his or her name is "Beelzebub" (another name for Satan), and that alter says it in a menacing voice, should we assume that "Beelzebub" is really a demon and not an alter? The truth is, I don't know. But in my lack of expertise in this area, I take comfort in the fact that God knows. I cannot explain how all of this works, but I do know the One Who can. As He is in control of the spiritual department, I leave these kinds of questions to Him.

There are cult alters who have been programmed to lie about who they are and/or for what purpose they were created. I assume that it just might be possible for a cult alter to act as if he or she is a demon just to interfere with the healing of the survivor.

At the opposite end of the scale, I can envision how frightening and confusing it might be to a cult alter for a professional to address him or her as a demon. Can you imagine how the treatment of that alter might drastically be hindered?

I feel strongly that this issue calls for prudence and caution before one applies labels of "demonization" or "demon possessed" to an alter and/or the survivor. Unfortunately, I have been witness to as much havoc as healing as some who are working with survivors have plunged blindly into the arena.

This is not a game for amateurs or people who do not know what they are doing. Survivors are already casualties of war. They don't need to sustain more wounds. The best of intentions is not good enough if those intentions are not accompanied by considerable experience and knowledge. On-going consultation with an experienced therapist is vital for a therapist's first case.

Cult alters in time will respond to a welcome mat, when it is set out for them by someone who has earned their trust and respect. And as a result, survivors will be less vulnerable to being stripped naked.

9

David and the General

Walking through the door of Dr. Lady's waiting room, I headed for her office. "Would you like to hear the recording David put on my answering machine yesterday?" Dr. Lady asked. David is one of my alters who has been trained by the cult. He is tired of being so abused and is working hard to cross over to the "good side."

I had never heard the voice of any of my alters before and I had no idea what to expect. I was a little apprehensive, but my curiosity got the best of me. "Okay," I answered, "but I'm not sure this is a good idea."

"Oh, it's funny," Dr. Lady responded. "I think you'll enjoy it." Bracing myself against the wall, I waited. I already was beginning to feel embarrassed and humiliated, and the tape hadn't even started. Dr. Lady pushed the "play" button.

"Dr. Lady, this is me, David. Me and the General had a race. My car is faster. It's a race car with fire coming out of it. I should have won, but the General didn't play fair. He kept shooting my car with the gun on his jeep."

I couldn't believe my ears. I didn't know this voice. It wasn't mine! The voice was considerably higher than mine and sounded much more excited than I ever get. And I certainly can't talk that fast! I began to fidget, and I turned my face away so Dr. Lady couldn't see how embarrassed I was. I didn't have the nerve to look at her. I felt as if my body was melting into the floor.

This "other" voice continued non-stop. "Dr. Lady, the General don't play fair. How can I win when he keeps

shooting me? He should get in trouble 'cause he's a bad
boy. You need to talk to him, Dr. Lady. You need to send
him to his room. I'm never going to play with him
again."

There was a slight pause. I think it's the first time he
stopped long enough to take a breath. Then there was a
hurried, "Bye." David had hung up the phone.

Even though I was still totally embarrassed, I have to
admit that David was irresistible and captivating, not unlike Baby. I couldn't help but smile. I had been hearing
about David for over a year, but I had never really "met"
him. Not like this, anyway. He had remained just a
name, nothing more. Now, he was a real person. Dr.
Lady had chuckled several times as David was talking.
She turned to me and asked, "Is this the first time you've
heard one of your alter's voices?" I managed to get out a
feeble yes, but I was still too embarrassed to say anything
else. I hastily turned to walk into Dr. Lady's office. I
stopped just short of the doorway. "Dr. Lady, this is
weird, just plain weird! I think it's crazy."

Just Who Are David and the General?

David and the General are two of my cult alters. David
was created by me many years ago as I was abused by
cult members trained in techniques of sadistic sexual
abuses and torture. As the years have passed, I have had
to take very little of the pain in such abuses. (I still tend
to dissociate in the face of trauma, although I am dissociating less and less as my therapy and healing progress.)
In the face of danger, an alter would emerge to take the
actual abuse and the memory of it. The dissociation
would begin the moment I saw the cult perpetrator or
when I heard a programmed pattern of knocks on the
door or a programmed tone on the phone.

The alter who emerges from the abuse and/or the programming is always given a name by the cult. Sometimes

the name is a common name such as "David." At other times the cult gives new alters names that designate the purpose that they are to fulfill when the cult triggers them at a later time, e.g. "Killer."

Sounds crazy? Yes, I know. If it had not happened to me, I would put this book in the freezer! But it *did* happen, not only to me, but to countless other survivors. So there is a critical need for those of us who are able, to write and talk about it. The fear of rejection and being disbelieved is immense, but someone has to be the forerunner in making a path for others to follow.

Immediately after David emerged, the cult programmed him to do one job and one job only. David was unaware of any other alters and knew nothing of the jobs the others had been given. Remaining isolated and frightened, he was committed to performing his job to avoid being punished. David was the "designated driver." None of the other cult alters, not even I, knew where David had been programmed to take charge of my driving. David's job was to take over and direct me to places that I would be unwilling to drive myself.

After many talks with my therapists, David finally confided that he really hated taking me places that I did not want to go, but that he really, really did like to drive. The emergence of David and the knowledge of his cult-programmed job called for innovative thinking by my therapists. After some brainstorming, David was approached with the possibility of being given a new job.

"No. I don't want a new job," he replied adamantly. "I'm the driver, and I'm a *good* driver!" Little by little it became clear that there was another element to David's driving job. He had also been programmed to crash the car and kill me. Remember, he was convinced that a car wreck would only destroy me and not hurt him. David's other job was to dispose of me so it would not look like a murder, but it would appear that I had committed suicide! How does one prepare oneself for that kind of news? I didn't know then, and I'm not all that sure that I know now.

Dr. Lady asked David, "How would you like a new job? You can still be the driver, because you are such a good driver, and I know that your job is important to you. You just shouldn't drive to places that aren't safe for everyone."

"But I don't know any safe places to drive to," he objected strenuously. "Where can I drive?"

(This is a tricky area—that of figuring out just how much the cult alters do the jobs for which they have been programmed and how much they just *influence* the host personality to fulfill those jobs. It is not reasonable to assume that a four-year-old or a seven-year-old has the ability to drive a car. But it does appear that the cult alter has the ability to make the host personality so compulsive about doing his job that, in truth, the "credit" must go to the alter for a job well done. But as much as David believes that he has total control of my car, and I don't mind him thinking that, I do believe that the body and the mind who does the driving is really mine.)

Getting back to David's question, "Where can I drive?", I imagine that Dr. Lady had to do some fast thinking. I think she had previously pursued this subject with my other therapist. "David, you can drive Lauren to her next therapy session with me. Do you know how to get there?" she asked.

"Oh yeah. I can do that!" he exclaimed excitedly.

"And if you do that job well, David, I'll give you another place to drive." When Dr. Lady told me that, I remember thinking that I hoped his next driving assignment wasn't to go cross country! Who would be around to stop him then? I wondered.

Much to my amazement and relief, David's trial run to Dr. Lady's office was uneventful. The word "uneventful" was music to my ears, and, I'm sure, to Dr. Lady's ears as well.

David is no dummy. He knew he had passed the trial run. Now, he was ready for bigger and better drives! My next therapy session was at New Lady's office, and the drive to her office is a much longer one. Once we were inside and well into the therapy session, New Lady commended David on how well he had done on his trial driving assignment to Dr. Lady's office.

"Yeah, but that was boring. I don't have anywhere else to drive now," he lamented.

I can envision New Lady taking a deep breath before she suggested the new driving assignment to David. She and Dr. Lady had conferred with each other on the possibility of giving David safe places to drive to. They decided that perhaps he could handle the drive home from New Lady's office. "David, do you know how to drive back to Lauren's home? You know, it's a long way from here."

David jumped at the suggestion. "Oh boy! Sure I know. On the freeway with lots and lots of cars!"

After hearing his response, New Lady wasn't so sure about the wisdom of having mentioned the possibility. But once David heard it, there was no turning back. David was going to drive me home! Period! When David retreated and I was myself again, New Lady informed me, not without some reservations, that she had given David permission to drive all the way back home. "Of course, Lauren," she said, trying to reassure me, "*both* you and David can call me if you get in trouble." Such reassurance fell on deaf ears. I only remember thinking as I left the office that maybe this would be my last good-bye to her.

Well, "we" arrived home safe and sound. And I thought, Maybe there's hope after all. Maybe these alters who have been programmed to hurt me or perhaps even make me want to commit suicide can be won over.

Dr. Lady's maxim was becoming more self-evident from week to week.

"The promise of reward with positive
reinforcement is a must when dealing with
cult alters."

Such a Crazy Name, "General Phoenix"!

Well, it sure beats the name the cult gave him when he emerged—"**Destroyer**." I'll never forget how I felt when New Lady told me that a cult alter named "Destroyer" had come out in a therapy session. A "David," I could handle. But "Destroyer"? No way! The last thing I needed to add to the list of alters in my life was one called "Destroyer"!

It is difficult for the therapist who is working with a survivor of ritual abuse to find out if and when a new cult alter has emerged from cult abuses. Virtually all cult alters have been programmed not to talk to anyone outside the cult—ever! They are uniformly told that if they talk to *anyone*, and that includes other alters who are inside, they will again be put through the torture of the initial abuse.

Thus, cult alters remain isolated and terrified. They function as robots, knowing only of the job they were programmed to perform. It does seem, however, that as they observe therapy sessions from their hidden vantage point, they slowly begin to feel welcomed to make themselves known.

During one of the sessions, when New Lady was finished talking with other alters, she asked if anyone else wanted to talk. An alter who had never spoken before said, "I do." New Lady, knowing that she had never heard the voice before, said, "Hi. I'm New Lady. Who are you?" This alter glanced at her face for only a moment, then stared at the floor. "Do you have a name?" she asked, trying to keep contact with him before he retreated.

There was a slight hesitation. Finally, the words came.

"I'm Destroyer." He spoke in a tough, macho tone of voice which is typical of many of my cult alters when they first speak. Their attitude is defensive, and they seem to want to give the impression of being unapproachable.

"Oh, you must have a very important job with that name," New Lady said, trying to establish at least a tentative relationship with him.

"Yeah, I do. My job is *real* important," he answered. New Lady was trying to find opening statements with which Destroyer could agree, a crucial first step in establishing an initial trust with every alter who presents himself for the first time.

"What is your job, Destroyer?"

Using his rough, tough, macho voice, he said proudly, "My job is to destroy Lauren."

It was not as difficult as one might think for New Lady not to be startled for it seemed that most of the cult alters who had made themselves known thus far had been programmed with similar jobs of getting rid of me in one way or another.

New Lady was quick to respond. "How are you going to do your job?" That question proved to be invading on territory that Destroyer was not willing to talk about yet. With a hasty, "Bye," he was gone.

At the end of each therapy session, both of my therapists have been careful to fill me in on what has taken place during the times they were talking to alters. That was a condition I had initially stipulated with each of them before I was willing to cooperate in their work with my alters. (That is, of course, with the exception of Baby, who comes out anytime she wants whether I agree or not!) Losing time and having no knowledge of who the therapist has spoken to or what the alter has said is too scary for me. I have yet to become comfortable with "others" talking and my having no awareness of it.

At the end of this particular session, New Lady filled me in on the alter she had spoken with for the first time.

All she needed to do was mention the name "Destroyer," and I went into a tailspin.

I thought, Whoa! We don't need his one! In a no-nonsense tone of voice, I asked New Lady, "How can we get rid of him?" I was always for getting rid of alters whose jobs were to get rid of me. It sure seemed only fair! But I knew things just didn't work that way. I knew that Destroyer, like the alters who had come before him, would have to be won over slowly and carefully. I had to remember the pain of his isolation and all he had endured in my place. I had to sit tight. Easier said than done! I had to at least try to be patient and allow my therapist to work with this one who called himself "Destroyer."

In ensuing sessions, Destroyer was given a new name. Don't laugh. I know it sounds a little "out there," but it works. After all, the original name was given to him by the cult who meant neither him nor me any good! New Lady gave Destroyer the new name of "Phoenix." She explained to him that he had risen from the ashes to give life, not take life.

At first Destroyer liked his new name, but in a later session with Dr. Lady, he said that his name didn't sound impressive or official enough to him—that it just didn't live up to the name "Destroyer."

When Dr. Lady shared that bit of information with me, I was ready to throw up my hands and say, "That's it. I quit. We're never going to win with this one."

Dr. Lady solved the problem a few weeks later. "Phoenix, how would you like to be a general?" Bingo! That was music to his ears. He acted as if he had just been given a shot of adrenalin.

"A general?" he asked excitedly. "Me, a real general?"

"Yes," answered Dr. Lady. "A real general."

"Wow! Can I have lots of troops under my command? Can I wear a uniform? Can I have medals and stars on it?" The new general was really revved up. It seemed that the chance to have a job that was even more important than his former one was very enticing. Dr. Lady was making him an offer he just couldn't refuse.

Ever hear of job perks? Well, if there was ever a job that had plenty of perks built into it, it was that of being a general in command of an army! The possibilities were as high as the sky. Thus came the name "General Phoenix." And most often, he referred to himself simply as "the General."

Every once in awhile, the General slipped back into Destroyer's modus operandi. Those times came when he felt threatened and unsafe. Just like David, he was most tempted to revert to his old job when he feared that if he didn't fulfill his role as Destroyer, he would be hurt again.

Ironically, it seemed that it was the most difficult for cult alters to stay on the good side during the times they were doing their best work, for then they feared that the bad guys would find out they weren't doing the jobs for which they had been programmed. Once they felt that the bad guys knew they were working for the good side, there was no convincing them that they could stay safe if only they didn't open the door when the bad guys knocked.

My therapists have repeated this reality over and over and over again, and are still repeating it, not only to David and the General, but to all of the alters. Another inventive device my therapists have used to keep the alters from reverting to their old jobs is to promise them job perks or incentives I mentioned earlier that come with their new jobs.

Food is a numero uno, big-time incentive. The reward of a cheeseburger tops the list for every new alter who makes himself or herself known. No matter what age the alters think they are, they are usually immature and childlike in their behaviors and in their likes and dislikes. And let's be honest. Most adults don't mind a cheeseburger and fries every once in a while!

My alters have an easier time deciding to work for the good side when they know that a cheeseburger will be waiting for them in the next therapy session—even if it is a little cold from the drive from McDonald's to the therapist's office! A cold cheeseburger, fries, and a Coke are better any day than getting hurt.

I began this chapter with my listening to David's message on Dr. Lady's answering machine. Remember him talking about his race car and the General's jeep? Job perks! David doing a good job in driving only to safe places earned him a toy race car that he is absolutely wild about. After all, it has big numbers on the top and fire painted on the sides. To David, his race car is hot stuff! And the General's jeep? It has a gun mounted on the back that can be aimed in any direction—much to David's dismay.

We leave David and the General playing with their toys. They are getting to know one another. Their interaction is a crucial step in the integration process, and even if such interaction is causing arguments and the cries of "foul play" from David, it is, nonetheless, a victory for all of us.

I'm sure there will be more crises for David and the General as the bad guys continue their threats and tricks. As Dr. Lady remarked to me when I asked if she would save the message David left on her answering machine so I could listen to it again, "I'm sure there will be many more to listen to, Lauren."

I was already imagining David's next cry for help. "Dr. Lady, I need new tires and a bigger engine." Or would it be the General's voice? "My jeep turned over, Dr. Lady. Would you call a tow truck? And I need an armored tank that David can't turn over with his race car."

And the saga continues.

10

Winning the War

The additions to my toy box are growing with almost every therapy session. Yes, I did say *my* toy box. Come to think of it, my toy box also belongs to Baby, and David, and the General, and all of the others. I never had a toy box until I found out that I was a multiple. Come to think of it, there are several things I've never had until I found out that I was a multiple! (I'm trying hard to smile.)

It all began with the racing car for David and the Army jeep for the General. Remember the message that David left on Dr. Lady's machine? ". . . Me and the General had a race. . . . I should have won, but the General didn't play fair. He kept shooting my car with the gun on his jeep. . . . How can I win when he keeps shooting me? . . . I'm never going to play with him again."

David's race car and the General's jeep fit nicely into an empty shoe box. I can handle that. Small enough to hide, yet within the reach of "the boys" who appear to be about seven and nine years old. But then the toys began to increase in number. I knew that my therapists had given them toys either as an incentive to keep them from responding to their old programming or as a reward for doing their new jobs so well.

Guess what David got recently? An Army tank with a gun mounted on top! I'm certain he was thrilled. Now, he and the General are on even terms. They both have guns.

As for me, I'm not quite so thrilled. The thought of sitting on the floor or scooting on my hands and knees pushing an Army jeep and an Army tank around just doesn't seem the proper thing for me to be doing.

In the first place, I'm not used to "walking" on my hands and knees. I always know when David and the General have been playing. My knees are always red, and all too often I almost trip on one of the toys. (I must remember to ask Dr. Lady to instruct the boys to put their toys away when they're finished playing.) Isn't being a multiple fun? I can tell you one thing. There's never a dull moment!

Back to my, excuse me, *our* toy box. Oh, I forgot something. The General now has an Army camouflage scarf to wear around his neck. No kidding! Also, and this is most important, Dr. Lady moved him up in rank. The General is now a "five star general." He has a badge with five stars on it as proof. Can you imagine a friend walking into my apartment, only to find me on the floor playing with a toy jeep and an armored tank with a camouflage Army scarf flying in the wind? You know what I'd do? Yep. I'd die right then and there. You can be darn sure that my front door is always locked. No slip-ups. It's not just for *safety's* sake. Now, it's also for *sanity's* sake.

Okay, I think I'm ready to get back to the toy box. With the addition of not only an Army tank, a badge, and an Army scarf, but also of more cars (most of them being race cars for guess who?), I had to move up in size to a small cardboard box. I kept it hidden in a shower I don't use. The box fits in nicely with the other ones I have stored in the shower. No one would notice anything out of the ordinary. (By the way, in case you're wondering, I do have another bathroom with a bathtub!)

As I was planning for this chapter this morning, I thought it would be a good idea to get out the ol' toy box and see what new things had been added. I was surprised that I couldn't even close the top of the box. It was full to overflowing. Little toys were spilling onto the floor. After picking them up, I realized that the toys had outgrown their box once again. Now, the books from one big box have no home, but our toys do.

When I saw my books stacked neatly on the floor against a wall, I thought how nice it would be if all of my alters were integrated and I could get rid of the toys. Then I thought, I will never throw them away. They're symbols of the steps I've taken and am continuing to take towards healing. Guess I'll just have to find another box for my books. There simply are too many toys to list, but some of the ones that caught my attention as I was sorting through them, are—get this—**twenty-one** racing cars, a motorcycle, a plastic container of fat crayons called "Chubby Crayons," a drawing pad, and, oh yes, a toy water pistol that I don't think any of my alters have figured out how to fill yet . . . and I hope they never learn! Guess who uses the crayons the most? The most welcome news is that Baby no longer draws on clothes and walls and . . . and . . . and . . . Thank God for small blessings!

I'm going to have to tell the members of my support team that either they're going to have to slow down in their toy buying or they're going to have to finance a bigger apartment.

After one of the members of my support team read this page of the manuscript, she wrote, "Don't you dare discount the loss of your childhood! The toys are a symbol for that, and being able to play with them is an important aspect of Baby's healing and David's and the General's and yours!" I think I get the message!

The Battle Plan

The work to be done is often difficult. It can also take some time—weeks, months, or even years. It is the job of finding and identifying the cult alters. They aren't all standing in line impatiently waiting to come out and be heard in the first therapy session.

Cult alters do not trust. They have learned just the opposite: trust no one. They usually stay in hiding where they feel safe. They are isolated from each other. They feel they are alone. As time passes, they may begin to have some amount of awareness that others are being talked to. If that does happen, they may take the risk of coming out, but it may be no more than emerging long enough to take in the surroundings and glance at the therapist. If the therapist is aware that a new alter has emerged, the therapist might introduce himself or herself. The alter may retreat without saying anything, but it is a beginning, a beginning of winning the alter's trust.

As alters venture out of hiding, they may begin to talk and eventually may even give their names. In time, they may let the therapist know what their jobs are. There is no pressure put on the alters. They call the shots. To pressure or to rush them might only serve to make them go into hiding once again. They will begin to trust the therapist and reveal more important information about themselves at their own pace.

My therapists have told me that all my cult alters share similar characteristics. At first, they don't want any physical contact. But in time, they will allow the therapist to give them a short hug. New Lady teaches the boy alters how to give "high five." They like that. After doing some work with the alter, she'll say, "All right, David (or whomever), give me a high five," and the alter will put up his hand and slap New Lady's hand. I guess that's the alter's way of showing that he has machismo!

Once initial communication is made between therapist and alter, the battle plan can be put into full gear. Winning over cult alters is an absolute necessity for the elimination of recontacting, revictimizing, and reprogramming, which all leave the survivor feeling powerless and helpless.

Cult alters do their jobs automatically. They are like mechanical entities, methodically going about performing the jobs for which they were created and programmed. They know nothing else. They will even do the unthinkable without realizing they are doing it. They have not been allowed to think, to rationalize, or to choose. They do not have a voice in decisions. If they were to voice their dislikes, they know that harsh retribution would be swiftly meted out with precision.

A good way to sum up the life of a cult alter is to compare it to a survivor of the Holocaust. Filip Mueller, a Czech Jew and an unfortunate member of the Auschwitz "special detail," had the job of stirring the bodies and ashes in the crematorium ovens in order to keep them burning.

Mr. Mueller was aghast at the job. When he hesitated, a fellow Jewish prisoner, Fischel, told him, "Do as I'm doing, or the SS will kill you." Mr. Mueller remarks that, "At that point, I was in shock, as if I'd been hypnotized ready to do whatever I was told. I was so mindless, so horrified, that I did everything Fischel told me."[1] Horror itself has a way of blocking out the horror or else the mind would not survive. It is a way of coping.

Cult alters do not perform their jobs with the anticipation of receiving rewards. Cult alters do their jobs first, to avoid being hurt, then second, because that is what they have been programmed to do. The performance of their jobs has nothing to do with the job per se. It has everything to do with what will happen if they don't do it. They don't know it, but it is a matter of automatic conditioned responses.

Again, the word "fear" is an essential part of the cult alter's programming. Alters may pretend to go along with the therapist to keep her approval while they are still following the cult's programming. The alter tries to be compliant with the therapist and with the cult, but he feels torn in two directions. On the one hand, he feels the need to do the job for which he was programmed because he is fearful. On the other hand, he wants to yield to the nurturing of the therapist. Fear pulls him to the cult, and genuine caring and nurturing pulls him to the good side.

Going Back to Square One

When a child is confronted with overwhelming trauma, he or she will often break down the experience into manageable pieces. This is referred to as "dissociation." Some examples of dissociation are a patient describing a horrendous experience without any feeling, or an incest survivor first experiencing body memories of vaginal pain before knowing what happened. In order to fully process the experience all the dissociated pieces of it need to be associated for the first time. Only then can the pieces become a memory that makes sense to the patient.

During programming, alters will divide the trauma into pieces, often sharing these pieces with other alters. One alter may hold the pain; another will hold the terror; yet another might hold the effects of drugs if they were used in the process of programming. It is because the programming experience has been dissociated that it holds such power over the alters. All they know is that they must have a certain response to a certain trigger. They don't know *why* they have that response, because the *why* has been split off. By doing the very hard work of going through memories, and by bringing all the pieces together and re-associating them, alters come to understand *why* they do *what* they do.

After they have walked through the hell of the memories, the alters know both the mechanics and the trauma of the program. Once they are no longer captive to separate components, they can look at that program and make their own decision about whether they want to follow the program or not. Now the cult alters are freed from being robots recognized by the cult just for *what they can do*. They can be appealed to for *who they are*. Alters who have only been able to think of themselves as *somethings*, are now able to see themselves as *somebodies*. The alters are enabled to function like people, to have needs and wishes, and to express them verbally.

For the first time, the alter has options! Prisoners have no options. Alters live like prisoners until the walls begin to come down. The walls of coercion! The walls of intimidation! The walls of threats! The walls of fear! The walls of isolation! The walls of submission! The walls of no choices! The blocks of the walls begin to tumble, and access to a whole new world opens up.

New Names and New Jobs

Alters come from the programming department with names such as "Killer," "Destroyer," "Viper," "Predator," "Terminator," and a host of other names that are *not* conducive to peace of mind. All of these are names which need to be changed. Others that are not as offensive or destructive may simply be given a different meaning.

One of my alters, "Terminator," was first given the name of "Savior." Savior decided he didn't like his new name. So he was allowed to choose his own name. "What would you like to be called," Dr. Lady asked. There was absolute silence for a minute or so. Savior was thinking. Suddenly, the name "Bob" was blurted out. ("Very loudly," Dr. Lady remarked.) I guess he wanted to be just a regular guy with a regular sounding name, and "Bob" seemed to fit the bill.

And I have already shared with you about the name changes from "Destroyer" to "Phoenix" to "General

Phoenix" to (finally) "the General." I'm a little surprised that the General's playmate, David, hasn't asked for a new name, perhaps the name, "President." So far I don't think he knows that the President could give the General orders. (I hope David doesn't know how to read or he may come up with a request for a name change at my therapy session tomorrow!)

Now, for new jobs. Is this ever important! This involves my safety as well as everyone else's. Cult alters certainly were not told by those who programmed them that they could have new jobs. David was delighted by the redefinition of his job that let him still drive without endangering anyone! But even with a new job there may still be some vacillation between the old and new job for a while.

Punishment is never an option. Punishment is what an alter expects, and we could never win the war in a contest of cruel punishment with cult perpetrators. Punishment instills fear, the main element of the prison in which the alter has been trapped. It is far wiser and more productive to show understanding rather than to threaten or punish. Far better to say something like, "I know it must be really hard not to go back to your old job. I know that you don't really want to follow the orders from the cult, but I can understand how afraid you must be not to follow them. We'll keep working with you on your new job."

Do you know what usually follows next in the therapy session? When I return, after one of my therapists has been working with an alter who is just plain having a hard time, I usually see an empty paper bag with those famous "Golden Arches" on it and an empty bag that french fries come in, and sometimes, a paper cup that is partially filled with Coke. If McDonald's ever goes out of business (not a great risk!), we're in big-time trouble! My alters are becoming addicted to McDonald's cheeseburgers and fries.

What are these new jobs? I'll be only too glad to share them with you. Bob's new job is to help to keep me safe instead of trying to get rid of me! The General's new job is similar. He is in command of troops, the number of which neither I nor my therapists know. He gives orders to his troops to keep me safe. And David has promised to call either Dr. Lady or New Lady if he ever feels he has to drive somewhere against my wishes.

Then there's wonderful Baby who keeps her ears and eyes open. If someone is about to do their old job, she is certain to call for help. She is aware and always vigilant. Baby has always been there to protect me, and that, she has done well. She has done a job that most grown-ups would be hard pressed to do.

Positive reinforcements are a must. Toys help. Burgers and fries help. Stickers are a big hit with almost everybody. Dr. Lady has an assortment of stickers that won't quit. When a cult alter has done something well, or perhaps I should say, has refrained from doing something bad, she gets out her sticker sheet and lets the alter pick one to put below all of the other stickers he has earned. I've come home to find stickers on my T-shirt or on my bag or anywhere else my alters have decided to put them. I've learned to smile. I know that progress is being made.

Safe Rooms

For me, the "Battle Plan" has also included the building of "Safe Rooms." Safe rooms are places within me where alters can go to feel protected and secure. When in their safe rooms, no one can harm them. Dr. Lady draws pictures of safe rooms for every alter who wants one tailored to their wishes. More opportunity for choices! I'm glad that Dr. Lady is a talented artist as well as one heck of a therapist. No alter would want to live in a safe room that *I* would draw, I can assure you!

When going through our toy box, I looked at the drawings of the alters' safe rooms. I had fun charting a graph of who had what in their room. So far I have drawings of ten safe rooms. If Baby were to talk to you right now, I'm sure that she would loudly and proudly tell you that her safe room is the only one that's in a frame. What can I say? I can't afford frames for all of them.

I had to chuckle when I discovered who wanted what in their very own private room. Only one of the ten wanted an exercise bike. That's my kind of alter! He must have inherited some of my genes. Can you hazard a guess what one thing all ten of them wanted in their room? All of them take after me on this one. A refrigerator! There goes my plans for losing weight. That must be why I find cracker crumbs in my bed when I awaken in the morning. Which reminds me. Nine of the ten wanted beds. I don't know what "Communicator" does. He must have a job that demands staying awake twenty-four hours a day.

One alter had Dr. Lady draw a picture of an Army jeep and his medals. I don't have to tell you whose room that is. It was interesting to note that one alter had asked Dr. Lady to draw him a box so he could put bad memories into it and then close it tightly so they couldn't get out. A noteworthy comment, and, I must add, one that concerns me, is that only two of the ten felt a need for a bathroom. I'm not sure what to make of that, so I won't venture to draw any conclusions. Maybe you can help me out on that one. I really do take a bath every day. Honest.

Baby's room is very special. She has more things than anyone else:

There's a fireplace.
    And a big rocking chair.
    Both mommies are in the room.
    There is a separate nursery room.

There's a bed,
   and a phone (of course),
   and a refrigerator which is well-stocked!
There's a table with food already on it.
And a television,
And one balloon with XOX on it
   and two teddy bears.

Not bad, huh? If I ever get to where I can't make my rent payments, I'll just move into Baby's safe room! (Just kidding, Baby.)

Since I've been glued more and more to my writing desk and computer as the deadline for this book nears, my therapists tell me that my alters have been more quiet than usual. Baby says they're staying in their safe rooms for now so they won't be a bother to me. Boy, are they smart or what?

It Helps If Your Therapist Is Creative

It sure does come in handy. In treating survivors of sexual abuse who have multiple personalities and even more so with survivors of ritual abuse, creativity is almost a basic necessity. Toys, stickers, burgers, fries, Cokes, and peanut bars are creative. Teaching a "macho" alter how to give "high fives" is creative. Taking Baby to the park is creative. It's also very embarrassing.

I found a multi-colored paper clip bracelet on my wrist at the end of one session. When my therapist saw the inquisitive look on my face that read, "Oh, no. What's this for, and how long do I have to wear it?" she was quick to tell me that the bracelet was magic.

"Where's the magic?" I asked dryly.

"Can't you tell? It's to keep the bad guys away."

"How long do I have to keep it on?"

"Oh, just as long as Baby feels safer with it on."

Let's get with the program, Baby, I thought silently. You're safe. *You really are safe.* I think the magic paper clip bracelet stayed on until I went to bed. I took it off and laid

it on my nightstand. I've not seen it since. Baby probably
has it hidden somewhere so I won't throw it away.

Empowering the Powerless

As has been discussed previously, both the victim and
the other personalities, especially the cult alters, have
had their power base stripped from them. The cult has
usurped the victim's power and has used it for their own
purposes. An emotionally naked person feels helpless. It
is not possible to heal without regaining a sense of
power. In the regaining of power, the victim can move
from victim to survivor.

Each human being has a uniqueness all their own.
Cults seek to strip them of that uniqueness. Cults strip
their victims of the qualities that all humans need—
unconditional love, respect, and free will. Cults make everyone feel that they have no options, no choices, no
rights, and no "say-so."

But then:

> The cult alters begin to take on new jobs,
>   ones which are positive rather than negative.
> The barriers between alters begin to crumble.
> They begin to communicate with each other,
>   maybe even to play with one another.
> They will begin to feel more and more powerful
>   as they feel less and less alone.

The Bible has a verse that has meant much to me as I
have tried to build positive relationships, not only in my
personal life, but in working with my alters. I think this
proverb lends itself well to the success of a survivor in
regaining the strength of which they have been stripped.
The verse reads:

> ". . . one standing alone can be attacked and
>   defeated, but two can stand back-to-back and
>   conquer;

three is even better,
   for a triple-braided cord is not easily broken."[2]

There is power in numbers when communication replaces isolation. When alters begin to communicate and interact with each other, and the host personality learns to keep from dissociating and gains an awareness of others, an empowering of a once powerless system will occur.

Baby is a good example of such a beginning. Bob had expressed a desire to tell me something, but he told New Lady that he didn't know how to talk to me. Remember that Bob's old name was "Terminator" and his old job was that of getting rid of me. So I am especially fond of what followed. New Lady asked Baby if she could talk with Bob and then tell her what Bob said.

What Bob relayed to me via Baby via New Lady put a lump in my throat. Baby said in the grammar of a four-year-old, "Bob say he here for you. You no be alone. He always be with you." Wow! I was blown away. All from an alter whose name had once been "Terminator" and whose job had been to get rid of me. I'll take that any day!

New Lady asked Baby how she had talked to Bob. In her own inimitable way, Baby answered, "Me no know how me do it. Me smarter than all the others."

As the hard work continues, Dr. Lady calls me every once in a while, and, with tongue in cheek, asks, "Lauren, do you know where your alters are tonight?"

PART FOUR

11

The Macabre

Viewing the video of a walk-through crime scene for the first time, I found it impossible to get through it without closing my eyes more than once to escape the pictures of its heinous nature.

Three teenage girls had nervously plunked down a garbage bag onto the front desk of the police station. "There's a head in here," one of the girls said. I can only imagine what the desk sergeant thought to himself: Sure, and I'm Santa Claus! After all, how many heads get brought into a police station?[1]

When I saw the head on the video, I became a horrified believer of the reality that I was looking at not only a *severed* head, but a *skinned* head as well.

I couldn't run to the kitchen sink fast enough. Once in the kitchen, I took a deep breath and drank a glass of cold water. "There," I said, trying desperately to compose myself. "I'm all right. I'm not a sissy. I can do this."

Walking back into the living room, I realized all the more why people want not to believe this sort of thing. The proof is just too difficult to assimilate. If *I* did not want to look at any more of the video—and I knew this kind of atrocity happens more often than even I cared to believe—how much more would others who had never dealt with these horrors not want to believe, much less view the evidence?

The head was ultimately determined to be that of a fifteen-year-old runaway. It had been skinned and severed just hours before. It had then been put in a ziploc

bag and placed in the freezer compartment of the refrigerator. It was still partially frozen. I wasn't looking at
a typical white skull we are more familiar with. I was
looking at a skull with reddish flesh covering it. Only the
top layer of skin had been cut away. The teeth were
clenched together, evidence of the excruciating pain the
victim must have suffered.

After I got over the initial shock of what I was viewing,
I was quickly drawn to the eyes. Still in their sockets, they
were a stunning crystal blue. I turned away. It was eerie,
as if they were watching me. It was too macabre, straight
out of *Friday, the Thirteenth* or a Steven Spielberg movie. I
pushed the stop button on the VCR sitting in shock. I
felt as if I was stuck in a freeze-frame of space and time.
I just wanted it all to go away. I wanted to push the play
button and find the severed head to be but an appari-
tion. Perhaps my eyes were playing tricks on me.

Starting the video again, I vainly hoped to see *anything*
else but that ghastly looking head. But there it was—the
same head with the same crystal blue eyes. It validated
everything I already knew to be true; there are those
who do commit such heinous crimes. Later in the video,
it became apparent that this murder had been a sacrifice, a sacrifice to the devil by Satan worshippers. The
perpetrators were doing Satan's bidding in exchange for
rewards they had hoped to receive. I became even more
horrified as I could only imagine what fear and agony
the victim had endured.

But then, I learned that she had been prepared for
the sacrifice. One of the three girls who had brought the
victim's head to the police station said that she had been
at the house of the perpetrator when the preparations
for the ritual were being carried out. She stated that the
victim's hair had been cut against her will. The hair
would be used for other ritual purposes.

The girl had been forced to recite Satanic incantations. The perpetrator also chanted incantations in

preparation for the final sacrifice. A death chant, written in a *Book Of Shadows*, had been chanted most likely before, during, and quite possibly, after the sacrifice.[2] Following are the words of the chant. The message is chillingly plain:

"Would you like to play a game?
This one is simple and without a name.
Would you like to take a chance
to play this game and hold a stance?

The rules are simple as you can see.
There's only one rule—that you play with me.
I play this game at any cost.
This game I've played I've never lost.

I'll tell you now the game has already started.
You probably knew this before we parted.
The game is sad and also fun.
But you never know when it's done.

With the flip of a card and a roll of the dice,
this is one game you will never play twice.
You play with a heart and with another soul.
When the game is over, I'll let you know.

So play with me now and be my friend.
But never be afraid of the game you can't win."

(Signed by one of the perpetrators)

I do not know how many times this death chant was recited to the victim, but I can imagine what fear those macabre words must have instilled in her. I can imagine the voice the words must have been chanted in. I can imagine the grim seriousness, the dead seriousness, if I may, in which the perpetrator must have chanted the words over and over again, gaining more power and nerve until finally the sacrifice was completed.

No one but the perpetrators really know what happened next in the basement of that suburban middle-class home. Sadly, the victim cannot be a witness for the prosecution. Her tightly clenched teeth are perhaps the most telling sign of the horrors that must have ensued.

After taking the severed head up to the medical examiner's room, the police immediately went to the crime scene. Neighbors had called, telling of foul smells that were coming from garbage bags that had been hurriedly buried in the back yard of the house. Dogs had sniffed the body parts in the bags and had dug up pieces of the bags.

Upon arriving at the crime scene and entering the back yard, the police found four garbage bags protruding from the ground. One contained the victim's clothing. The others were filled with the body parts of the victim. Another bag containing body parts was found on the front seat of a car parked in the garage.

I was drawn to a close-up shot of one of the bags. I saw what appeared to be a blouse or a T-shirt. It was covered with cut marks. I then realized that these must have been made as the victim was stabbed repeatedly in the back with a knife. I shuddered as I wondered at what point mercy took over and allowed her to die. It was too late to pray for a miracle. All I could do was hope against all hope that death had come quickly, for at that point, death would have been more merciful than life.

It was difficult to view the remains of a fifteen-year-old girl which had been dumped into garbage bags and buried in dirt, knowing that just hours before, these body parts had been the whole body of a living young girl. It didn't matter how mixed up, sad, and alone she had been. No one could tend to the wounds of her hurting heart now. She was dead.

What I was viewing simply did not fit my image of a teenager. She should have been at the beach playing volleyball in the sand with her friends. She should have been roasting hot dogs and marshmallows around a campfire, laughing and joking. That's where I wanted her to be. I couldn't accept the fact just yet that she was chopped up into pieces and thrown into garbage bags like so much meat. I couldn't accept the fact just yet that some of her body parts had been stored in the freezer compartment of a refrigerator. She was, after all, a human being, not a wrecked car! Knowing that human body parts, especially the heart and the skull, sell for anywhere from five hundred to a thousand dollars on the black market didn't help my viewing of the victim's body parts. Grimly, I wondered just how much automobile parts sell for at a junk yard.

The walk-through crime scene video then moved from the back yard to the inside of the house. The police went into the kitchen first. Upon opening the refrigerator they found a bread bag in the freezer containing the severed left hand and the right index finger of the victim.

The saving of the left hand was uniquely important as the left hand represents the left-hand path, otherwise known as the path of Satan. The index finger could have been saved to be ground into powder for use in later rituals, perhaps mixed in a potion for human consumption, or it might have been severed, frozen, and dried to be used as a necklace.

The skin from the victim's head was drying. It, too, was uniquely important. When thoroughly dried and the cut hair of the victim was glued back onto the skin, it could be used as a mask. Such human skin masks are extremely valuable and have a significant importance and purpose. They are worn at rituals by the Satanist who sacrificed the human from whose skin the mask was made. They are believed to have the power to summon the spirits of the dead. Such a practice is known as "The Satanic Rebirth."

Next to be viewed was one of the perpetrator's bed-rooms. Of particular interest was the music albums he listened to. They were all heavy metal, black metal, and death metal from such groups as Metallica, Judas Priest, Black Sabbath, Venom, Slayer, and Possessed.

"Into the Coven" typifies Merciful Fate lyrics:
> Howl like a wolf and a witch will open the door.
> Undress until you're naked.
> Take this white cross. Now curse it, crush the
>   cross.
> Say after me, "My soul belongs to Satan.
> Now you are in my coven. Now you are Lucifer's
>   child."

"Welcome to Hell" by Venom speaks to the Satanist's desire to triumph over God:
> We're possessed by all that is evil.
> The death of you God we demand.
> We spit at the virgin you worship,
> And sit at the Lord Satan's left hand.

Lyrics from "A Lesson in Violence" by Exodus:
> I'm guarded by Satan. I'm riding on a baphomet.
> I'll teach you a lesson in violence you soon won't
>   forget.
> The pleasure of watching you die is what I will get.

Lyrics from "Show No Mercy" by Slayer:
> In Lord Satan we trust.
> I tear your flesh to shreds.
> Your eyes now filled with blood.
> A victim of my force.

Lyrics from "Holy Hell" by Possessed:
> Kill the people, kill them dead. Take their soul.
> Blackened masses, Blackened crosses, Ritual—
> Cut the heads. Cut the throats. Take the fall.

Lyrics from "Kill Yourself" by Nihilistics:
> This method is effective, tried and true.
> It's the only solution left for you.
> Kill yourself—kill yourself.
> It's about time you tried.
> Kill yourself—kill yourself.
> It's about time you died.
> Kill yourself—Heed my advice.
> Kill yourself—Take your life.
> Kill yourself—It's all for the best.
> Kill yourself—It's time for a rest.

I challenge you to put on a set of headphones, turn the volume up as loud as your stereo can get, and listen to the words of songs such as these for several hours a day for just one week and see how *your* mind is affected. Perhaps then you will begin to understand how strongly young people are affected, and for some, even changed by the words of such music, of which only a few examples have been presented here.

As I looked at the stereo in the bedroom and thought of the lyrics the perpetrators had been listening to, it seemed that they perhaps had become like fodder, feeding their minds with heinous thoughts, and perhaps, even encouraging them to commit acts of ritual murder.

Thank God, the moderator said that the video was cutting to a news report. I was ready for a break—a very *long* break! I already felt battered and bloodied, and the moderator warned that the second half of the walk-through crime scene was even more grisly.

Do I understand why it is easier for people to deny that such horrendous crimes occur in the name of Satan? Of course I do. I was tempted to stop the video. Even I didn't want to watch the remainder of the tape. Even I don't want to believe that such crimes happen. And even I, one who has witnessed ritual crimes, would like to be able to say, "Hey, folks. This is crazy. This is too bizarre to be true. I am out of here!" Unfortunately, the evidence was in front of my eyes. There was no denying it.

The news report had been edited out and the story of the macabre continued. Thinking back on my first viewing of the video, I'm thankful that I managed to get all the way to the end. It gave me a renewed determination to carry on, warning the public of the dangers of dabbling in Satanism in the light of those who have so desperately tried to get out.

The Second Half

To those of you who are feeling ill from the first half of the descriptions on the video, it might be wise to discontinue reading the rest of the chapter. If the second half was almost too graphic for me, I understand why you might choose not to read on, but please read the last page in this chapter as it contains important information for everyone.

The video cam moved into the basement where the sacrifice took place. The perpetrators had tried to mop all traces of blood that had spilled onto the floor by using Clorox. Clorox is a cleaner of choice with people who are trying to remove blood. It works well as it destroys the effectiveness of ultraviolet lights that detect traces of blood. However, small blood spots were still found on the floor. The perpetrators had been in too much of a hurry to clean all evidence of the sacrifice.

Raymond Buckland's *Complete Book Of Witchcraft* was lying on a table. The teenage girl who had snatched the severed head and taken it to the police station admitted that she was into witchcraft and had previously spent some time in the perpetrator's home before the day of the sacrifice. She stated that she had been suspicious that Satanic activity went on in the house. She went so far as to arm herself with a knife before driving to the home. Although most Wiccan groups worship nature, the detectives noted that they have seen some beginnings of crossovers between the pagan community and Satanism—especially of Wiccans who practiced Black Witchcraft.

The video then shifted to the crime lab at the police station. I was looking at close-up shots of the body parts. The first shot was of a tatoo on the right breast. Although not clear enough to make a clean definition of the tatoo, The Mark of The Beast, 666, was surrounding what appeared to either be the symbol for The Cross of Confusion or the symbol for The Cross of Nero. The Cross of Confusion is an upside down cross with an upside down question mark meant to question the existence of Christianity. The Cross of Nero is an upside down cross with the cross member broken downward to signify the defeat of Christianity.

The tatoos (there was an identical tatoo on the left breast) were determined to have been done several days before the ritual, clearly suggesting that the victim had taken what she thought was a safe refuge in the house for at least one week before her murder. She could not have been more mistaken. Her house of refuge became her house of death. This lost and desperate fifteen-year-old runaway had unwittingly become the victim of a tragedy the scope of which cannot adequately be described. No pen could portray even a part of what I felt as I watched and then looked away.

The medical examiner had put the dismembered body parts together in their approximate correct positions as best he could. Not only had every part of the victim been severed with a knife and every bone joint been cracked apart with a hammer, but the victim had been gutted or disemboweled. The organ parts were viewed piled on top of the matching body parts.

The words that continue to haunt me are those made by the medical examiner when he referred to the perpetrator who had mutilated and dismembered the corpse: *"He had to start somewhere. Perhaps it was with animals."* Let that remark be a resounding warning to teenagers who think that their sacrificing of animals is only for fun; something different to do; not really bad; and not of any real consequence.

There was the teenager who practiced witchcraft, but chose to spend time with Satanists because she felt accepted by them. She had no way of knowing that with her choice, she would one day find the freshly severed and skinned head of the fifteen-year-old she had met at the house. The victim who dared to dabble in Satanism for just a few days in her newly found house of refuge had no way of knowing that she would pay with her life for spending time with committed Satanists. And the perpetrators who perhaps began their destructive path to ritual murder with the sacrificing of animals surely did not know the ultimate end to their choices.

I hope the teenager who was already into witchcraft and had begun to spend time with two men who were into Satanism was frightened and shocked enough to convince her to abandon her occultic practices. I hope the perpetrators, one of whom had a large pentagram within a double-ring circle enclosing a baphomet (a goat's head which represents Satan), realize that their god, Satan, tricked and deceived them. They didn't get power. They didn't get money. They got prison for murder in the first degree.

Do you think this fifteen-year-old runaway thought in her wildest dreams that she would pay with her life for her "innocent" involvements in Satanic tatoos, incantations, chantings, and whatever else went on in that house before she was murdered? I think not.

It has been my perception born from my own experience and from talking to teenagers across the country, that when teenagers make the decision to run away from home, in their mind there is nothing worse "out there" than what they have already gone through at home. All too often, however, they are wrong. There *are* worse things out there!

I wondered about the young victim. I wondered what *she* was running away from. I wondered how many times she had whispered to others of her desperate effort to make some sense out of a senseless world. And I wondered how many had failed to hear her whisperings. Grievously, one night, her whispers turned into one big scream, and now, many are listening, but it is too late. She is gone forever, and her scream has been buried with her.

To some who have accused authors who write about such events of writing pornography, I offer no apology. To some who have accused authors who write about such events of exploiting and sensationalizing, I offer no apology. If it takes the sharing of this heinous crime to save one teenager from starting down the road of occult involvement, the inclusion of this chapter has been worth every graphic word and every graphic scene that has been depicted.

There is no exploitation here, nor is there pornography or sensationalism. **These are the facts!** You lived this walk through a crime scene with words that were written in black and white. You are fortunate. I, and others, have viewed the remains of a brutally murdered young girl in vivid color. I pray that I never view such a macabre crime scene again. But most likely I will, for ritual murders continue to take place in the United States, and will, in all likelihood, continue to take place until the public grows out of their denial of the dangers of Satanism and the fact that ritual abuse and ritual sacrifice do happen in our society.

I wonder what explanations I will hear as evidence offered as proof this girl was not ritually sacrificed to Satan. I think I already know. "Just another isolated case," they will call it. How many more teenagers will suffer an identical fate before we ban the words, "It's just another isolated case," and get down to the business of warning teenagers of the very real dangers of dabbling in the occult and Satanism?

When I read the sentence, "The average teenager who dabbles with the Goddess religion is at little risk for destructive occultism," I was concerned.[3] That may be true for many teenagers, but as we see more and more young people escalating from the worship of nature into more serious and dangerous occult and cult practices, I am hard pressed to accept the validity of such a blanket statement. The words "at little risk" somehow don't assuage my fears. My mind goes back to the medical examiner's statement that "[they] had to start somewhere." And "somewhere" just might begin with innocent dabbling in the Goddess religion.

Tell "The teenager . . . is at little risk . . ." to the teenager who was only into witchcraft, but ended up finding the severed and skinned head of a girl she had come to know. Tell that to the perpetrators, one a minor, the other in his early twenties. And tell that to an unsuspecting fifteen-year-old girl who went along with them innocently enough at first—that is, until her involvement became deadly.

Most teenagers don't jump into Satanism head first and suddenly, abracadabra, become full-fledged, hard practicing Satanists who are signing contracts in blood giving their sole allegiance to Satan, willing to torture, kill, and mutilate animals, and even humans. There are, however, many teenagers who are committing suicide as the only way they know of to get out of Satanism.

I just heard of a young woman whose husband is a Satanist. She left a handwritten letter addressed to her mother in an attempt to help the mother understand why she had to kill herself as the only way she knew to escape the terror of her husband's involvement in Satanism.

How long will it take for those who choose to label each ritual abuse and/or murder or sacrifice an "isolated case" perpetrated by just another "psycho" either as an escape from dealing with the reality of Satanic abuse or as a determined effort to ban this subject from the face of the earth? There is something very wrong here!

"Self-styled" ritual sacrifice? Probably, as some ritual murders are, especially in the United States. But *just* or *only* another self-styled murder? Absolutely not! "An isolated case," you say? You're wrong. Dead wrong!

12

The Devil's Workshop

Byline—The Philippines:

"Communist soldiers of the New People's Army spent two hours killing a Sunday school class." And I, Lauren Stratford, am looking at a four-by-four color photo of a soldier holding the severed head of the pastor by his hair as he looks for the pastor's body. On the ground are the mutilated bodies of the children who were in the class.[1]

Do we believe this story? We don't want to, but yes, we believe. We know such crimes happen in *other* countries.

Byline—Iraq:

"At least thirty different forms of torture have been used in Iraq's prisons. They range from beatings, including falaqa [beatings on the soles of the feet], to burning, administration of electric shocks and mutilation. Torturers have gouged out the eyes of their victims, cut off their noses, ears, breasts, penises and axed limbs. Some of these methods have been used on children. The torture of whole groups of children have been recorded."[2]

Do we believe this story? We don't want to, but yes, we believe. We know such crimes happen in *other* countries.

Byline—Rio de Janeiro:

"I am fourteen years old. The police get hold of us and start torturing us. . . . They burn us with cigarettes. Standing with our heads up they throw hot water on us,

187

beat us with truncheons [billy clubs] on the head, on the hands . . . and they make us eat shit and cockroaches."[3]

Do we believe this story? We don't want to, but yes, we believe. We know such crimes happen in *other* countries.

Byline—Guatemala City:

"The police photographs clearly showed that the boys had been tortured; their ears and tongues had been cut off and their eyes burnt or gouged out. Salvador Sandoval also appeared to have had boiling liquid poured on his chest and chin. According to the Attorney General's office, the mutilations the four had suffered are consistent with the treatment the police normally meted out to those that inform against them. Mutilation of the ears, eyes and tongue signifies that the person had heard or seen something and then talked about it."[4]

Do we believe this story? We don't want to, but yes, we believe. We know such crimes happen in *other* countries.

Byline—South Africa:

"South Africa's jails hold many children: an estimated 9,800 were detained. . . . Many have said they were tortured in detention. They describe being beaten with whips, hooded, given electric shocks, and partially suffocated with plastic bags or rubber tubing pulled over the face."[5]

Do we believe this story? We don't want to, but yes, we believe. We know such crimes happen in *other* countries.

Byline—Turkey:

"A sixteen year old girl was arrested. . . . She was accused of belonging to an illegal organization. . . . She gave a detailed account of how she was tortured. . . . 'I was interrogated by policeman. . . . They took off my coat, blouse and bra. They made me stand on a chair . . . tied me to a cross with ropes. When they took away the chair, I was hanging by my arms. Then they gave me electric shocks on my fingertips and nipples. . . . All the policemen continued touching and squeezing my breasts and vagina. The naked policeman assaulted me with his sexual organ. . . . The torture continued for 15 days'."[6]

Do we believe this story? We don't want to, but yes, we believe. We know such crimes happen in *other* countries. As long as it has happened in *another* country, we have no difficulty believing such heinous accounts of torture. We find such stories ghastly, but then, aren't such ghastly atrocities always happening in other countries? We tend to believe that people in other countries are more primitive, less sophisticated, and perhaps, even less human.

Turning the Tables

Okay. We've dealt with these "other country" stories. Let's turn the tables around and see how we do when confronted with equally as ghastly stories of events that have taken place on our *own* soil.

Byline—The Loconia Ave. housing project, South Bronx, New York:

One little five-year-old boy. For almost an hour, defenseless Adam Mann is being brutally beaten. The blows shatter his skull and break his ribs. Finally, one blow is so violent that his liver is split in half and little Adam loses consciousness. He is taken to Our Lady of Mercy Hospital and admitted as DOA. The doctors cannot revive him. The official cause of death? *Fatal child abuse.*[7]

Do we believe this story? Well . . . we don't want to, but yes, we resign ourselves to believe.

Byline—New York City:

One little girl, six-year-old Lisa Steinberg. Lisa is

beaten over a several hour period by either both parents or by her father. She is rendered unconscious. She is left in the bathroom for several hours before the police are called, but it's too late. Little Lisa is dead.

Do we believe this story? Well . . . we don't want to, but yes, we resign ourselves to believe.

Byline—An upscale, fashionable Philadelphia neighborhood:

Edward Savitz, or "Uncle Eddy," as hundreds of boys called him, is a pedophile of the worst kind. Not only is he a pedophile, but he has AIDS. Teenagers, most of them under sixteen years of age, have come out to make stark and repugnant allegations of going up to Mr. Savitz's apartment and getting paid for oral and anal sex, for giving him their dirty socks and underwear, and for even giving him bags of their own excrement. Many of these boys went dozens of times to his apartment for the sole purpose of being paid to fulfill "Uncle Eddy's" deviant desires. The horror of Mr. Savitz passing on AIDS to hundreds of boys is almost incomprehensible.[8]

Do we believe this story? Well . . . we don't want to, but yes, we resign ourselves to believe.

Byline—Los Angeles:

After six years under the Los Angeles County Department Service's protection in a foster care situation, precious little Jesus was found lying in a puddle of mud. "Jesus was unconscious, his windpipe clogged with dirt and water. The near drowning left him spastic, quadriplegic, brain damaged and nearly blind. At the hospital, Jesus had evidence of being tortured, beaten, sodomized and drowned. His rectum was severely damaged with injuries of old and new lesions. He had scars everywhere. He had severe head trauma. He had this horrible through-and-through laceration of his ear that was becoming gangrenous. Jesus' testicles had been burned.

His buttocks had been burned. There was a gouge in his chest. There were whip bruises on his back."

Jesus lived, or I should say he existed, in such a violent, torturous, and unforgivable environment between the ages of five and eleven. Something had gone terribly wrong with the Children's Services Department. Jesus was removed from the foster care giver and "placed in a state institution called Lanterman Developmental Center which cares for some of the most disabled children in California. Jesus lived in a near vegetable condition." The Department of Children's Services filed a waiver in court so they wouldn't have to visit him every month! Precious Jesus never had a chance. He died.[9]

Do we believe this story. Well . . . we don't want to, but yes, we resign ourselves to believe.

One could go on and on citing countless examples of the severest abuses and neglect of helpless and defenseless children in our own country. We find them as ghastly and unacceptable as the stories from other countries. However, we somehow believe them. Why? Because we've been learning and accepting, however slowly, that severe physical abuse, sexual abuse, and even incest do occur in our country, and we are somewhat pacified in remembering that there are laws to punish offenders who commit such abhorrent crimes.

Matamoros

When the remains of thirteen men were discovered in a shallow grave near Matamoros, Mexico, I was curious to how we would explain them away so we wouldn't have to confront the reality of ritual murder in America. One of the murdered was one of our own, Mark Kilroy, a twenty-one-year-old pre-med student at the University of Texas. Sara Maria Aldrete, a twenty-four-year-old Mexican national had an apartment in Brownsville,

Texas, and was an honor student at Texas Southmost College. Sara was the girlfriend of Alonso de Jesus Constanzo, the twenty-six-year-old Cuban national who was known as El Padrion, or "the godfather," the male leader of the cult. On top of that, the murders were plainly ritual in nature.

A cauldron boiling in the shack next to the burial sites contained victims' brains which had been cut out and mixed with blood, herbs, rooster feet, goat heads, and turtles. A wire had been looped around the spine of Mark Kilroy. It was protruding from the ground so the spine could be pulled from the rotting remains of Mark's body to be used for necklaces.

At first, I entertained the unrealistic hope that maybe, just maybe, Americans would wake up. I didn't have to wait very long to find out how we would squirm out of this one. It took not more than a couple of days.

Rationalization number one: Matamoros was in Mexico. Therefore, no one in the United States was involved. Rationalization number two: When it was learned that even though Sara was enrolled in a Texas higher school of learning, and was listed in the college's 1987-88 "Who's Who" directory honoring outstanding students, we determined that the fact she was a Mexican national was sufficient reason to dismiss her either as a victim or a perpetrator of ritual abuse in America. Rationalization number three: When we learned that the ritual murders were probably perpetrated as part of a cult called "Palomayombe," the idea that Satanism was involved was promptly dismissed. Rationalization number four: We tended to describe the Mexicans who were involved in the ritual murders as poorly educated and ignorant. It was easy for us to say that such a grisly crime would only be perpetrated by uncultured people. Therefore, we found enough evidence to thoroughly dismiss the Matamoros ritual murders as having nothing to do with the United States, because, after all, they were not perpetrated by Americans and they did not take place on American soil. Perhaps most importantly, we found a reason to negate any hint of the dreaded word "Satanism."

It so happens that the cult leaders, Constanzo and Sara, were intelligent and well-educated. Upon further questioning of the cult members who committed the murders, it was found that they knew exactly *what* they were doing and *why* they were doing it. And, although ritual crimes can be committed under the auspices of any religion, whether it be Satanism, Santeria, Voodoo, Palomayombe or "Mumbo Jumbo," they *all* are connected with devil worship of one kind or another.

Do we believe this story? We don't want to, but yes, we believe. We believe, because we have found a way to wash our hands of any connection to it.

Ritual Crimes in the United States?

Before we are too quick to protest that it is irrelevant to cite an example of a ritual atrocity in *another* country, let us cite examples of such atrocities in our *own* country. "Ritual crimes in *our* country," you ask? "No way. Absolutely not!" Well . . . let's see.

Two days of banner headlines in the *Los Angeles Times* stunned the city in which it is hard to stun people. Headlines which read: "Dead Pets to a Human Sacrifice." "Boy's Death Tied to Devil-Worship." "'Fun' Killers Now Paying Devil's Dues." "Hapless Youth Became Human Sacrifice."[10] In a city which is used to articles, radio shows, and television programs on Satanism, Los Angeles still read such headlines with bewilderment and horror.

Three teenage boys—Jim Hardy, Ron Clements, and Pete Roland—each seventeen years of age—each sitting in prison for terms of life without parole—each charged with murder in the first degree of one of their classmates, Steven Newberry.

JIM HARDY: "Student body president by a landslide victory!" the school paper exclaimed. Jim's classmates remember him signing their yearbooks, "In Satan's name we pray." Many of them heard their new student council president announce that his life would not be complete until he had killed someone. "The ultimate goal," Jim boasted, "was human sacrifice to Satan."[11]

Jim had been asking Satan for more power, and he began hearing what he described as a voice inside his head. "Maybe it was all the drugs and the suggestive music . . . but it was also the evil force growing inside me."[12] Or, maybe he was a victim of early childhood ritual abuse and programming, experiencing an urgency to act upon the compulsions of his alter personalities.

Jim's favorite bands were heavy metal groups whose lyrics told of seances and Black Masses, of torture and destruction, of Satan and of sacrifice. Jim repeatedly declared that Satan was his Lord.

RON CLEMENTS: Ron had formed a blood-brother friendship with Jim Hardy. Their common bonds were heavy metal music, drug use, and, eventually, Satan worship. The occult became an obsession with the two teenagers. They began devouring library books on witchcraft and Satanism. They learned of chants to summon demons. They drew pentagrams and other Satanic symbols. They greeted others with the horned hand sign, raising their index and pinkie fingers.

Ron was praying to Satan as he spread his body on his bed in a position that represented an upside-down cross. Ron would say that believing in Satan could give you so much power that you could kill someone with the blink of an eye. He and Jim proclaimed that Satan did indeed rule the world.

When Ron went to spend the summer of '87 with his father, his mother finally got up the nerve to go into her son's room. "Ghastly heavy metal posters were plastered across every spare inch of wall space. Black cloth covered the windows. A stuffed wolf's head hung from the ceiling."[13]

PETE ROLAND: Pete's mother finally entered *her* son's room. The posters on Pete's walls were just as ghastly as the ones on Ron's walls. The album covers in his record collection were equally frightening. One album cover showed a singer drinking blood from a human skull. Pete's mother was horrified when she found a Satanic Bible.

Jim and Pete began to grow closer together. They tortured so many animals to death that they lost count. Each sacrifice brought a higher thrill. From the sacrificing of animals, they moved to the unthinkable. "In exchange for a *human* sacrifice, Pete believed Satan would appear and reward him with supernatural powers."[14]

THE FOURTH PERSON, THE VICTIM, STEVEN NEWBERRY: Jim, Ron, and Pete became inseparable. They began to think of someone to sacrifice. A teenage girl nominated Steve, since Jim and his buddies were always boasting about how much they hated him. "Overweight and with poor hygiene, Steve was what the kids called a 'wannabe'. And what he wanted to be was a part of Jim Hardy's crowd."[15]

Jim, Pete, and Ron began to sketch a human sacrifice to Satan. Their victim of choice: Steven Newberry, someone who was just eager enough to do anything for them. The three boys accepted Steve into their little group and began plotting Steven's demise. "We just had to have that experience [referring to a human sacrifice]. I know it had to be from Satan."[16] They started the machinery of their grisly plot.

Jim called Steve and asked him if he wanted to go out later in the day. Steve was quick to agree. A few hours later, Steve climbed into Jim's truck. The tools of Steve's demise lay on the floor of the truck—four baseball bats. Ron held up his bat for Steve to see. The word "Ultraviolence" was written on it. Music blared from the tape deck. "A line from one of the songs would later haunt Pete—the one that went, 'Dying time is here'."[17]

The boys arrived at their destination. They got out of the truck, each armed with a baseball bat, and hiked to a well they had found earlier. They had named it "The Well of Hell." Ron asked Jim what they were going to do. Jim replied that he heard Satan's voice inside his head telling him to do it now!

Jim instantly raised his bat and struck Steve in the face. Steve began to run, all the while asking why they had chosen him to be the sacrifice. Pete later admitted that they hit Steve about seventy times. His skull was fractured so severely that one of the bats broke. When the insanity was over, Steve was still groaning. "Jim Hardy took a bloody bat and nudged him in the shoulder. '*Sacrifice to Satan*', he said."[18]

The boys dragged Steve's body back to "The Well of Hell," tied a two-hundred-pound boulder to his body and dumped him into the well. "Steven Newberry was dying proof, that winter's eve, of his young friends' faith in Satan. He had become a human sacrifice."[19] Once again, as with the two who had murdered the fifteen-year-old runaway, three more young men found out how costly it could be to become involved in Satanism.

Jim, Ron, and Pete sit in small, solitary cells now. They each have plenty of time to think about how dangerous it was to play into the hands of the one whom they had begun to worship. They have nothing to show for their Satan worship—nothing that is, except for their life sentences without parole. Jim Hardy sums it up best by repeating the words he said Satan whispered to him. "*Just open the door once and I'll never let you go.*" Unfortunately, Jim Hardy found that to be only too true.

How are we going to deal with this case? Is it fact or fiction? I think most of us will vote on the side of fact. *But*, were the boys just "psychos" who would have acted out their deviate behaviors even without their devil worship? Was this a ritual sacrifice, as Jim Hardy called it, or was it a murder with unrelated signs of Satanic worship? Is it just possible that this brutal murder was at least, in part, caused by the boy's involvement in Satanism?

Some of you will vote yes. Some will vote no. Some will mark this case with a rubber stamp that reads "isolated case." Some will say, "This is horrendous! I'm thankful that the same kind of thing couldn't happen in *our* town!"

If you need examples of some towns besides Carl Junction, Missouri, I will cite others. Sean Sellers began his death-row sentence at the young age of sixteen. Sean, who is in his early twenties now, was just a teenager when he became actively involved in devil worship. One night he awakened, put on his all-black underwear, loaded a shotgun, went into his parent's bedroom, and shot them each in the head at point blank range. Sitting in his cell on death row, Sean is quick to warn other teens. "You think Satanism isn't dangerous?" He holds up his handcuffed hands to the camera and says, "This is where it got me."[20]

This tragedy happened in Oklahoma.

At fourteen years of age, Tommy Sullivan penned these words in his *Book Of Shadows* before brutally murdering his mother, then taking his own life by slashing his throat from ear to ear with his boy scout knife.

"To The Greatest Demons Of Hell,
    I, Tommy Sullivan would like to make a solemn exchange with you. If you give me the most extreme of all magical powers . . . I will kill many Christian

followers who are serious in their beliefs. I will tempt all teenagers on earth to have sex, have incest, do drugs, and to worship you. I believe that evil will once again rise and conquer the Love of God."

TOMMY[21]

Tommy signed his name in blood.
This tragedy happened in New Jersey.

Steve and Linda Taylor are dear friends of mine. It was difficult for me to listen to their story as Steve told it once again over the telephone. Their eldest son, Dereck, was just thirteen years old when he became preoccupied with devil worship. It didn't take long for Dereck's preoccupation to turn into an obsession. His bedroom contained Satanic objects: The Satanic Bible; a black cape; candles; long knives; drawings of pentagrams; a plastic skull with the numbers "666" drawn onto the forehead; an upside down cross; and record albums that contained Satanic lyrics and imagery.

According to his father, Dereck went into a dark depression. He grew his finger nails long and painted them black. As Steve put it, "Our loving son turned into a dangerous stranger. He became not one, but three Derecks. One Dereck came to the supper table; one Dereck went to school; and one Dereck descended into his 'dark room'" as Steve described his son's bedroom in the basement.

Dereck's teachers saw him shoving bullets with the Satanic symbol "666" on them in his ears, up his nose, and into his mouth, but not one teacher alerted his parents. Dereck cut "666" into his hand so deeply that it never healed over. He tried to hit his sister with a rolling pin. He chased the family's pet dog with a butcher knife.

Steve and Linda sought help from six psychiatrists. Each one stated that it was just a fad Dereck was going through. They were told that it was *they* who had a problem, not their son. A family pastor provided support, but no other help was available.

Just prior to his suicide at sixteen years of age, Dereck phoned his girlfriend, who was also into the occult and Satanism. He told her that Satan had appeared to him in a blue light; that Satan warned him that he was coming to collect his soul. If he refused to go, Satan would come after his parents.

The fateful day arrived. February 5, 1987. Steve and Linda went to the grocery store, leaving their two eight-year-old sons and Dereck behind. When Steve and Linda came back and entered the house with arms full of groceries, they noticed small wood chips on the floor. They quickly dismissed it as something the family dog must have chewed up. They noticed that the dog was hiding behind a chair. The two youngest sons were hiding upstairs. They told of hearing a loud bang. The noise had frightened them. Steve and Linda began to sense that something wasn't right. Setting the groceries down, they apprehensively descended the basement stairs to Dereck's room. A parent's worst nightmare became an instant reality.

Dereck had put his hunting rifle to his head and pulled the trigger. The explosion was great. The force of the bullet was so strong that, after passing through Dereck's head, it continued in an upward direction, going through the ceiling, thus leaving the pile of wood chips Steve and Linda had noticed on the living room floor.

Dereck's casket remained closed for the funeral.

Steve attempted to fill in the Royal Canadian Mounted Policeman on the events of the three years of Satan worship that led up to his son's suicide. One of the Mounties told him that he was out of his mind; that he was just looking for something to blame his son's death on; and that, "This type of thing just doesn't go on."

Soon after Dereck's suicide, his ex-girlfriend became involved with another boy who was into devil worship. That young man also committed suicide. At the funeral, the girlfriend chanted, "Hail Satan. Hail Satan." She then picked up a copy of The Holy Bible and threw it on the floor in disgust and mockery.

This tragedy took place in Nova Scotia, Canada.

In a television interview by correspondent Connie Chung, Rosemary Loequano was bravely making her way through the story of her teenage son's involvement in Satanism. Steven Loequano became interested in devil worship at the encouragement of one of his friends, Metazul. The name "Metazul" was more than likely a self-given Satanic name.

In 1982, Steven became a statistic in one of Denver's police files. Steven's mother came home one day to find her son's body in a car in the garage. The garage was filled with carbon monoxide.

Rosemary went into Steven's room for the first time in a long while. She remarked, "I found evidence of a boy I never knew, one who was heavily involved in devil worship."[22]

During the interview which was held in the Loequano's kitchen, Rosemary brought in a box and set it on the kitchen table. She began to bring out the evidence of the boy she never knew. There was a snake-like curved ceremonial knife; a ceremonial sword; cult books on magic, witchcraft, and a well-used *Satanic Bible*; *Dungeons and Dragons* manuals; school notebooks filled with drawings of monsters and demons; and a small plastic bag filled with bones thought to be from small animals that had been sacrificed to Satan.

Then Rosemary brought out the most emotionally charged piece of evidence—a black-covered book in which her son had written his last letter. It was addressed to his friend, Metazul. Rosemary began to read . . .

"To Metazul, My Friend and Companion,
  Upon reading these words, you'll know that I am dead. I have now started the lonesome journey to the bowels of the earth. I have lived here a long time with you building a foundation for my future existence, but something went wrong. My plight for evil became stagnant. The only instinct was to act and act fast, so ending my life."

As Rosemary read her son's last words, tears rolled down the side of her face. She said that she felt he was at peace now.

This tragedy took place in Colorado.

The following is a letter written by a seventeen-year-old to his girlfriend in the spring of 1988.

"Dear Kathy,
  By the time you get this letter, I'll have already shot myself. I just wanted you to know I really love you. I know every time you told me about God, I'd tell you to go to hell and I'd pretend not to listen, but I really was listening.
  You're probably wondering why I killed myself after talking to you last night. The truth is—I was getting too deep into Satanism and the power I had was controlling me instead of me controlling it. I got really scared when I went before the committee. [The committee was a Satanic governing group within the boy's high school.] They said I couldn't get out. They said I must get deeper into Satanism or die.
  I really wanted to tell you everything, Kathy, but then they probably would have killed you, too, because I've already told you too much about them. I really wanted to accept your God into my life, but I'd already given myself to Satan, and besides, God

doesn't want or need someone like me. What good
would I have done for Him?

I love you and please forgive me. By now, I'm
probably with my god, burning in hell.

I really love you."
Ken[23]

Ken shot himself and was dead before Kathy received
his letter.

This tragedy took place in Texas.

Let's examine the case of another fourteen-year-old
teenager, Diana. Diana's mother wrote . . .

> I looked underneath Diana's mattress and found a
> Ouija Board and a copy of the Satanic Bible. Diana
> has over 30 crystal alpha symbols that look like the
> cryptic symbols of the Satanic alphabet. Then, I
> looked under her bed. I found a freshly severed
> chicken's foot. Course salt had been poured on it.
>
> Diana dressed in all black complete with black high
> heeled boots and black nail polish. She calls it her
> "Black Death clothing."
>
> Diana's creations [Diana is an accomplished artist]
> used to be of Disney characters. No more! Now she's
> into drawing monsters, dragons and skulls.

Diana wrote to me over a two-year period. I'm sharing
with you a sample of her writings. My hope is that you
will begin to see the progression of dabbling in the occult. Her first letter began with a telltale warning sign
that a fourteen-year-old teenager was looking for, as she
put it, "something else."

Letter One:

"Life is boring! I want to get a goblet with a dragon on
it. I went to a magic shop and saw candles, incense, voodoo dolls, cow's feet, deer's feet, crystals, skulls and caul-
drons. It was spooky! I'm getting this book on Satanism

and Witchcraft, but I'm not gonna get into it. This stuff is sick!"

Letter Two:

Diana prefaced this paragraph with the directions, "Write and understand this."

"You see, you have to want to get out. Nobody can make that choice for you. You have to understand that no matter how much you get hurt from Satan, you always get something good out of it. You can ask for power, money, love, beauty, to kill someone, etc. You'll think about it and go back to Satanism. See if you go into a coma because you tried to kill yourself. You'll look back and see it wasn't so bad and go back to him [Satan]. It sounds stupid, but hey, it's the truth.

"I know two kids who are convinced they are Satan's children. They have this place they call 'The Gates of Hell.' There are upside down crosses, skulls and dead animals. You feel as if you're being dragged down and being forced on this hand built wooden altar. It's all true. I was scared. But I don't worry. I'm still into Witchcraft and Satanism."

Letter Three:

"I've given up all faith and hope in God. I'm an atheist now. In the middle of the school year, I sold my soul to the Devil. I started into it with spells. I only got deeper in it. I went to places where they held the Sabbats.[24] I'm still a witch. I can't get out of it. I'm getting back some of my powers and my ESP."

Letter Four:

"I'm still involved in Witchcraft. On certain days I can swear the Devil is watching and calling me. I'm scribbling down some Satanic writings. I always think Satanism is bad news: I tell myself, 'Diana, don't fool around with it.' But there's always something that turns out and

I think I need to do it. It's only natural that I go to Satan since I refuse to talk to God."

Letter Five:
"I recently bought *The Satanic Bible*. I read it. I believe in it so badly that I can do things I never imagined. I can predict events, put out candle flames, levitate bottle caps, match sticks and buttons. It all seems so scary, but I know I can handle it. If I do become messed up to the point of no return, then I'll become a Christian again. I know it seems that I'll wait until I become possessed or something, but I just want to see how it all works out."

Diana wrote on the back side of her two last letters to me.

> P.S. If I die, I give you permission to publish or use my letters in whatever book you do next no matter what ANYONE says.

> P.S. If anything happens to me, I want you to know that you are one of the fortunate people who made it out of this to wholeness.

This teenage girl lives in New Jersey.

I ask you, "Is Diana at risk?" You make the decision. I made my decision a long time ago. I believe that Diana is at grave risk if she continues in the direction she has been going. She just might get herself into a situation from which she cannot escape.

John was a sixteen-year-old. He did well in school. John said, "I went to a party. That's how it all started. At the first party, my friend had drawn a star on the floor. At each point was a red candle. He stood inside the star and prayed to a picture of the Devil he had on his wall."[25] The parties grew into ritual-like activities. John's friends introduced him to Satanism. Peer pressure was heavy, and John gave in.

Not many weeks after, John's mother found him writhing on the grass in the backyard. He was screaming, crying, and beating his head on the ground. "Mommy, stop them. Make them stop."[26]

When John's mother got him to the hospital emergency room, his clothes were removed. To her horror, there were at least twenty upside down crosses cut into his chest and back. That was her first clue that her son was into devil worship. John told her that the crosses had been cut into his flesh with a scalpel as an initiation rite to indicate that the person belonged to Satan.

John desperately wanted to get out of his friend's Satanic group. He was told that he knew too much for them to let him out. Scared for his life, John's family fled to another state, but fleeing didn't remove his fear.

News correspondent Connie Chung asked him, "Do you still believe in Satan?"

"Yes, I still believe in Satan," he responded. "He still makes me do things I don't want to do. Like hurting people and hurting my family. He's pretty powerful. I fear him. I can't disobey him."[27]

John is fighting not only for his sanity but for his life. This happened in Ohio.

I'm Afraid of My Own Son!

Several months ago, I heard of a mother who went into her son's bedroom only to find her son and three of his buddies sitting around a Ouija board. Black sheets had been hung on the walls. Candles were burning on the floor in the corners of the room.

When the mother asked her son what he was doing, she got the scare of her life. She said that he looked up at her with an expression in his eyes that she had never seen before—a frightening look of evil. "Mom," he said solemnly, "I love you, but a spirit has just talked to me through the Ouija board. I have been ordered to kill you. I don't want to, but I have to obey the spirit."

The terrified mother called the police. "Ma'am," the officer told her, "we can't do anything until a crime has been committed." She called a psychologist. "Don't worry," he said. "It's just a fad. He'll grow out of it." In desperation, she called a church. "I'll be praying for your son," the pastor said encouragingly, "but I really don't know what more I can do."

Left to her own creativity, she asked her husband to buy a dead-bolt lock. She had him install it on the *inside* of their bedroom door. The mother sighed with relief. "At least I will be safe from my son in the middle of the night."[28]

I have written only about glaring cases which ended in the most serious of consequences. I believe that the thousands of teenagers who are into devil worship of one kind or another are at high risk either to themselves or to others.

Dare I ask whether these teens should be ignored as, after all, it has been said that they are just into a fad which will go away in time? Should we ignore the telltale signs that indicate our sons and daughters are beginning to dabble in Black Witchcraft and/or Satanism? If you answer in the affirmative, how long should we continue to pass off their involvement as just harmless fun? Where do we draw the line? Where is the point of no return? Dare we risk looking the other way? If we take that risk, I can assure you that the price for our decision will be high, perhaps *very* high.

I certainly acknowledge that teens who are not involved in Satanism commit acts of violence upon themselves and/or others. But when there *is* an involvement in Satanism, that involvement often becomes critically dangerous and, at the very least, that involvement fuels acts of violence and destruction.

Eeek! A Mouse!

Dave Roever, a survivor of the Vietnam War, who had over sixty pounds of his flesh blown off when a white phosphorous hand grenade accidentally discharged in his hand, has a ministry to teenagers in the public schools that won't quit. His talks have changed the lives of literally thousands of young people.

Not long ago, Dave was doing a program in one of the junior high schools in our country. At first he thought that perhaps his eyes were playing tricks on him so he continued with his talk . . . that is, until he just couldn't ignore what he was seeing any longer. The shirt pockets of some of the boys were wiggling. Dave had to find out what it was that was wiggling in the boys' pockets.

"What do you have in your shirt pockets?" he finally asked. One boy near the front of the auditorium put his hand in his pocket and pulled a tiny mouse out by its tail. Only God knows how fortunate it wasn't me standing in Dave Roever's shoes. I would have been long gone — probably into the next county within two minutes flat!

Watching as other boys began to pull out similar rodents from their shirt pockets, Dave was dumbfounded. Surely these mice weren't all to be dissected in biology class, were they? So Dave finally popped the big one. "What are the mice for?" You can bet that Dave wasn't expecting the answer he got.

"Satan demands a blood sacrifice," one boy yelled out. Every day at lunch time, we kill the mice for our blood sacrifice." I can just imagine the shock that must have registered on Dave's face, but knowing Dave as I do, that answer probably inspired him all the more as he picked up his talk where he had left off.

"Come on," you ask with a hint of doubt in your voice. "This isn't really happening with our twelve- to fourteen-year-olds, is it?" You bet it is! And if you ask Dave, he will tell you more stories — not just of junior high kids, but of *elementary children* who are seriously dabbling in Satanism. It's here, and it's getting worse!

Public health departments are reporting that teenagers are walking in off the streets since AIDS became a household word and they are asking three questions:

"Can I get AIDS from drinking human blood?"
"Can I get AIDS from eating human flesh?"
and, "Can I get AIDS from having sex with a corpse?"

It doesn't take too many smarts to know that these teens are involved in Satanic rituals. It just takes guts to assimilate it and do something about it.

The Deadly Deception

It is difficult to relate to such tales of bizarre activity until it hits one of your own. It is difficult even to believe that such heinous activities and crimes happen until it affects someone you know. Then you become a believer. Even then, many of us try to find reasons for denial, because we can't cope with the information. That's the deadly deception. The very things that should make us sit up and take action are the very things we want to close our eyes and ears to.

One might think that a boy, let's say he's a high schooler, goes the way of the crowd. The crowd is into drugs, sex, and heavy metal music. The crowd is willing to try anything at least one time. I tend to think that many of the boys who want to belong, to be accepted, to be somebody, but just aren't able to fit into the crowd, find themselves filled with anger, resentment, and frustration. Rejection is a painful thing for anyone, and more so for a teenager. Teens call them "nerds," "duds," "losers," "dead heads," or "wannabes."

On the other hand, we have a teenager who is a rebel without a cause. He's popular with just about everybody, that is, with the exception of the principal and the teachers! He craves attention and adulation, and he's always looking for something more.

These two boys, coming from opposite directions, are more alike than it would appear on the outside. Looking from within, one can begin to see things that initially were not apparent. There may be secrets. There may be secrets of in-home childhood abuse, physical, sexual, and perhaps even ritual abuse. Perhaps there are secrets of neglect and/or abandonment. Perhaps there are secrets of sexual or ritual abuse at a day care center, a preschool, or by a baby sitter, a Big Brother or a Boy Scout leader, or, God forbid, by a pastor or a priest.

What if both of these boys, as children, dissociated the abuse and/or developed multiple personalities? What if some of these boys were in an on-going situation of ritual abuse, but it never came to the attention of anyone else, because the boys continued to dissociate it? And what if, even *the perpetrator* was a victim of childhood abuse, as the statistics tell us many of them are? Even the perpetrators may then have dissociated their abuse as children.

What do we end up with? We end up with dissociating or multiple personality perpetrators who pass on their abuse to young children who then dissociate the trauma. Sounds farfetched? Not as much as it would appear to be.

I talked with a mother whose child was a victim of in-home ritual abuse. The more I listened to her, the more I really began to believe that she was not aware of her abusive actions. She was desperately seeking an answer as to how the courts could say she had committed these awful acts, yet she had no memory of them. It can and does happen more often that you might think.

Let us say that these two boys have endured such traumas in their childhoods. To the naked eye, their family upbringing would pass anyone's scrutiny. One of the boys has ended up as the popular rebel without a cause.

The other boy has ended up not being accepted by any of his peers. The rebel will do anything to find a cause of which he can be the leader. The "wannabe" will do anything just to be accepted.

These two boys begin dabbling in Satanism. They each think they're doing it for different reasons—the one to organize a group, even if it's just four or five boys; the other, because he's finally found somebody who will include him in a group. But there is a hidden reason why perhaps *both* of these boys find themselves heading towards the darker side. It's called early conditioning and programming to keep them tied to the cult. We discussed this in the chapter on mind control. As you've read previously, ritual abuse is not done for fun, not just for the heck of it. There is a carefully designed plan that will follow these children into their teen years. For both of these boys, the irony is, that though each thought they were becoming involved in Satanism for a different reason, in reality, they were reacting to the unresolved abuse in their early childhoods; one boy, because of severe physical and/or sexual abuse; the other boy, because he was being triggered by the cult to respond to cult conditioning and programming.

We are now seeing teens who have been involved in Satanism, committing suicide or taking another person's life, because, as they describe it, they "heard the devil" tell them to do it. The "voice of Satan" which speaks to them and instructs them to commit these violent acts is, in some cases, the programmed voice of an alter who has been given the name "Satan" by the cult.

Many teens dabble in Satanism and get out. Others get a high and a thrill of excitement out of it and stick with it until the high wears off. Then, there are those who are lured, entrapped, and, ultimately, the victims of Satanism. Those who become the victims may have travelled divergent roads, but they arrive at the same destination. Many of these teens have been on this road since childhood, but no one ever paid attention. We might give serious thought to listening to the little ones who, in their own voices, sound a loud alarm of sexual and ritual abuse. If we offer the child victims the help they need *as children*, perhaps many of them will not be so apt to become involved in harmful practices in their teenage years.

We must give serious attention to our children as they are growing up. Are we listening to them, or are they just another part of the household furniture? Then, all of a sudden, they're grown up, and they're gone. Then, and only then, do we wish we had paid more attention to them. Are we addressing the issues of Satanism, of the occult, and of sexual and ritual abuse, or are we hushing it up because we're uncomfortable with them? "Besides," we're quick to notice, "most people say this kind of stuff doesn't happen anyway. It's just a hoax. It's an 'urban myth' that creates hysteria. Let's leave well enough alone."

Well, we can leave it alone. We can ignore it. We can deny it. We can refuse to address it. But one day, any one of us could wake up to find it in our community or, perhaps, in our house with our own son or daughter. Then the words "hoax," "urban myth," and "hysteria" will no longer describe Satanic cult involvement and ritual abuse. Those words will be replaced by the word *reality*. It will become the order for the day.

Reality Hits Home

I'll never forget the remarks of then Attorney General of Texas, Jim Mattox, on "Larry King Live." Referring to the Matamoros ritual murders, Mr. Mattox told of a seminar that had just been held in Texas. He said that several of his men had attended the seminar and had come back joking about it, saying how this stuff just doesn't happen, that it's just too bizarre. Mr. Mattox

admitted that he had joined in the laughter. His appear-
ance on "Larry King Live" was just one day after the ritual murders had been discovered. He had just hours
before returned from the Matamoros grave site. There
was no joking this time. I was on the show, and I wasn't
joking. Pat Pulling, whose son's suicide had, at least in
part, been influenced by his intense involvement with
the game *Dungeons and Dragons*, wasn't joking either.
None of us was smiling when the Attorney General of
Texas looked squarely into the television camera and solemnly said, "Folks, I saw the sacrifices. I'll never laugh
about this again."[29]

Satanic ritual abuse almost has to happen to someone
you know—your child, your nephew, your niece, your
neighbor's son, or perhaps your youngster's playmate in
a preschool or day care center—before you become a believer. Then, this insane evil shakes you to the core of
your being.

I am reminded of the large red block letters that
greeted me when I entered the Los Angeles Simon Wiesenthal Center for the Study of the Jewish Holocaust.
The blocks spell the word **REMEMBER**.

Is it possible that anyone could forget the Holocaust?
Is it possible that anyone could forget Jonestown?
Is it possible that anyone could forget Tiananmen
Square?

And is it possible that anyone could forget the story of
the severed and skinned head of a frightened and lonely
fifteen-year-old runaway? **Yes!** Because if it doesn't in-
vade our own life, we Americans are good at forgetting
. . . *too* good at forgetting. Denial doesn't just happen in
other countries. We in the United States are experts at
that, too!

Let us remember—

Little Adam Mann, *stripped naked.*
Lisa Steinberg, *stripped naked.*
The victims of "Uncle Eddy," *stripped naked.*
Little and alone, Jesus Castro, *stripped naked.*
Mark Kilroy, *stripped naked.*
Jim Hardy, Ron Clements, Pete Roland,
and Steven Newberry,
stripped naked.
Sean Sellers, *stripped naked.*
Tommy Sullivan, *stripped naked.*
Dereck Taylor, *stripped naked.*
Steven Loequano, *stripped naked.*

The devil's workshop has been very, very busy.

13

Fact or Fiction?

**"You can tell the world what happened here,
but they will never believe you."**[1]

IDAHO: An Act relating to ritualized abuse of a child;
. . . by the addition of a new section 18-1506A . . . To
provide a felony offense for specified abuse of a child as
part of a ritual . . . Passed 1990.

"A person is guilty of a felony when he commits any of
the following acts with, upon, or in the presence of a child
as part of a ceremony, rite or any similar observance:

18-1506A

    (a) Actually or in simulation, tortures, mutilates or
        sacrifices any warm-blooded animal or human
        being;

    (b) Forces ingestion, injection or other application
        of any narcotic, drug, hallucinogen or anaes-
        thetic for the purpose of dulling sensitivity, cog-
        nition, recollection of, or resistance to any
        criminal activity;

    (c) Forces ingestion, or external application, of hu-
        man or animal urine, feces, flesh, blood, bones,
        body secretions, non-prescribed drugs or chem-
        ical compounds;

    (d) Involves the child in a mock unauthorized or
        unlawful marriage ceremony with another per-
        son or representation of any force or deity, fol-
        lowed by sexual contact with the child;

(e) Places a living child into a coffin or open grave containing a human corpse or remains;

(f) Threatens death or serious harm to a child, his parents, family, pets or friends which instills a well-founded fear in the child that the threat will be carried out; or

(g) Unlawfully dissects, mutilates, or incinerates a human corpse."

This almost sounds like an amendment to the Ten Commandments, doesn't it? Am I reading right? Am I to understand that one of our states has found it necessary to pass legislation in order to make it a punishable crime to torture children; to mutilate or to sacrifice a human being; to force someone to ingest feces, flesh, and blood; to place a living child into a coffin containing a human corpse, etc.?

Section 2 of bill 18-5003 actually is headed by the following words: **"CANNIBALISM DEFINED"**

(1) Any person who wilfully ingests the flesh or blood of a human being is guilty of cannibalism.

Honest, I'm not making this up. I thought most of us already knew what cannibalism was, but, if we need a law to spell it out and make it a felony, I'm all for it.

What a startling sign of the state of affairs in our country that we should even have to consider such a crime bill, but thank God, those in places of high position are realizing the need for these kinds of bills.

I am a survivor of ritual abuse. There are those in our country who are only too ready to state from any forum they can find to declare that ritual abuse simply does not happen. It's a myth, an "urban folk legend," if you will. As a survivor, I feel validated when the courts of our land find this issue serious enough to enact legislation against ritual abuse, spelling it out word for word. That indicates to me that our court system is saying that ritual abuse does indeed take place, and ritual abuse is absolutely not acceptable. Therefore ritual abuse will be punishable by law.

I gave a talk to a room full of attorneys and judges several years ago. A bill such as the Idaho bill was virtually non-existent at that time. Part of what I said was:

"Judges and attorneys are being inundated with heretofore unheard of cases of ritual abuse. The legal ramifications of ritual abuse cases are far more involved than sexual abuse cases. The more bizarre the ritual crime, the less apt the court system is to successfully gain a conviction.

"When a law becomes a hindrance; when existing laws do not relate to or possibly may even do harm to the new crises; or when there simply are no laws to cover a certain type of abuse; then those laws need to be changed and/or new laws need to be passed. Laws must fit the crime, and presently, our country has no laws to fit crimes of ritual abuse and/or ritual murder.

"Laws do not necessarily remain effective laws forever. As our nation changes, and as the crimes of our nation change, so must our laws be revised, modified, or new ones need to be passed. Our laws should not be carved in stone to remain forever as they were one hundred years ago.

"Hundreds of children have been taken into the underground by their mothers to protect them from their fathers who have ritually abused them. Surely this is not good for the child, but, for them, it has seemed to be the only solution. I cannot think of much else that would match the trauma of a child not being able to live a normal life, rather having to exist in the underground . . . nothing, that is, other than the ritual abuse continuing if the child remains at home.

"There is something drastically wrong when anyone in our nation feels driven to resort to this type of safeguard in order to protect a child. The choice of mothers to hide their children in the underground is a devastating choice for all concerned, but until all fifty states pass new legislation to accommodate the specific and unique crimes of ritual abuse, the underground will remain, and no one wins."[2]

I was especially moved, when, after I finished my talk, an attorney came up to the podium. He whispered so softly that I could barely hear what he was saying. The gist of his disclosure was that his wife and children had been ritually abused and they needed help. He apologized for speaking so softly, but he said that he didn't want his colleagues to hear what he was saying. He ended by whispering a sentence I've heard over and over again. I've heard it from people from all walks of life who have been touched by ritual abuse. "It's a secret," he whispered. He gave me his business card and immediately blended into the crowd of his colleagues. Ritual crimes know no boundaries.

At the time of this writing, four states have passed such crime bills: Idaho, Texas, Illinois, and Louisiana. The state of Utah is working toward forming a task force to determine the need for such a bill. The United Kingdom is following suit. A state senator from California is authoring new legislation, in the form of a Senate Concurrent Resolution, to set up a Ritual Child Abuse Advisory Committee. The purpose of this committee will be to look into the problem of ritual child abuse.

I am especially gratified that the state of Louisiana has, in its subsection of Crime Bill 107.1, B3, included a section that is needed in every crime bill across the country. To my knowledge, Louisiana is the first state to include this sentence:

B.(3)

No person shall commit ritualistic psychological abuse of children or of physically or mentally disabled adults as part of a ceremony, rite, initiation, observance, performance, or practice.

The operative word here is the word *psychological* abuse. Most physical wounds heal in time. Psychological wounds do not. Physical wounds are oftentimes apparent. Psychological wounds may not be. For most victims of ritual abuse, the most lingering of wounds are those that have been made to the person's mind. These are the wounds that must be carefully tended to if a victim is to be restored to wholeness. Louisiana, I applaud your insight! I also applaud the State of Idaho for including the word "simulation" in referring to tortures, mutilations, and sacrifices of animals or human beings. Many children have seen just that, a *simulation* of animal or human tortures, mutilations, and sacrifices. The child, in *thinking* it is real, is just as traumatized as the child who has witnessed an actual torture, mutilation, or sacrifice. However, I must still add that there are children and adults who have witnessed in actuality such grisly atrocities.

Hear Ye, Hear Ye!

To the doubters; to the unbelievers; to those who have closed their eyes and ears; to those who snicker about people who actually believe the stories that survivors tell, calling them "gullible," or "true believers," or some other put-down, I would pose a question: *If* there is no such thing as ritual abuse; *if* there are no "real" survivors of ritual abuse; *if* there is no evidence of ritual abuse and/or sacrifices — then why in the world would intelligent, successful, and clear-thinking politicians, those whom we have voted into office, work so tirelessly to get bills passed through the legislature making the ritualized abuse of a child a felony? *If* there were no crimes of ritual abuse and/or sacrifices taking place, doesn't it stand to reason that legislatures wouldn't give such bizarre nonsense the time of day? Legislatures don't go through the agonizing and time-consuming process of fashioning bills, laboriously pushing them through the House and the Senate just for fun. There must be a proven reason for such bills.

As far as I am concerned, the very fact that states in America and states and provinces in other countries are beginning to establish task forces on ritual abuse and others have already passed laws making ritual abuse and sacrifice a felonious crime, tips the scales in favor of *fact as* opposed to *fiction*.

Jean-Jacques Gautier writes in his treatise on "The Case for an Effective and Realistic Procedure," "It is hardly meaningful to demand of governments who deny the existence of torture within their frontiers that they abolish it in their own countries."[3]

That which *does not exist* needs no laws abolishing it. Only that which *does exist* needs laws abolishing it. Obviously, the various states whose laws have been presented here give acknowledgement to the fact that ritual abuse does occur in the United States.

"Where's the Evidence?" You Cry

I have before me a copy of a judgment handed down by a county court in Mississippi that specifically states ". . . that while in the custody of [the parent], [the child] was subjected to mistreatment and Satanic ritual abuse." The judgment is signed by the chancellor and dated October 20, 1989. Did you get that? Lest it pass the naysayers by, allow me to reiterate the crucial words in the judgment again. The child was subjected to "Satanic ritual abuse."

As more laws are passed by state legislative bodies like the ones cited in this chapter, the words "ritual abuse" will be found in more and more court judgments. And in the cases where the specific accusations of ritual abuse cannot be proven, we must remember that in no way does it mean the abuse didn't happen or that ritual abuse and sacrifice do not exist.

A private investigator worked on a case of alleged Satanic sacrifice in Texas. The case was shown on a television program.[4] A private detective found six trash bags containing letters that had been written between cult members. Each member had a code name. There was an ominous tone to one of the letters. "See you at 9:30. Please bring Gwen." Gwen was but a youngster.

There was cause for grave concern that perhaps Gwen was to be used as a human sacrifice, for in the trash among the letters, was found a "recipe" for killing and dismembering bodies. There was a photo of Gwen's mother who had been mysteriously ripped apart and died. There was also a photo of Gwen's father in a clerical robe of some sort.

Investigators also found a magazine on incest and a sheet of the names of Satanists connected with child pornography. Little Gwen was first and foremost on the detective's mind. He had grave concern for her whereabouts.

The detective did not stop until he found Gwen. As he flew with her back home, his hand tightly held her hand all the way. Although specifics were not given, the detective commented, "I believe the unspeakable things they did to her."

"Where's the evidence?" you cry. I quote Raul Hilberg, the great historian who spoke on Claude Lanzmann's epic film, *SHOAH, An Oral History Of The Holocaust.* "In speaking of the Nazi Germans and their hideous atrocities, Mr. Hilberg says, '. . . they did not copyright or patent their achievements, and they prefer obscurity'."[5]

This is also true of those who are the perpetrators of cult crimes. They do not copyright or patent their achievements, and they prefer obscurity. Just because the evidence is often difficult to find, do we throw out the baby with the bath water? Do we throw in the towel? Do we throw up our hands in resignation? Or do we begin to take a stand as several of our states are doing in forming task forces and passing new bills? I think some of those in authority have made a start in the right direction. My fervent hope is that others will follow.

Isolated Cases?

"Oh, it's just an *isolated* case," we say. We have a unique way of isolating every situation that we find uncomfortable. That way, the numbers of those isolated cases don't add up to a large number that we cannot avoid any longer. Nice and neat. No fuss. No muss. No sweat. Just another "isolated case."

Tell that to the mother who lost her teenage son in a gang-related shooting ten years ago. She was interviewed by a television reporter after the L.A. uprising began to cool down. "They [the police] called it an isolated incident then, and they're still calling it an isolated incident." Her voice grew louder, and she cut loose! "Just how many sons do we mothers have to lose before they stop calling them isolated incidents, and they become what they *really* are—a major problem?" I was raising my arm in the air and yelling, "Preach it, sister. Preach it!" That mother told it like it really was with enough conviction and fervor for herself and me put together.

I ask, How many fifteen-year-old runaways have to be ritually abused, tortured, and perhaps even murdered before we recognize it to be a major problem, and not just isolated cases? How many teenage boys will murder in the name of Satan before we recognize it as a major problem? How many teenagers will commit suicide as their only foreseeable way of escape from their involvement in Satanism before we recognize it as a major problem? And how many survivors of incest and ritual abuse will have to tell their stories before we lay down our denial and recognize it as a major problem?

We Have a Major Problem Here

Evidence of ritual abuses, murders, and suicides have been cited throughout several chapters. However, to the skeptics, I could never cite enough examples to convince them that we do have a major problem with ritual abuses, murders, and ritual suicides. For myself, I need look no further. To those who need more body counts, my feeling is that it is likely that no evidence will be sufficient for them. There are those who will not accept *any* kind of evidence as proof that acts of criminal ritual abuse occur. Staunch nonbelievers will continue to resort to the argument that has been stated in previous chapters, that all survivors are lying, or that our parents, therapists, or the books we read and movies we see are brainwashing us. It is not to those of you who are impervious to evidence that ritual abuse is real that I provide the following cases. It is for those of you who are sincerely listening, and struggling to integrate this hard-to-digest information.

The Little Rascals Day Care Center case is one of the most recent publicized cases of ritual abuse in day care. According to *Time* magazine, Robert Kelly, Jr. has been sentenced to twelve consecutive life terms (one for each victim) after being found guilty on ninety-nine counts of sexual molestation involving twelve four- to seven-year-olds. Disclosures of ritual abuse were included with descriptions of rape, drugging, and photographing a child as she was forced to perform sexual acts with another child. Ritual abuse acts, involving animal sacrifice, fire, and snakes were also made. One boy claimed that Mr. Kelly prayed to the devil.

Please hear this. "Though some of the children's tales

verged on the fantastic, their testimony proved strong enough to convict Kelly."[6] I do not know whether this judgment included the words, "ritual abuse," but even if it didn't, the allegations were made and, unlike so many cases in the past, this one was not thrown out of court *because* of them. This is a victory in itself!

I have said it over and over again. If a case is thrown out of court because of bizarre allegations of ritual abuse, or if the allegations of ritual abuse are omitted from the courtroom in a carefully planned strategy to assure a conviction of at least sexual molestation, it does not mean that ritual abuse did not happen. It simply means that the court was not able to handle the allegations of ritual abuse. This is precisely why our states need new laws.

I noted in the *Time* article that special mention was made of the massive expense ($1.2 million) of the trial of the Little Rascals Day Care Center. Since when do we equate money with the safety of our nation's children?

I have heard some "experts" who repeatedly say that ritual abuse simply does not exist, and that our court system has "wasted" millions of dollars on trials of innocent people who have been accused of ritual abuse. These millions of dollars, they say, could better be used to bolster our nation's sagging economy. Hogwash! I'm certain that the parents of these children, and most thoughtful Americans, would take great exception to the idea that economics are more important than the safety of young children.

Now, That's Bizarre!

I am quoting from a book whose author I did several talk shows with on the CBS network in the summer of 1988. ". . . experts, like Dr. Lee Coleman, argue that the bizarre nature of the stories is proof that they did not occur."[7] Excuse me? Am I reading correctly? Is psychiatrist,

Dr. Coleman, actually saying that bizarre stories cannot be true?

Was the cult of Jonestown not bizarre in nature? Let me remind you, first of all, that Jonestown had its beginnings in *our* country and in one of *our* cities, San Francisco. We tend to dismiss it, because, once again, as we did with the Matamoros incident, it happened on foreign soil, not on ours. Second, let us remember that 276 children were murdered, yes, on foreign soil, but each one of those children was born in the United States. When President Jimmy Carter responded to the Jonestown tragedy by saying, in part, that we should remember that Jonestown did not take place in our country, I wonder what kind of message he was trying to give to us. Can we excuse the murder of 276 children and their parents just because the Jonestown tragedy occurred in another country? God forbid!

U.S. Attorney General Griffin Bell had in his possession the murder/suicide cassette tapes found at Jonestown. He, however, chose not to listen to them saying, "I do not suffer from morbid curiosity. . . . Jonestown was an aberration that is not likely to occur again."[8] Come again? Have we yet another example of burying our heads in the sand to protect us from hearing disquieting facts? Perhaps Jonestown was an aberration on the grounds that it substantially departed from the standard or the norm. So was the Holocaust!

Ritual abuse and murder certainly depart from the norm. Should we call it an aberration on that basis? I think not. Thank God, such tragedies are not the norm, but that does not mean that they are not continuing somewhere. And that they will more than likely continue until we pull our heads out of the sand, listen to those victims who are screaming to be heard, and take actions to insure the safety of all our citizens. We may not be talking about 276 children being murdered at one time, at one location. But we are talking about such abuses and murders happening one at a time and one at a time and one at a time . . . Each one counts, and each one adds to the count of the one before and to the one before that.

It is a fact that Jonestown occurred *in spite of its bizarre nature*, just as the Holocaust occurred *in spite of its bizarre nature*.

Dr. Michael Durfee, child psychiatrist and medical coordinator for the Los Angeles County Department of Health Services child-abuse prevention program remarked, "We have a problem in acknowledging that people kill kids; that there are those who methodically torture and kill babies. It's not a *technical* problem. It's a *cultural* problem for we who live in America. We just can't handle such information."[9] As long as we remain insulated to these shocking facts, the horrors will indeed continue, yes, even in *this* country.

To the red block letters at the Simon Wiesenthal Center that spell out the word **"REMEMBER,"** I would add the words, **"LISTEN, LEARN & DO SOMETHING!"** A country of "do nothings" we do not need. The word **"DENIAL"** is not acceptable. Myra Riddell, a member of the Los Angeles County Commission for Women, and Chairperson of the Los Angeles Task Force on Ritual Abuse, mirrored the feelings of many when she stated emphatically, "The concept of ritual abuse, that groups of people in cults would terrorize and torture children in order to control them, is frightening and controversial, raising for us problems of denial and fear of the consequences of such information. We do not need more examples of this denial."[10]

The Unspeakable Was Finally Spoken

There was The Country Walk Babysitting Service in an upscale suburb of Miami—the perfect place for children to be, reasoned the parents, because the babysitter called her little charges "bundles of love." Then, there was The Country Walk Babysitting Service in an upscale suburb of Miami where those "bundles of love" were abused in ways that were almost too heinous to speak about.

Five-year-old Jason was the abused product of The Country Walk Babysitting Service. He had been telling of horrors, horrors that made his parents feel like they were walking around in a fog that never lifted. Their world had almost become surrealistic. At times, they just wanted to die.

Jason told of his penis being put in Iliana's [the babysitter] mouth. He told of being forced to play with another boy's penis and of being forced to kiss a little girls "gina." He said that he had to kiss Iliana's butt, and that Frank [Iliana's husband] peed in his mouth.

"Jason describes a game called 'Who's gonna lose their head?' Frank played it with a knife. Jason said, 'I don't want to die. I'm only five years old, and dying is bad . . .'"[11]

The Prayer

> "Devil, I love you.
> Please take this bird with you
>   and take all the children up to hell with you.
> You gave me the grateful gifts.
> God of Ghosts, please hate Jesus and kill Jesus
>   because
> He is the baddest, dammnedest person in the
>   whole world.
>
> Amen.
>
> We don't love children because they are a gift of
>   God.
> We want the children to be hurt.
> Signed, Iliana and Frank
Amen."[12]

"Suddenly, he blurted out a string of words that sounded to his astonished father like the cadence of a prayer. Jason knew it backward, forward, and sideways. His father stared at the piece of paper on which he had written the words dictated by his five year old son and knew with stark clarity that in his hands he held the one piece of the puzzle that, for him, connected all the rest."[13]

The outcome for all the children and all the parents who were so devastated? The Dade County, Florida, Country Walk Babysitting Service Trial. Frank Fuster, an already convicted child molester was once again arrested and convicted. The sentence? One hundred sixty-five years in prison. Frank Fuster will be eligible for parole in the year 2150.

The parents heaved a sigh of relief. They clutched each other. They cried. Their agonizing nightmare was finally over. Or was it? The children continued to tell of unspeakable acts long after Iliana and Frank Fuster were convicted and the trial was over.

"Only time will tell how scarring are their wounds. That depends largely," say the Bragas, "on their willing-ness to keep cracked the 'window of disclosure'."[14] Drs. Joe and Laurie Braga were development psychologists who worked with the DA's office so forensic questions could be asked in a three- and four-year-olds' language. They gave some of the most crucial testimony for the prosecution. Some of the children testified. They were believed. Score one for our side!

What scarring wounds are the Bragas referring to? The wounds Jason described. He described more . . . of having to kneel on the floor while Frank pushed his pe-nis in his behind. Jason was believed. And the wounds the other children told? They told of having to eat shit, of having to poo-poo after which it was rubbed on their hands and face by Frank and Iliana. The children were believed. They told of having to sit in the bathtub while

Frank peed on them. The children were believed. They told of having several fingers stuck in their anus and their vagina at the same time. The children were believed. It gets worse. Much worse! But you get the picture.

Then, there was Chip, one of the children who was horrendously abused, physically and psychologically, who could not be pacified when his mother told him that Frank and Iliana were sent to jail for what they had done to him. Chip kept insisting, day after day, that Frank and Iliana would get out. No amount of reassuring swayed his fear.

Chip then made what to me is one of the most heart-wrenching sentences I will ever read. To his mother, he screamed, "'But I called for you! I cried for you to help me and you never came! . . . Why did you leave me there'?"[15]

In referring to the Frank and Iliana Fuster case, Jan Hollingsworth, the author of *Unspeakable Acts* which chronicles the events of abuse and the ensuing trial, makes a poignant observation. "But for every Chip, there are two others for whom the door is nailed shut. There are Fuster babysitting customers scattered all over the map . . . whose parents continue to deny themselves the dignity of acknowledging the truth. These children might never learn the lessons of a 'burden shared' as have the children who were allowed to dignify their pain."[16]

As long as we continue to deny the truth of reports of ritual abuse, even those from our own children, the survivors will be denied the chance to heal. We are often half-heartedly on the side of the whole truth. If the truth is still positive and gives us a good feeling, we become champions of that truth. *But,* if the whole truth hurts our consciences or makes us feel uncomfortable, we find a way to put it aside or deny it totally. Then it doesn't exist, and we can get on with our lives. Can we afford to do that with our little ones, to those who look to us for protection?

Children in Terror

Jonathan, Three Years Old

Jonathan came home from preschool one day and said emphatically, "Mommy, I don't want to eat anymore, because I don't want to grow older. Something bad is going to happen to me if I grow to be six years old." Since Jonathan's disclosure, he has gone on a starvation diet, refusing to eat anything.

A few days later, Jonathan came home again and said "Mommy, I want to get rid of my 'boy parts' so I can't be hurt again." Jonathan had been toilet trained and had graduated to drinking from a glass. He reverts back to wearing diapers and drinking from a baby bottle.

If you were the parents of Jonathan, what would *you* do?

Jimmy, Four Years Old

Jimmy used to love going to preschool. For no apparent reason, he began to cry every morning, saying that he didn't want to go to preschool any more. Then he began crying the night before school. After his mother would get him to sleep, Jimmy began to have nightmares from which he would wake himself screaming, "Teacher, don't hurt me!"

If you were the parents of Jimmy, what would *you* do?

Jimmy began to talk about his pee-pee hurting. When his mother asked him why it was hurting, he said that his teacher hurt him there with her mouth. Jimmy's mother was horrified. She didn't know what to think or do.

Wouldn't you be horrified? Would you know what to do? Or would you be tempted to ignore it and hope that your child's disclosures would go away as suddenly as they had appeared?

Jimmy attends Sunday school. He has always been excited about getting dressed up for his teacher. But one Sunday, after the class was over and he was on his way home with his parents, Jimmy blurted out, "Jesus is bad. Jesus hates little children." Nothing his mother and father said convinced him that that wasn't true. Jimmy began to color all the pictures of Jesus in his coloring book in black. Even when his mother gave him other crayons, he would throw them down and pick the black crayon up again.

Then Jimmy began talking to the rocking chair in the living room. When his mother asked him to whom he was talking, he answered, "My teacher said that there would always be a person sitting in a chair in the living room. I can't see him, but I know he's there. My teacher told me that he is always watching me, and he will tell the bad people if I tell what happens at school."

After being put to bed one evening, Jimmy came running out of his room and into his mother's arms. "What's wrong, honey?" Jimmy answered. "Mommy, my teacher said that a stranger would always be hiding in the closet, and at night he would come out and hurt me when I'm in bed."

The last straw came when Jimmy and his parents went over to one of their friend's homes for a barbecue. Jimmy always liked to go over there, because he could play with the other kids. He was especially excited this evening, because Jimmy loves hamburgers. It is his most "favortist" food.

Both families sat down at the dinner table. The children's eyes were on the plate of hamburgers which had been placed right in front of them. They were all a little reluctant to close their eyes when it came time for the blessing to be said, but they did. No sooner had Jimmy's father gotten out the words, "Dear Jesus," than Jimmy screamed at the top of his voice, "You can't pray to Jesus any more. He's bad. He hurts children!" The clincher was to follow. "*You can only pray to Satan now!*"

What would be *your* reaction?

Jimmy's parents were aghast. The host's parents were aghast. All eyes were on four-year-old Jimmy. There was no blessing of the food that evening. There was only bewilderment, frustration, and questions, so very many questions.

Sally, Four years old

Sally came home with a story about "The Big Bad Wolf," one of the many stories about The Big Bad Wolf her family was to hear. Sally talked about The Big Bad Wolf who could change into a man and get into her house. Sally said that the Big Bad Wolf would stick pins in her bottom to make blood come out. She covered her bottom with her hands as she talked. The Big Bad Wolf could also make her die. Sally said that The Big Bad Wolf wouldn't let kids eat if they told "the secret." Sally told. Both Jonathan and Sally have told the same secret. Now, there are *two* three-year-olds on a starvation diet.

David, Four Years Old

David came home from preschool one afternoon and announced that he wanted to die. He said that he wanted to shoot himself, but he couldn't find a gun. He said that he wanted to stab himself, so his mother hid the knives. As the last resort, David tried to drown himself in a way that only a four-year-old would think of. David filled a glass with water, held his head back, and tried to pour the water up his nose.

If you were David's mother, how would you assess your son's actions? Do you know who you would tell? Or would you tell no one? Do you know to whom you would take him for consultation? Or would you decide not to take him to anyone?

The Signs Begin to Add Up

All four children have shown similar behavioral changes and have made the same disclosures. Some of them are:

—not wanting to go to preschool.
—saying that bad things happen in the preschool bathroom.
—having continued nightmares of being hurt.
—talking about being threatened not to tell "the secret."
—saying someone would die if they told.
—using violent "death talk" against parents and others.
—using only black when coloring.
—coloring in aggressive and strong strokes.
—saying that Jesus wants to hurt children.
—saying that Jesus hates children.
—talking about group nudity.
—referring to people in costumes, usually black in color.
—talking about black and red candles being lit.
—talking about having to swallow pills they were given.
—speaking of being tied with ropes and being handcuffed.
—talking about seeing red liquid or blood in the glass.

I can hear the naysayer psychologists who are the "expert" witnesses against children. "The children were coached by their parents," they will say. No, it won't work. Not this time. None of the parents of these children had ever heard the words "ritual abuse." They were as naive about ritual abuse as naivety can get. They just knew that, suddenly, *something* was terribly wrong, but they had no idea what that something was.

I can hear the second accusation. "Surely it was the therapists who 'implanted' such bizarre stories into the children's minds." Remember Dr. Lee Coleman's statement that the bizarre nature of the stories is *proof* they did not occur? Excuse me, but that theory, or "proof test" won't work this time either. These children had yet to go to a therapist.

I guess then we just must have four children who held secret meetings at the preschool to devise an intricate plot to stir up some big-time excitement! The reason? I don't know, but I'm sure the children will tell you.

Well, our naysayers will say, "Four kids out of dozens of kids doesn't mean anything." First, let me tell you that if just *one* child showed such behavior and talked of such abuses, I would be deeply concerned. So would most people, for that matter. But these *four* kids have now been joined by *many* kids.

Oh, yes. I now hear the naysayers cry, "Cross contamination. Unfair!" Sorry. Not in this case. Up to this time, none of the parents had spoken to each other. Each was alone in their quandary. And I can't really buy the top-secret planning meeting by the three- and four-year-olds.

Do I hear another voice? "Well, the parents aren't very well-educated. They could be convinced of anything." Wrong again. Some of the parents of these children are, but not limited to, a judge's son, a lawyer's daughter, a pastor's son, a surgeon's son, and a policeman's daughter.

Well then, I guess we'll have to resort to our ever faithful explanation that children do lie, and children do make up fairy tales. I couldn't agree with you more. When the cookies disappear from the cookie jar, they often go into the stomach of a wide-eyed child. But when that child is questioned about it, seldom does he or she admit to it. It's always the *other* brother or sister who took the cookies. Are we to interpret that as proof that children and adults lie about *everything*?

But what about the scary things? Are they pretending when they wake up from a fitful sleep screaming, "Teacher, don't hurt me!"? Is David play acting when he tries to drown himself? I think not.

Let us not forget the dozens of other children who remain at the preschool. A medical doctor examined several of the children who were taken out of school when so many strange behavioral signs, symptoms, and allegations were first noted and heard by the parents. The doctor's findings, you ask? It was noted that signs of sexual molestation had taken place, and the doctor was concerned for the safety of the other children still attending the preschool.

Jonathan, Jimmy, Sally, and David, and quite possibly, other children who enrolled at the preschool—each have been stripped naked—in one way or another.

I bowed my head after writing this page and thanked God that it was summertime and school was out.

Is There No Justice?

What you have just read are true situations that parents have had to deal with. What would *you* have done if one of these children was yours? Would you have responded with a sense of urgency or would it have been easier for you to chalk your child's frightening disclosures to an overactive imagination as many of us tend to do? These are the kinds of horrors that parents across the country and in other countries have had to deal with. Some are living through nightmares like this one even now.

The parents cry for justice, justice for their own child who has been ritually abused. Their child doesn't understand why the bad people aren't in jail. They keep asking, "Mommy, don't all bad people go to jail?" The parents have no answers. *They* don't even understand why the people who did this to their child aren't in jail. It

seems that the perpetrators have more rights and protection under the law than their child has. Is this justice?

Even when other families who didn't have their children in that preschool joined the others in crying for
justice, and the powers that be said that they had no
right to talk because their children weren't involved, to
whom could they turn?

How does the community respond when one set of
professionals argues that these children indeed have
been victimized, and another set of professionals argues
that there isn't enough evidence to prove that the children had been victimized? How does the community respond when one set of professionals says that the school
should be closed until a full investigation has been completed and another set of professionals says there's not
enough evidence to warrant it? How does the community respond when the case is never brought to trial because the courts say that the children are too young to
give credible testimonies?

I know how some families have chosen to deal with it.
They are moving out of town just to get away. They feel
that their town has failed them. I know of one case of
ritual abuse where every child on the block on both sides
of the street was abused. All but one family has not only
moved out of town, but they have moved out of the state.
There is but one family left on the block.

What happens to the community when there are two
camps, and the chasm is wide and deep? Is it possible to
bridge the chasm? What happens to the ethos of the
community when there is no closure, one way or the
other, and the allegations continue to weigh heavily on
the people's minds? Where there is no closure, the ethos
of the community will always experience an existential
chaos, a disturbance of woundedness, of suspicions, and of
accusations. This is true especially of a smaller community.

However, I have been witness to parents, whose children who have been victimized in the same setting,

becoming divided and at odds with each other. They're frustrated and angry at the system. They feel the system has failed them, so they take their feelings out on each other. Do they press charges? Do they not press charges? Should the children be in therapy or should the parents try to heal their child's wounds with no external intervention? Should they even let their child's disclosures be known to anyone? Or should they discuss their plight with the press in hopes of putting pressure on the legal system to take notice?

Where there is no closure, the nagging doubts never go away. Did it or did it not happen? For frightened parents, this question does not fade away in time. It becomes permanently rooted in the very fiber of their being. Emotional pain, anger, and resentment will become their closest neighbor.

No community is safe and protected until its residents are willing to lay down their natural instincts of denial and take responsibility. If children are not to be believed, aren't we sending a signal to cult perpetrators that our children are fair game in our community? If a solid stance is not taken, then aren't we declaring, without putting it in print, that children can be victimized in our community?

Do we have children who are trying to tell the world, but the world will not listen, let alone, believe them? Could one of them be your child? Could these children be in your community?

But Why Our Little Ones?

"Satanic cults focus their initial efforts to achieve mind control most frequently and strenuously with children under the age of six. Like developmental psychologists, Satanists understand that people are most susceptible to having their character, beliefs, and behavior molded during this early period of development."[17]

Children stimulate our protective instincts. Their vulnerability and innocence demand special care. Little children don't know how to protect their minds from the evil plans of others. Their minds are open, uncorrupted, and wholesome. Yet minds with such innocence and openness are targets. They are like receptacles willing to receive anything, no questions asked.

To Believe or Not to Believe

The fate of victims, both children and adults alike, often hangs in the balance of how we measure *the credibility* of those who dare to tell us their horrendous stories. Child victims will continue to be abused. There will be no healing for them. Adult victims will continue to be abused. There will be no healing for them. And perpetrators will continue to abuse . . . that is, until we shed our systems of denial.

Dr. Michael Durfee disagrees with Dr. Coleman's belief that bizarre stories cannot be true. Dr. Durfee remarks that, "The reason kids talk about rituals and chanting and wearing robes and killing babies is because it happened. . . . I don't want to believe that people are doing these things to children, but the stories are too patterned, too consistent not to be true."[18]

"Delivering a lecture titled, 'The Child Sexual Abuse Backlash,' by Howard Davidson, director of the American Bar Association, Center on Children and the Law, Mr. Davidson said, 'Regarding the truth of children's reports, generally, what the child says happened is the best indication of what did happen. If the child spontaneously tells a trusted adult, then gives details, you can be almost certain that the child is speaking the truth'."[19]

The operative word here is "spontaneously." Uncontaminated, unrehearsed, spontaneous disclosures from young children can only be born from the truth.

Special care must be taken when treating children of

ritual abuse. Children are not eager, contrary to some experts' beliefs, to tell of such acts that have made them feel dirty, ashamed, and guilty. Many, if not most victims of sexual abuse and ritual abuse, tend to clam up. The horrifying threats that are made to these victims virtually insures that they will not talk. It may take months and months of building relationships of trust before they begin to make any verbal disclosures. The signs of what took place begin to come out first in changes in behavior, in play patterns, in disturbing nightmares, in unusual fears, in sudden insecurities, etc.

Sometimes, it is necessary to let the child know that it is okay to tell Mommy or the therapist about the awful things that happened. Sometimes a directive question such as, "Did anyone touch you somewhere and you didn't like it or it hurt?" gives the child permission to tell. Giving the child anatomically correct dolls is a less confrontive and less intimidating way of allowing the child to "speak without speaking." Often, the child's actions speak much louder than his or her words. Is this what the critics call coaching, brainwashing, programming, and fabricating for the child a story that never happened? I think not.

In an unpublished letter by the director of The National Center for Prosecution of Child Abuse, Patricia Toth states, "What [research] does show is that children are unlikely to reveal abuse unless they are questioned directly about it—confirming what experts have known for a long time—that children are far more likely to lie by denying abuse in order to avoid the horror of public exposure and family chaos generally accompanying disclosure. Prosecutors and expert witnesses face a dilemma: 'leading' questions may be necessary with young children to elicit the truth most effectively, yet their use raises the spectre of 'suggestibility' and can taint any information offered."[20]

Dr. David Young, clinical director of the Kempe National Center for the Prevention and Treatment of Child Abuse and Neglect, did an exacting study on the plausibility of children making false allegations. Dr. Young presented his findings at the seventieth National Conference on Child Abuse and Neglect.

"Children rarely make false allegations of being sexually abused even though the public generally will believe the adult being accused instead of the youngster." Dr. Young went on to say that, "Children who made such allegations were lying or incorrect less than 2 percent of the time. . . . I found that children make false or fictitious accounts very rarely."[21]

A more recent finding, printed in an article on incest, corroborates Dr. Young's findings. The study examined, among other things, the reliability of children's memories. Can they be made up? Do leading questions under directive therapy by parents, by law enforcement, or by therapists create false accusations?

Gail Goodman, a psychologist at the State University of New York, Buffalo, designed studies "to test the accuracy of children's recall under stress and how children respond to leading or strongly suggestive questions designed to bring about false accusations."[22] Dr. Goodman set up a scenario where children were taken into a dilapidated trailer where they encountered a man who talked to them using hand puppets. He put on a mask. He photographed the children. He played a game where the children tickled him. He played another game during which he and the children touched knees.

"Ten to twelve days later, the children were asked the kinds of questions that might lead to a charge of sexual abuse: 'He took your clothes off, right?' [The children] could not be led into sexualized answers. They became embarrassed by the leading question, looked surprised, covered their eyes, or, according to Goodman, asked in disbelief if we would repeat the question."[23]

Dr. Goodman even went so far as to use anatomically correct dolls to see if the dolls would encourage false reports of sexual abuse. The study's conclusion on this one point was: "Whether or not the children were interviewed with anatomically detailed dolls . . . did not influence their responses to the specific or misleading abuse questions."[24] One year later, Dr. Goodman re-interviewed several of the children. "Even after the children had listened repeatedly to leading questions, most persisted in reporting the incident [of one year ago] exactly as it had taken place."[25]

The conclusion of Dr. Goodman's study was that perhaps children would not remember superficial incidents, but "child abuse involves actions directed against a child's body. Such a violation is memorable."[26]

Sexual abuse assaults the body, the mind, and the emotions. The abuse is total. The abuse instills fear of the worst kind imaginable. Sexual abuse is an integral part of ritual abuse. Fear, control, reprisals, and consequences "if they tell the secret," keep the child quiet. If that child somehow manages to leave his or her world of fear to disclose even a sentence of what has happened, that bravery and risk taking is nothing short of a miracle. A child who risks everything, in their minds at least, to tell of sexual and ritual abuse, is not apt to be lying. A child has nothing to gain by making up a story and everything to lose by revealing true incidents of abuse. Believing the child will insure the safety of that little one. Disbelieving the child can mean more abuse, more brainwashing, more fear, and more secrets that spread like diseases in the mind.

The Naysayers

As long as we have those who maintain that—

"Ritualistic child molestation has suddenly become

the pop art of the child abuse field." (Aline Kidd, a Mills College psychologist.)[27]

As long as we have those who maintain that—

". . . the will to believe might not even stem from religious convictions, but from simple boredom. You kind of find yourself wanting to believe it. . . . You go through crime reports day in and day out, and you come across a statement like that, and it jumps off the page at you. It's something new and exciting." (Ray Verdugo, a Los Angeles Sheriff's Department homicide sergeant.)[28]

As long as we have those who maintain that—

"I haven't seen a single case yet where the fantasy wasn't first stimulated by an adult." (Dr. Lee Coleman, a Berkeley, California, psychiatrist.)[29]

As long as we have those who maintain that—

"It's the adult interviewers who are bringing these ideas to the children. . . . suggestive questioning by over-zealous interviewers has elicited false allegations of ritualistic abuse. In the name of protecting [children], these professionals are abusing them by putting fear into them." (Dr. Lee Coleman.)[30]

As long as we have those who maintain that—

"What is the justification for law enforcement officers giving presentations of Satanism and the occult to citizen groups, PTA's or school assemblies?" (Ken Lanning, FBI Academy, Quantico, Virginia.)[31]

As long as we have those who maintain that—

"There are sleazy people like me out there. . . . There are people out there who come off friendly. I cannot emulate people who come off friendly. There are people who are gracious. I've never been gracious in my life."[32] "The last time I had a four-year-old on the stand it took me less than forty-five minutes to break her down." (Michael Von Zamft, attorney for the defense in the Dade County, Florida, Country Walk Babysitting Service trial.)[33]

As long as we have those who maintain that—

". . . the same tactics used by the North Koreans, Red Chinese, and 'oppressive tyrants everywhere' had caused the children to tell these 'fantastic stories'." (Dr. Ralph Underwager, a key witness for the defense in the Dade County, Florida, Country Walk Babysitting Service trial in referring to the interviewing techniques of the children.)[34]

As long as we have those who maintain that—

"In a carefully documented article in the *Christian Research Journal* (Winter, 1992), the Passantino's report on their in-depth investigation of SRA, including conversations with therapists and 'dozens of alleged survivors,' among others. The article's conclusion: there are thousands of accounts, 'none of which (has) produced a single piece of corroborative evidence,' and to date there is 'no substantial, compelling evidence that SRA stories and conspiracy theories are true'." (Gary Collins, Ph.D.)[35]

As long as we have those who maintain that—

"To treat a child as if satanic abuse were real . . . is to reify a child's most terrifying fantasies and force a child to grow into an adult whose world remains at the level of a constant night terror. It is to run the risk of training a child to be psychotic, not able to distinguish between reality and unreality. It is to irrevocably and likely irretrievably damage a child and induce a lifelong experience of emotional distress." (Dr. Ralph Underwager.)[36]

As long as we have those who maintain these positions we will forever remain a camp divided. This is not only sad, but tragic, as our children, teenagers, and adult victims of ritual abuse need all of you (us), working side by side for one common goal—the safety of our yet unharmed children and the healing of our nation's child and adult victims.

But . . .

As long as we have those who maintain that—

> "I can't see how in this day and age someone can say this is not going on. We've taken down [arrested] priests and ministers for molesting kids. Why not practicing Satanists?"(John Rabun, Deputy Director for the National Center for Missing and Exploited Children.)[37]

As long as we have those who maintain that—

> "Ritual abuse is a serious and growing problem in our community and in our nation. Ritual abuse is not a new problem, but society is only just beginning to recognize the gravity and scope of this problem. We are all in need of education on this issue." (Catherine Gould, Ph.D. and Lyn Laboriel, M.D.)[38]

As long as we have those who maintain that—

> "Despite the Passantino's conclusions, Satanic ritual abuse has been reported so frequently and observed in the practices of so many counselors, that we cannot pretend this does not exist. And we cannot ignore police investigations that have led many law enforcement officers to conclude that crimes have been committed in the context of Satan worship." (Gary R. Collins, Ph.D.)[39]

As long as we have those who maintain that—

"For these four children, this case will never end. They will live with it every day of their lives. Although they walk and talk like normal children, their souls have been poisoned by these defendants. The children are four broken people, condemned by the past to a nightmare." (Andrew Gindes, Prosecutor for the District Attorney's Office in his closing remarks to the jury in a case which centered around Satanic ritual abuse allegations.)[40]

As long as we have those who maintain that—

"Only an extraordinary effort and a strong sense of coalition can empower us to hear the small voices and overcome the enormous pain." (Roland C. Summit, M.D., Head Physician, Community Consultation Service, and Clinical Associate Professor of Psychiatry, Harbor-UCLA Medical Center, Torrance, California.)[41]

As long as we have those who maintain their belief that ritual abuses do occur and there are, in fact, victims and survivors of these abuses, we who *are* the victims and survivors have hope, the hope of being believed and the hope of being restored to wholeness.

Some Final Words

Once again, I quote from Claude Lanzmann's film, *SHOAH*. And once again, I write the words of Raul Hilberg as he makes a stark observation. His words have stamped an indelible imprint on my mind. I share them with you.

". . . from the earliest days, from the fourth century, the sixth century, the missionaries of Christianity had said in effect to the Jews: 'You may live among us as Jews'. The secular rulers who followed the late Middle Ages then decided: 'You may not live among us'. And the Nazis finally decreed: 'You may not live'!"[42]

I would like to take a respectful liberty, if I may, in likening those of us who are victims and survivors of ritual abuse to Mr. Lanzmann's striking expression of the tragic truth of the Holocaust.

We, who are the victims and survivors, had to remain silent for too long. We finally braved the outside world and broke our silence in cautious whispers. Now, some of you are listening to us, and some of you are believing us. But there are many who do not listen, and there are many who do not believe. There are a few of you who do not even believe that we exist! This is a tragedy.

A philosopher once observed that truth is first ridiculed. Then it is violently opposed. Finally, it becomes self-evident.[43]

My fervent prayer is that the reality of ritual abuse will, one day, become self-evident. I can then lay down my pen.

PART FIVE

14

The High Cost of Survival

March 18, 1990

"Dear Lauren Stratford," the letter began.

"I was one of the tortured souls you wrote your book for. My name is Annie. I am twenty-eight years old. I read your book [*Satan's Underground*] about a year and a half ago. Getting better was and still is a long slow process. Before I read your book I was an emotional cripple. Reading your book planted a seed of hope inside my hard cold heart. Then I wrote to you and you wrote me an encouraging letter. That was the water for the seed that you planted in my heart."

In the ensuing months and for over a span of three years, I have found out just *how* tortured Annie's soul and body were. Annie has given me permission to raise the shades and let you look into a world that never should have been.

During her therapy, Annie had written down as many of the abuses as she could remember. She told me that it would be easier for her to read them to me; that perhaps she wouldn't have to re-experience the feelings of the memories then. But as Annie began to look at the pages, I could hear her breathing. It was faster and more pronounced.

"Annie," I said, becoming quite concerned, "I'm worried about how this may be affecting you. We don't have to do this."

"Yes, we do," she was quick to affirm. "Other survivors have to know that they can make it through this shit too."

"Okay, but remember, you can stop at any time."

"I know," she replied. I listened to her as she took a deep breath. My concern was that perhaps she was about to dive into the deep end of a swimming pool, not knowing how to swim.

"INCEST. I hate that word. It's hard to say, but I can say it now," she began. "It started with my mother. It went on and on."

"How old were you when it began?" I asked.

"From . . . I don't know. I was small. It went on forever . . . I think until I was about eleven. To keep me quiet, my mother killed bunnies, ripped their skins off, pulled the guts out, and told me if I ever told, she would do to me what she did to the bunnies." Annie took a deep breath and with a louder voice, added, "I believed her!" I remember thinking, That's enough, I hope you're through. But Annie wasn't through.

"Then my brothers molested me from the time I was a kid until I was seventeen. As a teenager, I knew no boundaries. If I couldn't say no to my mommy, who could I say no to? I never thought I had the right to say no to my brothers."

"Then there was my step-father." I held my breath. I feared what was coming next. "He molested me when I was fifteen." Annie paused. I was grateful. I needed a break to assimilate hearing traumas that had been per-petrated on someone who had, through the years, be-come a good friend of mine. If I needed a break, how much more Annie must have needed to pause and re-group. Annie began once again.

Annie always did as she was told. Her mother warned her never to tell anyone. To reinforce the warnings, An-nie's mother beat her with anything she could get her hands on. Pointing a gun at her or raising knives in front of her, Annie's mother threatened her with death if she ever told. As if that wasn't enough reinforcement, she forced a gun barrel up her vagina and into her mouth, threatening to blow her head off. Her mother held a lighted candle over Annie's arms, letting the hot candle wax drip onto her arms and burning her badly. Annie's mother also held her hands over the flame of one of the gas burners on the stove.

When Annie was in first grade, she made a terrible mistake. She raised her hand to answer the teacher's question. Annie's long sleeve slipped to her shoulder, revealing the telltale signs of child abuse. One of her classmates saw the black and blue marks that covered her arm. The classmate told the teacher. The teacher took her into the teachers' lounge and called the police. A policeman came, looked at the bruises, and admonished her to be a good girl and do every thing her mommy told her to do. "Then," he quipped, "you won't get punished."

When Annie got home from school that day, her mother was gone—gone to a mental institution. She remained there for six months. Upon her return home, she began to give ominous warnings to the already frightened Annie. "If you tell anyone about this, I will kill myself and you. Then there won't be anyone to look after your younger brothers and sisters."

Annie already felt guilty for telling the school teacher. She felt that it was all her fault that her mommy got sick and had to go to the hospital. It was at six years of age that Annie became a self-mutilator and a cutter. Self-mutilators hurt themselves for a number of reasons. For Annie, she hurt herself because she felt that she was to blame for her mother having to go away. Annie began to cut herself on her arms with razor blades in an effort to punish herself. Annie, at the tender age of six, was also filled with hurt and anger. She couldn't hurt anyone else to get back at them, so she hurt herself. Hurting herself was one of the ways she used to discharge her anger and frustration. It was also a way to feel real. If Annie could feel pain, then she knew that she was real.

A large percentage of abused children self-mutilate. The act of self-mutilation often continues on into the victim's teenage years and adulthood. It is one of the common ways victims characteristically handle their abuse. Six-year-old Annie was no exception.

Over the course of Annie's life, the acts of self-mutilation and other types of hurting herself, including a number of suicide attempts, began to grow in nature and in number.

Please keep in mind that Annie is only talking about these incidents with you and me because she wants her sharing to make a difference in other survivors' lives. Through her sharing these extraordinarily painful times with you, she is saying, "If I can make it through all of this craziness, so can you!"

Annie's self-injuring behaviors lasted for twenty-two years. She is now thirty years old. She has been completely free, or as she puts it, she has been "clean," for three years and "completely clean" for two months. Clean from alcohol, drugs, burning her arms with a hot glue gun, dripping hot candle wax on her arms, cutting herself with razor blades and knives, and poking needles through her skin. For two months, she has been "completely clean" from standing in scalding hot showers.

I wanted to yell from the highest housetop, "Good for you, Annie! You're coming out the other side. I am so proud of you!" And I am!

I'll answer the question before you ask it. Annie did these abusive things to herself *not* because she derived pleasure from them; *not* because someone else forced her to do them; *not* to get attention; and *not* because she liked living "on the edge." She did these abusive things because she was trying to numb herself to the never-ending mental pain that had been accumulating for almost her entire lifetime. The intense *physical pain* helped, if only a little and if only for a brief period of time, to numb the *emotional* pain that her memories brought her.

Annie began to tear at pieces of skin on the soles of her feet until much of the skin was gone. Annie ripped the nails off her thumbs. Annie allowed herself to mushroom to four hundred pounds. There were other things that Annie did to herself that she had written down on the piece of paper from which she was reading that she just couldn't get out. "Annie, it's okay. We don't need to know everything," I said. "You have told a world of survivors that they aren't the only ones who have done these kinds of things. You've already made an important contribution."

"But, Lauren, I need to say more."

I knew that Annie was in weekly therapy and was attending a support group. She also has an absolute treasure for a husband who supports her all the way, in the really bad times as well as in the good times. Though I wanted to protect Annie from speaking of more memories, I knew it was important for me to allow her to talk. Annie is the real writer of these pages. I was but the listener.

"You know, Lauren, I quit burning and cutting myself three years ago. I had been trying to outrun my pain, but I found out you can't do it. The pain runs with you. And I didn't quit standing in a scalding shower until two months ago. I've tried so hard to make myself clean. I wanted to make all the 'icky' garbage go away. I wanted all the 'yucky' stuff to leave. I wanted to be worth something. Nobody ever told me that I was worth something. It's hard, man. It's so hard!" Annie paused momentarily.

I took the opportunity to say something that I needed to say for myself. "Annie, I know how hard it is. I know what it's like to feel that life has passed you by. That's tough, Annie. I know. I've felt the same way. In fact, I still feel that way sometimes."

Annie's momentary respite from talking didn't last very long.

"I've been in and out of psychiatric wards for fifteen years. Most of the time, I was kept doped up, not so much for treatment, but just to keep me restrained, less anxious, and less abusive. I had two sets of electro-shock treatments. There were twenty-five shocks in each set. That sucks!"

"And you know I tried suicide—more than once. If the *pain* wouldn't go away, then *I* would go away."

I remember thinking, Wow, what a statement.

Annie continued to unburden her heart. "Suicide almost became like a challenge. It got so bad that I tried to self-destruct almost on a daily basis."

"Annie," I asked, almost hoping that she wouldn't answer, "how did you try to end your life?" Annie began. I think she must have had a list for that, too. But, oh, how hard the words came.

"Well, I played Russian roulette with a nine-cylinder twenty-two more than once. I guess I got lucky. When I'd put the gun to my head and pull the trigger, the chamber was always on the one cylinder that didn't have a bullet."

"Thank God," I said, although I was sure she didn't feel the same way at the time.

"And then I ran my car into a concrete wall going at a high speed. I didn't even hurt myself."

Again, I said, "Thank God."

"Then I cut the veins in my wrists with razor blades. The docs would just stitch them up and either send me home or on to the psych ward, but I'd be fine. *I just couldn't die, Lauren. I just couldn't die.*"

And once again, I could only say, "Thank God, Annie. Thank God!"

The Hero Emerges

"We made it, Lauren. We made it!" Annie said emphatically. I had the feeling that in Annie's going through the garbage of her life on the phone, from one piece of garbage to another, like bam, bam, bam, she saw in a matter of just a few minutes that yes, it was horrible, it did "suck" as she put it, but hey, she was making it!

"Lauren, I'm not there any more. That was then. I live in the now, and I know I can make it."

I remember thinking that that is what heroes are made of. Guts, blood, pain, horror. The hero comes out still fighting. Never quitting. Stumbling, but getting back up.

"And you know what?" she asked.

"What, Annie?"

"The change in my life has been noticeable to everyone who has ever known me."

"I can certainly second that, Annie. I really can."

I asked Annie if she would write me a letter in summing up the pain of her past and what helped her to keep on going. With her permission, I respectfully share it with you.

"I spent a lot of years trapped in the pain of the past.
It hung over me like a cloud of toxic gas,
seeping into everything I did or saw.
It clouded my vision.
The turning point for me
came in the form of my last suicide attempt.
I remember feeling helpless and hopeless.
I took an overdose.
I don't remember how long it took
for the pills to take effect because I lived in a daze.
What I will never forget
is the feeling in my heart beating wildly
and knowing I was going to die within minutes.

That is when my fight for life began.
For the first time I knew that I didn't want to die!
I just needed a break from the pain.
I stumbled to the bathroom and made myself
throw up.
The next thing I remember is waking up
in intensive care
feeling very grateful to just be alive.
I have spent the last four years fighting for my life.
Today, I am a Survivor and a Thriver.

My life is no longer controlled by the pain of my past."

F. Scott Fitzgerald once wrote:

"Show me a hero
and I'll write you a tragedy."[1]

Annie lived through two decades of tragedy. Her physical and emotional scars are proof of that tragedy. But Annie came out on the other side a survivor. In my book, Annie is a real hero! She is a hero who is triumphing over her tragedies in every sense of the word!

But I Don't Know Any Survivors. Where Are They?

You think you don't. You're convinced you don't. But the fact is, you probably do. You know them. You just don't *see* them.

I spoke at a seminar in Atlanta several years ago. At its conclusion, several of us had been promised a tour of the city that was billed as "the ride you will never forget." I was anxious to get started. We piled into the van, eager to find out just what we were going to see that was so unforgettable. A young couple from "Safe House Outreach" who were our tour guides looked back at us all squashed together and asked with a glint in their eyes, "Ready?"

"Yes!" we yelled in chorus. "Let's get going." The van lurched forward, and our unforgettable ride began.

The van circled blocks of inner city Atlanta. We saw men dressed as women and women dressed as men. We saw gay and lesbian prostitutes standing on the street corners and their pimps sitting in their limos keeping a watchful eye on their "workers." Among the "workers" were eleven- and twelve-year-olds standing on the street corners waiting for a pick-up. We saw the homeless sleeping near the warm air vents on the sidewalks and drunks who had passed out "wherever." But these, we were told, were not the people our tour guides had especially wanted us to see. They kept telling us, "Just wait. Hold on. Be patient, and you'll see." We had no idea just what it was we were waiting for.

It was getting hot and sticky in the van. We were all for going back to the lot where our cars were parked. We'd seen enough of the "other" side of life. Our tour guides heard us mumbling to each other. The driver pulled over to the curb and stopped. Turning around, he said, "Look folks. This is not easy for any of us, but we work down here every night, and you haven't seen the people we want you to see yet." He spoke so seriously that none of us mumbled another word.

The van pulled onto a dirt road and stopped in front of an old abandoned two-story building. The windows had been broken out. The building had no electricity and no running water. We all stared at it wondering why our tour guides had taken us here. I have to admit that I was a little unnerved, and even a little frightened.

"Jim, why did you stop here?" one of the passengers asked. "Nobody is here. What are we supposed to be seeing?"

Jim quietly opened the door of the van and got out. It was pitch black out. Not a sound could be heard. Jim put his fingers to his mouth and sounded a shrill whistle that pierced the blackness like a sharpened knife.

Suddenly, like from an eerie Stephen King movie, ghost-like images began to appear in the doorways and windows. We were startled. The empty building was full of people. Jim began his greetings. "Hi, Joe. Hi, Tom. Tom, how's your wife? Does she need any medical attention?"

The ghostlike images began to answer back. "Hi, Jim. Where's Jane?"

Jane got out of the passenger side and called, "I'm here, you guys. Do any of you need anything tonight?"

"No. We're okay for now, but thanks for dropping by."

A lady's frail voice could barely be heard. "Thanks for caring. You're the only ones who know we're here."

When Jim and Jane got back into the van, Jim said, "That's really not true, We're not the only ones who know these people are here. We're just the only ones who care enough to help them."

The van lurched forward and made its way around huge pot holes, broken glass, and other objects. Once back onto the smooth street that was well-lit, we began to calm down. "Now this is more like it," one of us exclaimed as we drove by the OMNI Hotel, one of Atlanta's show cases. This was definitely much better. It took only a few seconds to pass the OMNI and cross the street that ran behind it. The block on the backside was nothing more than a large plot of undeveloped and rugged terrain. Tall grass covered the ground, some of which would reach over our heads if we were to stand next to it.

To our surprise and to my horror, Jim made a sharp left-hand turn, driving right into the grass. There was no road. There were no lights except for the headlights of the van that shined into the thick, swamp-like grass. Jim honked the horn. Once again, human beings began to pop up. I was stunned. People living in the ruins of vacant buildings was one thing, but people actually living among the tall grass? Anticipating our reactions, Jim made it clear to us that these people were not just *sleeping* here. They *lived* here.

One man towered above the rest. "Hi, Cowboy," Jim yelled.

"Hey, Jim. Good to see you!" he yelled back.

"Are you all bedded down for the night?" Jim asked.

"Yeah, Jim. We're doin' okay."

"See you all tomorrow night," Jim yelled as he pulled himself back into the van.

Then Jim gave us a tour of the entire plot of ground that, I remind you again, was not more than fifty yards from Atlanta's finest, the swanky OMNI. The grass had been cleared for a lean-to that was about eight feet square. It was made of cardboard. "A baby girl was born here a few weeks ago. No one would even have known she was here if we hadn't come by. She wasn't doing well so we took her to the county hospital to get her checked out. She's back now."

"You mean to tell me that an infant is inside that . . . that dirty cardboard lean-to?" I asked incredulously.

"Yes," Jim answered. "Along with her mother and father."

"You see that car over there?" Jim was pointing with his finger. One could hardly call it a car. It was the shell of a car. No tires. No window glass. The springs of a front seat. That's about all. "A family of four lives in that car," Jim announced.

"You mean twenty-four hours a day?"

"Yep, twenty-four hours a day and seven days a week. They cook over a campfire; they go to the bathroom in the tall grass; and they sleep in the car." It sounded so simple until you took into consideration that Jim was talking about human beings.

This was really too much for any of us to grasp. When Jim got us back to the parking lot, no one moved, and no one spoke. Jim and Jane sat quietly, knowing that we were having to absorb the human sights and sounds of the ride that lived up to its billing. None of us would be apt to forget it.

Finally, one of the tour members broke the silence with the question most of us were thinking. "Why don't these people ask for help?" Before Jim could respond, another tour member asked, "And why don't people help them?" I seconded the question.

The answer was simple. I really already knew it. I just didn't want to acknowledge that I knew it. The dwellers were afraid to ask for help, because people would be hard-pressed to believe them, and besides, nobody wants to get involved with people who have problems like theirs. We comfortably put such people into the government's lap.

Do You Wish We Would Just Go Away?

Survivors are not unlike the human beings I just described. Survivors of ritual abuse are everywhere. There are probably some of us in every city, in every state and, perhaps, even in your neighborhood. We look like you. We act like you. We talk like you. We work alongside you. We are normal people who have problems just like you have. The only difference is that our problems are different from yours.

Ritual abuse is not an illness. It is not a disease. It is not contagious, but it may be life-threatening, not to you, but to us.

We talk just like you, because we're afraid to share our secrets. We act like you, because we've learned that we're only acceptable to you if we blend in with the crowd. Our very survival has depended on our ability to keep our traumas hidden. You don't know we're survivors, because we don't tell you. We're afraid of being disbelieved and rejected. So we keep our not-so-fine personalities hidden away where no one will be able to see them. We learned how to do that a long time ago.

Some of us have come out of hiding, and you disbelieved and rejected us. You ridiculed us and accused us of seeking unwarranted attention. We have either been accused of lying or of really believing stories that are untrue. We've heard you say that. So you see, we can't win. We feel much safer if we just remain silent and hidden. Silence has become our only friend.

We have a difficult time surviving in a world from which we have to hide. Our problems are so many. Sometimes they get so big that we become fearful that we won't be able to keep them hidden any longer. Then we really don't know what to do.

Maybe the only way to get rid of our problems is to get rid of us. Is that what you want? If there were no more of us, would you feel more comfortable? We hope not, because we are fighting so hard to stay alive and get on with our journey to wholeness. But how can we ever hope to do that if you won't listen to us, if you won't believe us?

We hear that help is but a stone's throw away. We hear that if we come out of hiding, there will be someone to reach out and take our hand. But then we hear some of you say terrible things about the person who is reaching out to us. That person is usually a therapist. You say that he or she will brainwash us to believe things that never really happened. I wonder why anyone would want to do that, but it keeps us wanting to stay hidden. That way, we'll be safe from everyone!

We hear you say that we want to make lots of money from telling our stories. You say that we want to become celebrities. You say that we tell our stories to cover up a bad past that was our fault. You say that we are like those who tell stories about being UFO abductees or those who claim they have lived in reincarnated past-lives. In fact, some of you even infer that "alleged" survivors of ritual abuse are one rung lower that those who claim to be UFO abductees or those who believe that they are past-life regression individuals. You say that we crave an overabundance of attention by trying to get on television talk shows and getting reporters to write newspaper articles on us. To be quite frank, we've read many of the articles on ritual abuse that the press has written, and for the life of us, we don't know anyone who would want to be written about in such a negative light.

You call us "professional victims," as if we wanted to become victims in the first place. And now that we are victims, you infer that we want to remain victims, as if it were something to be enjoyed. I wonder, have *you* ever been a victim of something or someone? Did it make you feel good? Didn't you want to become a non-victim as soon as you could, and didn't you seek healing from your trauma in one direction or another? Why do you think we are any different? But then, your wounds were probably ones that showed on the outside, and everyone could readily see them. Our wounds are on the inside, and no one can see ours. So it seems to be easier for you to pretend or to deny that our wounds even exist. Why do you do that?

We who are survivors are like the homeless ones living in those old abandoned buildings and among that tall grass. Oh, we're there all right. You just don't see us. If someone told you that we were there, would you stop and search us out to lend us a helping hand, or would you go on by?

We have found a few who call for us, and we dare to come out from our hiding places. We feel like we're braving the whole world when we come out of hiding. We reach out to those who are calling for us, and our hands clasp firmly. Only then, do we dare to share our secrets and our wounds.

Sometimes we cry. Sometimes we sit silently. Sometimes we even laugh. We feel safe. Some of us are learning to trust for the first time ever. It's scary to trust. Some of our wounds just hurt too much to talk about, but that's okay for now. We'll talk about them some other time. Do you know what? Some of us have healed enough to reveal who we really are, victims of sexual abuse, of incest, and of ritual abuse. Why does that bother you?

Do you think we're crazy? We've heard some of you say that we are. Do you think we're something bad, not to be believed or trusted, just because we're finally getting the help we need? We've heard you say that we are. Do you think it's wrong to get help? If you had been a victim and had suffered some pretty horrible wounds, the kind that are on the inside, wouldn't you feel the need for crisis intervention, or maybe even a time of intensive therapy? Would your being in therapy make you any less a human being, a person of worth?

We've heard one of you refer to a victim of ritual abuse as "a specimen." Is that all you think we are — specimens? That hurts! Do you think it wrong of us to get ourselves into therapy so we can find out the whole truth so our healing can begin? Does a temporary time of emotional instability make our stories less believable? We've heard you say that.

Do you think we are dumb? Do you think we cannot hold down jobs? Well, some of us can, and some of us can't. Do you know that some of us are respected attorneys, physicians, teachers, scientists, real estate managers, social workers, and politicians? You feel comfortable with us. You see us as credible persons. And yet, if any one of us was to say that he or she is a victim of ritual abuse, would your assessment of that one fall short of the acceptable norm? Would you then find that person *less than credible*?

I had an interesting phone conversation with a uniquely refreshing person. Her responses were full of energy. Dr. Noemi Mattis has both a doctorate in law and a doctorate in psychology.

She has an interesting perspective on the believability of survivors' stories. "We have doctors, teachers, college professors, nurses, and others in whom we value their input. We deem them to be totally credible for everything else to which they would testify. But if any one of them then said that they were a survivor of ritual abuse, we would not believe them. We would dismiss their story altogether." Dr. Mattis went on to evaluate this perplexing and pervasive problem. "I have a law degree. So I have the ability to look at a problem from a lawyer's point of view. I also have a psychology degree. So I have the ability to look at a problem from a psychologist's point of view. There is one level of proof that is called for in court. Findings in a court of law are based on the provability of the story detail by detail. There is a different level of proof that is called for in the therapy setting. The therapeutic community believes in and works with the *substance* of the story."

She likened this perplexing problem to an automobile accident. "Each witness will more than likely give a slightly different report of the accident. The mind is complex. The memory that comes from the mind is complex. Because *one* memory does not check out does not mean that *all* the memories are false. Just because one detailed memory of the automobile wreck doesn't check out does not mean that there wasn't an automobile accident. We as mental health professionals must listen to the *substance* of survivors' stories."[2]

Coming from a person who has training in both law and psychology, Dr. Mattis' perceptions seemed to me to be extremely helpful.

I am reminded of a sentence that is not to be taken too seriously, but one which I have entertained often as this subject of credibility and believability is bantered about. "Our puzzlement is partly based on your puzzleheadedness." The arguments go back and forth, back and forth. I have heard some of our critics say, "I can't help my doubting. I am a lawyer, and I have to demand evidence that would meet a court of law's approval. I won't believe that ritual abuse happens until you can meet the criteria for acceptable evidence." Well, such evidence may not be available. However, that does not mean that the car wreck (or the ritual abuse) did not happen.

We have heard you say that, "Many of the survivors entered into therapy to treat illnesses related to multiple-personality disorders" and that, "These are the same people who act as 'experts' on television shows—even though their sanity may be in question."[3] We want to repeat that multiple personality disorder may just possibly be the only *sane* response to an *insane* environment.

I have a very rare and life-threatening blood clotting disorder called Anti-Thrombin III Deficiency. Because I have lived with this disorder for many years now, I have been asked a number of times to speak to support groups whose members also have life-threatening medical problems. Applying the same reasoning that you apply to survivors of ritual abuse, I should not be allowed to talk about my illness, and I should most assuredly *not* be considered an expert on the problem. I have never called myself an expert and personally, I don't know of any other survivors who have called themselves experts. But . . . who better to talk about a problem than the person who has the problem? Who better to reach out and take another survivor's hand and say, "I know how you feel, because I've been there too," than another survivor? Showmanship is not the issue here. Helping others by listening to them and caring for them is.

Very few of us ever go public. We go to our therapist for help and some of us are fortunate enough to have a small support group to attend just to be with others who understand. For most of us, that is the extent of our coming out of hiding. We would be terrified to appear on television, or, for that matter, even give a newspaper interview. We don't want recognition, nor do we want publicity. We just want to be healed. Why do some of you seem to want to deny us our healing? Do we not have the right to seek help?

One of you has said that you would "do" anybody, referring to alleged survivors of ritual abuse.[4] The word "do" meaning to investigate us. We'll pass on that offer. None of us wants to be "done." We are living, breathing, and feeling human beings, and we are doing our best to remain that way. One of you made a remark on a television talk show that, "So far, we haven't had any takers."[5] Somehow, that doesn't surprise us. What we can't figure out though, is why it would surprise you.

You don't talk unfavorably about the person who has cancer and goes to an oncologist. Why do you talk unfavorably about those who have been abused and go to a therapist? Why do you talk so unfavorably (and that's putting it very mildly) of the therapists who are providing us a safe environment in which to heal? Do you talk badly of the oncologist who treats the patient who has cancer? I go to a hematologist for my blood disorder. I do not hear you accusing him of trying to convince me, or worse yet, of trying to brainwash me into thinking that I have a life-threatening illness. What would he possibly gain from such an unethical practice? Why then, do some of you accuse therapists of the same unethical behavior? What would be their gain? We have yet to hear an answer that makes any sense. Why then, do you try to convince us that therapy for our minds and for our hearts is wrong? We who are survivors find this situation baffling.

Taking the Walk Back to Hell

The walk back to recovery often first begins with a walk back to hell. Until all the pieces of the puzzle are found, the puzzle cannot be completed. *Webster's Ninth Collegiate Dictionary* defines the word "puzzle" as one which "implies existence of a problem difficult to solve." Although I know that Webster's dictionary is published by Merriam-Webster Publishers, I can't resist responding to the definition by saying, "You got that one right, Mr. Webster!"

The road to wholeness is not set in cement. There is no single plan that works for every survivor. We who walk that road make right turns and wrong turns. Sometimes a certain piece of the puzzle is found to fit by trial and error, just as you would try to match a real piece to a puzzle by placing it next to piece after piece after piece until you finally found the other piece that matches the one in your hand. The road for survivors and their therapists is often one of trial and error.

Before you take the time to complain about that statement, let me compare it with the treatments I have undergone which have kept me alive. Some of the treatments were experimental. I was the "guinea pig" for the FDA. Some of the treatments have been altogether unsuccessful. Others were mildly successful. And one was and continues to be my lifesaver, even though the cost is so prohibitive that I can only take it when my life is in danger. The process of trial and error has saved my physical life. Why then, would you call the process of trial and error in therapy unacceptable or unethical? Treatment issues for survivors, especially survivors of ritual abuse, is still largely unchartered ground. Does this mean that no therapist should take on a client who has been ritually abused?

In the "Afterword" of *Satan's Underground*, there is a paragraph which reads, "It [healing] is a process with starts and stops, with right turns and wrong turns, with circles and retracing. . . . Lauren herself is still dealing with dissociated memories. As she continues in therapy, the dissociative barriers become less, and more of her memories return. Some missing pieces of the puzzle that have baffled her are beginning to fit together. Other pieces may never seem to fit clearly."[6] This is often the case of persons in general. An anonymous quote reads, "Life is a jigsaw puzzle with most of the pieces missing."[7] The only difference between you and me is that I have more pieces missing and more pieces to retrieve.

The walk back to hell is one of the most difficult and painful things survivors will do in their lifetime. Neither the survivor nor the therapist derives pleasure from it. The pleasure for both the therapist and the client comes far down the road when the journey to wholeness is realized, when we are freed from the chains that have bound us for so long.

I remember an incident that happened about two years ago. I had become a friend of another survivor and his wife. Jack is a victim of sexual and ritual abuse. He was in therapy. He is a multiple, and he was being flooded with memories that still remained fragmented. The pieces of his puzzle were coming too fast. When that happens, the survivor feels like he or she is drowning. Every attempt is made by the therapist to slow down the remembering process, but for Jack, his mind was being bombarded by fragmented pieces right and left.

Let me tell you a little about Jack. Jack is an intelligent young man. Everything he did, he did well. I used to tell him that he should be a radio talk show host. His voice was one you could listen to forever. It was a low voice with a resonance that wouldn't quit. Jack was liked by everyone. He especially was looked up to by children. He just exuded that happy, upbeat personality to which children are drawn.

These accolades had not always been true of Jack. Jack had been into Satanism for a brief period of time. He became a self-appointed high priest of a small coven. They met in a cave among the rugged cliffs along the Pacific coastline. Memories of the rituals over which he presided began to haunt him. Ghosts from the past began lurking in every corner of his mind. They lived with him twenty-four hours a day.

Jack had been severely physically, sexually, and ritually abused as a child. I have read many pages of a journal he was writing. He writes brilliantly, but oh, the pictures he painted on those pages were almost too much even for me to read. Jack had a lot of horror stories to tell. I could begin listing them for you, but then, I could list every survivor's book of horrors. I choose not to do so, for my sanity, as well as yours. Just know that Jack's abuses were about as bad as bad can get.

Many of Jack's horrors had been neatly compartmentalized and stored away in his subconscious as a young child. But now Jack was an adult. The childhood abuse and the ritual acts he performed would not stay so conveniently locked away any longer. I had met his therapist at a planning session for a children's home. I talked with her briefly and came away with good feelings about her. I am always thankful when I meet a therapist who is willing to work with survivors of ritual abuse and is knowledgeable about treatment issues. Jack was fortunate to have her as his therapist.

One evening, someone knocked very loudly on my door. I looked out the peephole and saw Jack standing in the hallway. Upon opening the door, Jack came in and fell into a heap on the floor.

Obviously, something was very, very wrong. Tears were already filling his eyes. "I can't go to my therapist one more time," he cried. "I don't want to remember." Most survivors express similar feelings at one time or another in the therapeutic process. I have felt that way probably at least once a week, and sometimes, once or twice a day. So Jack's feelings didn't surprise me at all.

I liken a survivor to a prizefighter in a boxing match. Jack was in a fight for his life. If he did not deal with the trauma issues of his past, he would remain debilitated, and an emotional cripple, but in dealing with the trauma, he felt like he was going to lose his sanity. What was Jack to do? I could not make the decision for him. It was his and his alone to make.

I envisioned Jack sitting on the stool in one corner of the boxing ring. The demons of his past sat opposite him. Each time Jack went to therapy, the bell rang for another round. Jack had to get up, go to the center of the ring, and meet his demons.

About all I could do was to encourage him that the recovery process would, in time, get easier; that there was an end to his walk back to hell; and that if he hung in there, he would begin to see the light at the end of the tunnel.

I sat on the floor in front of Jack. "Jack, there is light at the end, but there are so many bends in the tunnel they obscure the light. As you round each bend, you'll be one step closer to the light." Jack just sat there. I didn't know if anything I was saying was getting through to him. No words seem to help when one is so far down. So I just sat silently with him. Finally, I said, "Come on, Jack. Let's get up. You can do it, Jack. You can make it."

Jack slowly lifted himself off the floor. As he went out the door, I whispered to him. "Jack, you're in a boxing match. You don't have many more rounds to go. You can make it to the end. Just respond to each bell as if it were the last round." Jack muttered something that I didn't catch and walked down the hallway.

I didn't hear from him for a couple of weeks, but on a Tuesday evening my phone rang. It was Jack. "Lauren!" Jack was yelling at the top of his voice. I had to move the receiver away from my ear. I feared for the worst. I tried to ready myself for anything Jack might say.

"Lauren, I went to my therapist today. I answered the bell like you encouraged me to do. I got off my stool, and I met my past in the center of the ring. You know what?" Jack was yelling louder and louder with each word.

"What, Jack?"

"Lauren, you've got to hear this."

"I can hear you, Jack," I said softly in hopes that he would begin to lower his voice.

"Lauren, I'm going to keep on going to my therapist. I'm going to keep on answering the bell. I'm a fighter, and I'm going to win!"

"Good for you, Jack," I exclaimed. I even found myself talking louder. I was ecstatic. "I'm proud of you. I knew you could make it."

Jack is making it. He moved to another state a year ago. He just called me last month. He sounded so good. He is continuing to answer the bell of each round. No longer does he cower in his corner. He bounces off the stool and meets the demons of his past face to face. Yes, he gets bloodied and black and blue from time to time, but he is nearing the thirteenth round now. I know that he is going to emerge as the champion. Jack is on his way to a complete healing.

Why Go to Therapy If It Hurts So Much?

After reading of Jack's courageous, but painful fight, you might wonder if he would have been better off to leave well enough alone. How often we who are survivors have heard the question put to us by a close friend or family member? "Why don't you just leave the past in the past and get on with your life?" All survivors who have never been asked that question please raise your hand. Do I see two? No. Do I see one? No. Not even one.

The answer is simple. First of all, *survivors cannot leave the past in the past, because the past does not leave them*. It follows them wherever they go, because the past is an integral part of their lives. Sooner or later, the past will either begin to seep ever so slowly into their consciousness, or it will explode in one big bang. Better for *you* to deal with *it* before *it* deals with *you*!

Second, even if you think you've beaten the demons of your past, you're wrong. There is no way of permanently sneaking off and leaving them behind, so far behind that they will lose track of you. That would be wonderful if it worked that way, but it doesn't.

Amaro Gomez Boix, a man who had been whisked off to the Cuban Havana Psychiatric Hospital for reasons he never learned, spoke eloquently of how he so desperately tried to keep his memories of ghastly tortures far behind in his subconscious.

Mr. Amaro Gomez Boix speaks. "There's a place sealed in my thoughts and memories which, like monsters, is best kept secret. We never dare open that chest which keeps hidden the most abysmal of experiences that can never be forgotten. Sometimes, however, a captured memory escapes and lodges itself in the core of every thought, every word." Listen well to Mr. Boix's next insightful expression.

"It can happen even after ten years and three thousand miles have passed, when we find ourselves reclining leisurely on the terrace of a beautiful restaurant watching the vast ocean float by. This happened to me recently one evening at a beach in Southern California, when I was visited by the ghosts of La Perrera."[8] La Perrera, "the dog kennel," was the walled courtyard of the Havana Psychiatric Hospital where new prisoners are drugged with five hundred milligrams of thorazine, sodomized, and given electroshocks on a continual basis.

Survivors of trauma cannot escape. They are prisoners of the past. Some are aware of it. Some are aware of parts of it, and some are aware of none of it until it comes lurking in their minds as ghosts from the shadows. All survivors, however much they remember or do not remember, will have to meet their past head on one day or another. It is best to remember in a safe environment. It is best to remember with a skilled and caring professional. And it is unarguably better to deal with it before the better part of your life has passed you by.

It's Okay to Feel!

The flooding of memories; trying to push them away; trying to push them back inside; trying to hold back the tears; putting your arms around yourself and squeezing really hard because the emotional pain hurts so much; holding your breath so the cries of your pain won't be heard by others; burying your head with your hands so your therapist won't see the anguished look on your face; digging your fingers into the arm rests of the chair and holding on for dear life because you feel as if you're about to explode; wanting to use every swear word you can think of, but you don't, because you feel it would be unacceptable; wanting to pound into mush everyone who frightened and hurt you, but not allowing yourself even to pound your fists into a pillow because it doesn't feel okay to do it; wanting to scream out, "It's not fair. It's just not fair!"—In one paragraph, that's the world of survivors in therapy.

I know. I know, because I've been there too, and in some situations, I'm still there. One of my therapists has tried to get me to beat the sofa in her office with a bataca, but I won't even touch it, let alone hit anything with it. My mind tells me it's not okay to hit; that it's not okay to cry; that it's not okay to yell; that it's not okay to do anything! But I am telling you and reminding myself that it *is* okay.

   *It's okay to cry.
   • It's okay for someone you trust to hold you when you cry.
   • It's okay to pound your fists into a pillow.
   • It's okay to remember.
   • It's okay to hurt.

- It's okay to tell someone you hurt.
- It's okay to be a person with multiple personalities.
- It's okay to let those important persons within you express themselves with someone you trust.
- It's okay to dissociate for now. When you're farther along in your recovery, you won't have the need to do so. But for now, it's okay.
- It's okay to go to a therapist. Going to a therapist doesn't mean you're crazy or that you're a weak person.
- It's okay to be wherever you are in your journey to wholeness. You can't go any faster. It will take time, and that's okay.
- It's *not* okay that you were sexually and/or ritually abused, but it *is* okay to tell someone about it.
- It's *not* okay that there are those who don't believe you, and there are those who say these kinds of things just don't happen. *But you know they do, and that's what really matters.*

Yes, my survivor and friend, it is okay to feel. In fact, it's therapeutic for you to feel. And it will be even more therapeutic when you give yourself permission to let those feelings be expressed in a safe way, one that won't hurt yourself or anyone else.

The Self-Appointed Apostles of Denial

I was watching "20/20" last night. Lynn Sherr, a reporter for "20/20," did a segment that got my attention. The segment was on the physical and mental problems that were unique to many of the men who had served time in the Persian Gulf War.[9]

Some of the men's symptoms were aching joints,

problems with their vision, memory loss, dizziness, back spasms, thick saliva, night sweats, ugly rashes, and hair loss. Scattered across the country, these men each went to their Army, Navy, or Air Force base hospital for a diagnosis and treatment. Each doctor came up with the same diagnosis—stress.

A dozen or so of these men had been gathered together for the "20/20" segment. When Lynn Sherr told them that all of the doctors and even the Pentagon had issued the same diagnosis of stress-related illnesses, the men laughed in unison. They weren't buying that diagnosis. Their physical and mental problems were much too bad to attach a single word like "stress" to their problems. They felt that it was an easy cop-out.

They talked about taking showers day after day that strongly smelled of diesel gas. They talked of breathing in air that was mixed with the burning of petroleum from the hundreds of oil wells that were burning out of control. They talked about things that we had not heard of before. Had Saddam Hussein put a poison of some kind in the payload of the Scud missiles? The men likened themselves to the men who had served in the Armed Services in Vietnam. It took over two decades for the powers that be to finally admit that their use of Agent Orange had caused cancer and other life-threatening illness.

These men were obviously in great distress over their conditions. Tears filled one man's eyes as he wondered if he would even continue to live. Another man had been hospitalized. Each soldier's life had been turned into a living nightmare. They all expressed their fear of never being able to lead a normal life again.

Two things caught my attention as the report neared the end. The Pentagon encouraged those who had served time in the Persian Gulf and were experiencing similar symptoms to come forward. President Bush was also asking that the White House establish a task force to investigate this problem.

What does this "20/20" report have to do with survivors of ritual abuse? The men who had served our country in the Persian Gulf were scattered from the Pacific Ocean to the Atlantic Ocean— yet each was telling a similar story. No one had implanted these stories in their minds. No veteran of the war wanted their story to be true, and no doctor listened because it was what he wanted to hear. Yet, this is what our self-appointed apostles of denial have espoused of survivors on an on-going basis. I have heard not once, not twice, but dozens of times, on television, on radio, and in print, that survivors of ritual abuse are saying what they want to be true and therapists listen because this is what they want to hear!

Our stories are unique, just as the stories of the veterans are unique. Our stories are complicated. Few there are who want to tackle these problems. It is far easier to label them stress-related or altogether fabricated so they can be swept under the rug. That way, no one has to take responsibility for them. "What we can't see, we don't have to deal with," is often the rule of thumb.

"Sherill Mulhern, an anthropologist, recently completed a two-year study of the most prominent MPD psychotherapists, MPD satanic-cult 'survivors' and police Satan-hunters. Mulhern came to the conclusion that the key factor in the acceptance of satanic-cult 'survivor' stories is the predisposition of psychotherapists to accept them in response to group pressure."[10]

Excuse me? That was the finding of a two-year study? . . . that therapists are "predisposed" to believe the stories survivors tell because of group pressure? That's a neat and tidy way to sweep survivor stories under the rug!

Dr. Jeffrey S. Victor, professor of Sociology at Jamestown Community College, Jamestown, New York, came up with his own reasoning. "The 'survivor' stories were first given credibility when leading MPD psychiatric authorities professed their belief in their plausibility. This happened at the first national conference of the International Society for the Study of MPD, in 1984. Once authority figures lent credibility to the stories, the process of consensual validation, operating through the psychiatric communication network, reinforced the credibility of the stories. In this network, normally open and public scientific criticism and dispute is discouraged."[11]

Don't we who are survivors like to see ourselves enclosed in quotes—"Survivors"—like the fact that we are survivors is open to question? Most of these self-appointed apostles of denial not only question our credibility, but they strongly reject it.

I have talked to therapists across the country. I have found them to be intelligent. They are their own bosses. I have not found them to be easily influenced pansies who can be intimidated into believing survivor stories simply because other more well-known and more influential mental health professionals believe survivor stories.

The theory that our self-appointed apostles of denial are only too eager to dole out that survivors are saying what they want to be true, and therapists listen because this is what they want to hear is outrageous and ludicrous!

Contrary to what these critics argue, survivors do not run into their therapists' offices and readily spill out stories of grisly torture. In opposition to those same critics, therapists do not eagerly await the hearing of such stories.

What I do hear are obviously agonizing and painful accounts from survivors who tell how difficult it is even to begin to make such disclosures. What I do hear from therapists is the heavy toll it takes on them to get used to such stories—if one can *ever* get used to them.

One therapist told me that she almost feels guilty about being able to hear such horrendous tales of abuse without collapsing herself. With a hint of guilt in her voice, she said that she has had to numb herself to the stories of ritual abuse. I ask you, does this sound like a therapist who eagerly awaits to hear the next gruesome story of ritual abuse? I think not!

My comment to her was that her numbing process was her way of enabling her to continue helping survivors of ritual abuse. If she took every story to heart, she wouldn't be of help to anyone. Police have their coping mechanisms that help them emotionally accommodate tragedies they encounter on their jobs day after day. They call it "cop humor." Their jokes, which would sound sick to others, enable them to cope and go on with their work. The critics' allegations simply do not hold up in light of the information both survivors and therapists have to tell.

In a letter written by a parent who has been accused by his child of sexual abuse we read: "The therapist has become the cult guru, the god who controls information received, controls the patient's mind, manipulates thru hypnosis, trance and meditation, and devastates the family and friends of the patient. The therapist then sends the patient thru the 'healing process' permanently detached from those who really loved them—their family and friends."[12]

I can well understand the devastation that this parent must be going through, but I cannot agree with his view of what a therapist does or becomes in the client/therapist relationship. The vast majority of mental health professionals conduct their work in an ethical fashion that leads the client to recovery and autonomy, not to a state of manipulation, controlled and isolated from others who genuinely care for him or her.

From another perspective, some parents who have had allegations of sexual and/or ritual abuse made against them may have been severely abused themselves as children and have dissociated the abuse. If, early on, Multiple Personality Disorder emerged as a coping mechanism, an alter of which the parent is entirely unaware may have abused the child.

I have read that many adults who have an extraordinary need for attention and who have read my book, *Satan's Underground*, and Lawrence Pazder's book, *Michelle Remembers*, have latched onto these stories and taken them on as their own. This supposedly explains why we are hearing so many accounts of sexual and ritual abuse which we had not heard heretofore.

Martin Smith, M.Ed., wrote a paper which critiqued the work of Dr. George Ganaway, Ph.D. (1989, 1990) who suggested that in considering the existence of widespread, interlocking cults that practice ritual abuse, we need to look at alternative explanations for clients who report these experiences in their background.

Mr. Smith writes, "He [Ganaway] cites the idea that widespread accounts of satanism constitute an 'urban legend.' Ganaway also notes the publication of books such as *Michelle Remembers* and *Satan's Underground*, extensive media attention, and the networking of clients and therapists nationally who share information and cross validate each other's realities. This all has presumably fueled an explosion of factitious accounts of ritual abuse in MPDs."[13]

It does seem ironic to me that someone actually believes I have the ability to wield such power and influence!

I have been accused in print of reading the book *Sybil*, and patterning my story after Sybil's life! I would like to make it clear, that although I had heard of the book, I had never read it. And even after seeing it in a video store and reading the description of the story, I put it back on the shelf because I don't like watching such stories. Only three or four months ago, when the story of Sybil was aired on television, did I make an attempt to watch it. After one particularly upsetting scene, I turned to another channel.

I do not eagerly await the next book, the next TV program, the next newspaper or magazine article on this subject. In fact, right now, I have probably five or six sets of information that I have neatly stacked in a corner on the floor in my study. They remain unread. When I have more time, I will go through the sets one at a time, giving myself plenty of breathing space between them.

The men who served in the Gulf War weren't wanting attention when they individually went to their base doctors for a diagnosis and treatment. The had not "networked" with other men across the country. They each had disturbing physical and/or mental problems. Why are more of these men coming forward now? Because they have found out that there are others who are suffering from the same kinds of problems. May I suggest that that is the reason survivors are coming forward now with their own stories?

The answer is unequivocally, "Yes." Their stories are not patterned after someone else's story. They do not "inherit" or "latch onto" a story, as some have alluded to, because it is the newest "fad" or "chic" emotional problem to have. They do not have these stories because therapists are brainwashing them or implanting such grisly stories into their subconscious. And survivor stories are not abounding because therapists are being pressured into conforming to a standard of acceptance set by another mental health professional.

Survivors are coming out, thank God, because they are hearing that there are others like themselves. They are finding out that they are not alone in their woundedness. My story or the stories of others has not been the impetus for imitators. Rather, they have been the impetus for giving other survivors the courage to break their silence to seek the help they so desperately need. Not unlike the veterans of the Gulf War who were encouraged to come forward because of the few who had already sought help, so survivors of sexual abuse, incest, and ritual abuse have been encouraged to break their own silence and come forward. Because a few others preceded them, crossing the barriers of fear and of being labeled "crazy," "a fraud," or "a Munchausen," scores of survivors are free to find help.

I think that for me, and other survivors, it boils down to the fact that we are not trying to convince anyone of anything. If some believe, we are most appreciative, and we take note of the fact that many are believing and taking the subject seriously. To those who doubt or deny, you cannot stem the tide of survivors who are now free to disclose and seek help.

Unfriendly Fire

Isn't it time to lay down the stones and pick up the burdens of our nation's survivors? We do not need more stone throwers. Stones are easy to pick up and sling at another. Picking up another's burden and sharing it is not so easy. Let us not pummel our own injured. Rather, let us pick up the stretchers and carry our injured to safety.

Words can burn like hot coals heaped one upon another. They can ultimately injure and take away life. Our tongues can be used to whip another into submission, then into silence. Unfriendly fire by those whom we have looked upon as friends is as unpowering a feeling as is the feeling of being re-victimized and stripped naked once again.

All survivors of ritual abuse have come under heavy attack. Our stories are simply not to be believed. Such figurative assassinations serve no purpose. The survivors know their stories are true. The therapists know their clients' stories are true. The only ones left are the critics whose agendas are hard to define.

Over a year ago, I listened on the radio to two people raise their voices at each other for two hours. One person was of the firm conviction that ritual abuse existed, and that there were indeed survivors of such abuse. The other person yelled, "Where's the evidence?"

Several months later, I had the opportunity to speak with the gentleman who had been on the talk show and who believes that there are survivors of ritual abuse. I asked him if he thought I had done wrong in remaining quiet, going about business as usual. His reply was well-taken. "Lauren, for me, the subject of survivors of ritual abuse is an issue. For you, it is your life. You've done right in remaining out of the fray."

I continue to heed his advice. I will not place myself in an adversarial role. Our answers will never meet the demands of the critics. Few first-person accounts will ever meet such rigid standards, especially of things that happened ten, twenty, or thirty years ago or more! No definitive proof may ever be possible for some survivors. When we haven't even been able to accommodate the voices of children who tell us of their own stories of molestation, mainly because it is the belief of the self-appointed apostles of denial that children do lie about being sexually molested, how can we even hope that they will ever believe the bizarre stories that we adult survivors have to tell?

Are the critics going to insist that Annie's story isn't true? Probably. Are the critics going to suggest that her therapist brainwashed her with a story that she [the therapist] had implanted into her mind, thus leaving Annie thinking a story about her life is true when, in fact, it was all concocted by her therapist? Probably.

Are you going to convince me that Annie's story isn't true? Not a chance! Are you going to convince Annie's therapist that her story isn't true? Not a chance! Are you going to convince Annie's husband that her story isn't true? Not a chance! Are you going to convince Annie's close friends that her story isn't true? Not a chance! Are you going to convince Annie to doubt her own memories? Not a chance.

The quote that has been running through my mind while writing this chapter is one which I would do well to cite as this chapter comes to a close.

"Ideas die hard,

and a mindset, unlike a computer chip,

is not easily altered or replaced.

Even fresh new evidence may fail to persuade.

The doors of some minds have rusty hinges."

Richard Wurmbrand[14]

15

Will We Survive?

**"When I think of the miracles in the universe,
I consider you.
You are a little miracle!!"**

These are the words my first therapist of several years ago wrote to me on her Christmas card this year. She continued. "My heart feels warm and glowing when I think of the timid Lauren sitting in a wheel chair at the support group I facilitated in the doctor's office asking if she could see me individually and the Lauren I see today seeking honesty, truth and concern for others."

My heart glowed with hers, and I felt a much welcomed warmth from such a caring expression. I needed this unsolicited affirmation in the wake of the difficult times I and other survivors have experienced as they have chosen to speak out about their own tragedies.

Those who have taken an unfriendly aim at survivors have made too many accusations for anyone to answer.

It is true that I wrote *Satan's Underground* under a pseudonym. I thought it would be fairly obvious to most why I chose to do so, and it was, but for some, it meant that I was trying to hide something. When asked if Lauren Stratford was my real name, I always answered in the negative. However, Lauren Stratford is my legal name now, and I am very comfortable with it.

Do I love to jet-set around the country? Hardly. Ask anyone who knows me. I hate to travel!

Do I love meeting celebrities? Sure I do. However, I would much rather talk to a group of survivors than to be on a TV show that is hosted by a well-known talk show host. TV producers normally encourage their guests to talk about the most sensational aspects of their stories. I seldom have been given the opportunity to say what I have really wanted to say. Celebrities are people with jobs that are geared to the almighty ratings system, and unfortunately, sensationalism is the key that boosts those ratings.

And limousines? I am embarrassed to death to ride in them. The limo arrives at our destination and I step out. People are gawking at me. I just know they're thinking, Who's she? I want to run and hide.

Financial gains? I'll trade my bank account for yours any day.

Famous? Not really, but more well-known than I ever wanted to be or will ever be comfortable with. I remember appearing on "The Oprah Winfrey Show" one morning in Chicago. We had just done the show, were whisked off to the airport in one of those limos, and barely made it to the plane on time. I was walking to my seat, when a man called to me and asked, "Ma'am, didn't I just see you on Oprah?" I thought, Now, this is not possible. I just left the set of Oprah not more than an hour and a half ago. I nodded in the affirmative and quickly scrunched down in my seat, hoping no one else would recognize me.

Believe it or not, I arrived at my apartment from Chicago to Southern California in time to watch myself on the show that afternoon. Later on in the evening, I was dressed in my usual comfortable jeans with holes in the knees and my slippers that had just about seen their last day. I was taking my garbage to the dumpster. I began to laugh out loud. Dragging my garbage sack behind me, I looked towards the heavens and said, "Lord, You sure do have a way of humbling a person. Don't you know that I was on 'The Oprah Winfrey Show' this morning?" I'm sure He must have chuckled. Walking back to my apartment, my feet were planted firmly on terra firma. It really didn't matter whose show I had been on. It only mattered that survivors who were still in hiding would know that it was safe to break their silence, some of whom had kept that silence for twenty or thirty years.

Do I fear for my life? Sometimes. Three years ago, the elevator was jammed. Looking back now, it would seem that it probably was jammed on purpose. For the first time, I had to walk down three flights of stairs to reach my car in the underground parking. The last set of stairs was on the outside of the building. They were made of concrete. I neared the landing and suddenly, I was pushed from behind. I fell forward, my head slamming onto the cement landing. I am blessed to be alive today. It took several months to recover from a concussion and a shattered wrist. I have a faint white scar on the side of my forehead, and my wrist sometimes tells me to give it a rest. But other than that, I'm almost as good as new.

A few months ago, I surprised a man who was on my balcony patio as I stepped out of the elevator. His hand was on the handle of the french door that opens into my living room. I now have a security and alarmed response system in my apartment. I have less reason to fear now, but I'm still cautious. Someone either travels with me or someone meets me at the airline gate and accompanies me wherever I go. All survivors learn to be careful. The ones who have gone public learn to take even more stringent precautionary measures.

Why did some have a problem with my first book? I have always been aware that there are time gaps, chronological errors, omissions, etc. Some were done purposely, to protect the anonymity of those involved, and some were omitted because I just wasn't able to fill in all the gaps. I'll give you an example.

I stated early on in *Satan's Underground* that my adoptive father left home when I was four years old. I sincerely believed that to be the truth. However, when I made a trip to visit my birth relatives for the first time, I asked one of my aunts and uncles to drive me to the town where I had lived as a child. We drove past a private school. It looked very familiar. I exclaimed out loud, "I went to that school when I was in kindergarten and first grade." Then I remembered that my father was still living with us.

As soon as I flew back to Southern California, I phoned my publisher and talked with the editor-in-chief. When we were connected, I said, "I have a problem. I wrote in *Satan's Underground* that my adoptive father left home when I was about four. I've just returned from my hometown. I found out that I must have been somewhere around seven or eight when he left. That should be corrected in the next printing."

I am still in the healing process, and will be for some time to come. I made that very clear in my second book, *I Know You're Hurting*. For that matter, probably all of us are in a continual process of healing from one thing or another. For survivors of abuse, the healing process is a major undertaking. I continue to take right and wrong turns, and I continue to start and stop. But will I quit and give up after having come so far? No. I dare not.

When I have questioned myself if I should have never spoken out about the subject of abuse, I have only to look at the boxes of letters survivors have written, thanking me for writing what they have been wanting to say, but were too fearful to say. They learned that they were not the only ones who went through these kinds of abuses. They learned that they were not alone in their suffering, and in their need to find healing for their emotional wounds. For this reason, I continue to write and speak. And I will write and speak of things I am now just remembering.

For instance, I have just recalled a good memory of my father that came to mind a few weeks ago. I was about five or six years old. I was sitting on my father's lap. He gave me his pocket comb, and he let me comb his thick, wavy hair for what must have been at least several minutes. I remember feeling a sense of caring, of love, and of warmth as I repeatedly ran the comb through his hair over and over again.

Even more recently, I remembered my adoptive mother taking me to a symphony program to see the world-famous composer and conductor, Arturo Toscanini. Being the budding musician that some thought I was, we attended many kinds of concerts. I don't remember enjoying it or not enjoying it. I only remember that I was there. These are but small pieces of the puzzle, but they continue to add to the bigger picture. As I continue on my journey to wholeness, I'm sure I will remember other things, some good, and some not so good.

Have I been tempted to give up? Yes. Many times. But I was given a priceless gem that has kept me going day by day, hour by hour and sometimes, minute to minute. A pastor and dear friend of mine who acted as a security person of sorts at a book convention a couple of years ago, became an instant encourager when I was near tears over something I had overheard.

He said, "Lauren, you have lit too may candles across this country and in other countries. The candlelights will never be extinguished no matter how hard some may try. When you get down and you feel like quitting, remember the bookstore owner from Puerto Rico who jumped up and down saying, 'Now, *all* my people can know how to get out of devil worship.' Think of each person who has found the way to freedom through reading your books. Close your eyes and see the flames lighting the darkness. Your work has not been in vain."

I closed my eyes and envisioned candles burning brightly in my own country, in Puerto Rico, in South

Africa, in Australia, in New Zealand, in Singapore, in Canada, in England—well, needless to say, my tears of sadness turned to tears of joy. I have the priceless vision of candle flames to keep me going through it all. I will always have my pastor friend to thank for sharing such a timeless gift with me.

There are times when I'm tempted to quit therapy. It is just plain gosh-darn hard work. Writing this book in between therapy sessions is like living with these issues every hour of the day with no break in between. I've said to myself and to my therapists, "I don't need this in my life right now," but then, in my gut, I know that "this" will remain in my life until I deal with it. Then I can release it and let it go.

Marilyn Van Derbur, Miss America 1958, shocked the nation in June of 1991 by saying, "I am an incest victim." Marilyn's high society millionaire father had incestuously molested her from the age of five until she moved away to attend college. Marilyn did not start therapy until she was forty-seven years old.

Her husband, Larry, likened her life in therapy as a person with a sliver in their finger. On a television program he said words to the effect, "Honey, it has been like each time you went to a therapy session, the festering wound was pried open a little more. Tiny pieces of the sliver were removed in each session. You would come home with that painful finger. Each session opened up the wound a little more. I watched your pain, and I applauded your courage in pressing on towards healing. The pieces of the sliver are almost out now. When they are all out, the wound that has been festering for fifty years will finally be healed." I remember Larry giving Marilyn's hand a comforting squeeze and saying, "Honey, I'm so proud of you."

Marilyn Van Derbur could have said, "I don't need this in my life. I'm a middle-aged woman." But Marilyn was desperate for the pain to go away, and there was no way it was going to go away until she allowed the wound to be opened as her healing began in therapy. It would be nice if all the "yuckies" would magically disappear, but healing simply doesn't work that way.

We Are Just What the Word Says—Survivors!

In his book, *Beyond Survival*, retired Naval Captain Gerald Coffee discusses his seven-year internment as a Vietnam POW. Captain Coffee was savagely tortured and constantly lived on the brink of starvation. I quote from his writing.

"Where does one go to give up? If we knew, would our answer be there? I think not. The answer comes from moving forward, even through confusion and fear. To give up on something you desperately want guarantees you won't get it."[1] For my benefit as well as for yours, I would like to repeat that last sentence again. "*To give up on something you desperately want guarantees you won't get it.*"

Captain Gerald Coffee is a survivor. He is proof positive that if we don't give up, even in the most severe and hopeless of circumstances, we have the inner capability to survive. If I did not believe that with every fiber of my being, I would not be writing this book. I only half-jokingly tell people that I'd probably drop out of society, move to a quaint little cottage by the ocean, and become a beach bum!

I do not say this lightly nor do I say it boastingly, but I am a fighter. Survivors are fighters, otherwise they would still be victims caught in a never-ending pattern of being re-victimized. We are fighters, and we are resilient. Survivors are but miracles in the making! We must never lose sight of our miracle!

I have fought for my life in many ways. There are over five thousand pages of hospital records on me. When my hematologist relocated to another state, his secretary mailed me copies of my medical records—four volumes and 470 pages. I've been given a rare drug three times to keep me alive when I've been near death. The cost? Hang on to your seats. Thirteen thousand dollars per dose! One dose lasts one day.

I still take an anti-clotting drug via intra-pulmonary inhalation. So far, it has worked wonderfully. After having been hospitalized over fifty times, until several weeks ago, I had not been in a hospital for my blood disorder for two and a half years. That's a miracle, a survivor's miracle.

I'm writing to let you know that yes, I have had to fight for my life, but I am a survivor, and I choose to continue to be a survivor.

Has there been a cost in writing this new book? Sure. There is a cost for anyone who writes about these kinds of abuses. As I wrote a few pages back, I have had to deal with my own issues of healing in therapy as I've been writing *Stripped Naked*. There have been sessions when we would ordinarily tackle a difficult issue, but because I needed to be off the emotional roller coaster on which survivors often find themselves while in therapy, my therapists have allowed me to avoid or to put aside issues that would be too difficult for me to take on until after I finish the book. I have some really neat therapists!

Also, I will probably get the usual response to *Stripped Naked* by those who do not believe survivors' stories of ritual abuse. This time will be different, though. I thank God that I am surrounded by a group of people who have given me five years of uninterrupted and undaunted support. I have been blessed with a team of mental health professionals, my pastors, and a few close friends who have consistently been my support, a shoulder to lean on, my advisers, and my safety team. They are always there for me. They are loyal, knowledgeable, and patient. I am only too aware that in dealing with me, one's patience can be severely tested, but my support team keeps hanging in.

How I wish every survivor had a support team. I realize just how fortunate I am to have this team each time I hear from a survivor who is lucky to have even one person to turn to. Then there are the survivors who have no one. That is where the rubber meets the road, and healing becomes impossible. Any survivor who reads this paragraph will surely identify with what I'm writing. Some survivors are hanging on by their fingernails, and there is no one to catch them if they can't hang on any longer.

One of the newest problems I have begun to deal with is that my life is more than half over, and I feel as if I haven't experienced life as I would like to have experienced it. Lost years cannot be recaptured. We who are survivors have all felt this same sense of loss. Grieving for this loss is a gut-wrenching, but necessary experience.

Recently, I heard someone give a quote on TV. The quote will have to remain anonymous, because I can't remember who said it. For me, and for many survivors, this sentence expresses how many of us would describe our lives with defined precision:

> "The tragedy in life was,
> when it came time to die,
> I discovered that I had not lived."

I choose life! This is the first day of the rest of my life, and I am going to do all I can to make it richer and fuller. I know many survivors who are beginning anew and are starting to build a meaningful and rewarding life. The rubble of the past is being left behind as we face the morning light of each new day.

The Rewards Are Already Beginning!

For the past five years, I have been rewarded in the things that really count in one's lifetime. The rewards of making a difference in someone else's life are awesome. George Eliot once said, "What is life for, if it is not to help another on his journey?" This is what gives my life meaning. Just to know that someone else has made it through another day because of something I shared with them makes me want to get on to the next day. Those days rapidly turn into weeks, months, and years. To experience a not-so-perfect past turning into one that can encourage another survivor in their struggle is the push I need to say to myself, "Yes! It's okay. You're going to make it today, tomorrow, and the day after."

If I can help survivors like the ones who have dared to break the silence of their own hells by writing to me, signing their letters, "From NOBODY," "From Box-holder," or with just their initials, I am blessed.

A fragile survivor recently shared the pain of her life with me. I obtained permission from this survivor to share part of her painful expressions with you. Some of you may find yourselves saying, "Me, too."

> "For a little while, please hold me,
> The suffering is so intense;
> For just a little while, please hold me,
> For a little longer than you're comfortable with;
> Hold me as you would a small child,
> For inside, that's what I really am.
>
> Please do not betray . . . only reach,
> To touch, to love, to understand;
> One who hungers for loving touch,
> For love, for peace, help me to believe;
> For just a little while,
> Please hold me, won't you?"
>
> — Karen, a survivor

To have the privilege of reaching for the hand of a lonely soul who braved the unknown writing, "All I'm seeking for is someone, somewhere, to understand that I feel so alone," that is my reward.

You're on Your Way to Recovery When . . .

- You have allowed yourself to tell the one thing you thought you'd never tell another soul.
- You can accept the fact that someone you loved and someone you thought loved you abused you.
- You are able to stop feeling guilty for the yucky things that happened.
- When you don't feel quite so weird about yourself.
- When you don't feel like SRA or MPD is stamped on your forehead for all the world to see anymore.
- When you don't want to dig a hole and hide when you begin to remember a yucky memory.
- If you have been diagnosed as being a multiple, you come to accept and even like those who are inside, instead of being fearful of them or hating them and wanting them to just go away.
- When you call your therapist or a close friend and say, "I was okay today." That's a victory! Even if you have a difficult night, you can remember that you made it through another day.
- When you see a tiny ray of light in the midst of your darkness, even if only for a minute—that is a milestone. To others it may seem insignificant, but then, we're not on this journey to impress others. We're on this journey *for ourselves!*
- It may be a simple thing, one that would go unnoticed by another. Like hearing the chirping of a bird; like feeling the warmth of the noonday sun; like observing the vivid splashes of color in a flower.
- When your will to live outgrows your will to die.

I write about these things, because they are signs of recovery that either I have experienced or I am working towards experiencing. Each one is encouraging and with each new one accomplished, I've taken one more step. I started to keep a journal of my steps. Some are tiny steps and others are gigantic steps, more like leaps. I encourage you who are on the same journey to keep a journal. It will be something to read and reread when the darkness begins to envelop you again. We need hope, not hopelessness. Our remembering of triumphs gained gives us that hope. Remember that the word "survivor" is *not* a four-letter word. *The very fact that you have survived and you are continuing to survive is a major, major accomplishment!*

What Survivors Need from You

- Acceptance. Allow us to be however we need to be at the moment.
- A little TLC (Tender Loving Care).
    A hug.
    A shoulder.
    A tear shared.
    A word of encouragement.
- Don't expect us to act courageous and brave at all times. We don't always feel that way. In fact, we're more apt to feel frightened, insecure, and unsafe. We need you to be a solid foundation for us.
- Let us know if we're becoming a little too much for you. We would rather know that and adjust our relationship with you than to have you suddenly pull away from us altogether.
- Allow us our humanity. We are not aliens from outer space. We have not appeared on your doorstep from a past life. We just have unique wounds from which we are working to be healed.

Sarah

I have a picture that I cut out of a *National Geographic* magazine. It caught my eye. After looking at it several times, I began to realize just why I was so drawn to it. It was an advertisement for the City of Hope. The City of Hope is a hospital that treats patients who have catastrophic illnesses.

This full-color ad was a picture of a young woman in a gorgeous bridal gown standing in the center aisle at the front of a church. Her husband-to-be was standing beside her. What mesmerized me was the caption alongside the picture. It read, "It Took 50 People To Get Sarah Down The Aisle." I looked again at the picture. Behind Saran and her groom was the usual entourage of bridesmaids, friends, parents, and other relatives. But something was uniquely different about this wedding photo. Standing behind the others were at least thirty-eight persons from the medical profession all dressed in their white hospital jackets. One of them even had a stethoscope hanging around his neck.

The writing underneath the caption read:

> "Most brides need only a helping hand from their father to get down the aisle. Unfortunately, Sarah wasn't like most brides. Sarah had just been diagnosed with cancer. Faced with an uncertain future, Sarah might have postponed her marriage plans and allowed the diagnosis to devastate any future plans for her life if it hadn't been for the reassuring support of a highly skilled cancer team.

> "Together, her support team gave Sarah the hope, strength and the chance she needed to start a new life. When it comes to conquering cancer, you need a special group of people to lead the way.

> "Thanks to those very special and highly trained people, Sarah is recovering and is on her way to the life she's always wanted."

My eyes moved back to the photo. I began to see Sarah as a survivor, not of cancer, but of sexual abuse, and perhaps, of other kinds of abuses as well. The people standing behind her had been replaced by highly skilled mental health professionals who understood the scope of sexual and ritual trauma.

I rephrased part of the advertisement to read:

> "Together, her support team gave Sarah the hope, strength and the chance she needed to start a new life. When it comes to conquering the devastation of abuse, you need a special group of people to lead the way. Thanks to those very special and highly trained people, Sarah is recovering and is on her way to the life she's always wanted."

I was handed a note from a survivor when I spoke in Salt Lake City several years ago. The survivor had no sooner handed it to me than she disappeared into the crowd. I hastily put it in my pocket without reading it. Back at my motel room, I rather nonchalantly took it out of my pocket and began to read it. "Lauren, bless you for your courage. The Satanists killed my mom and dad and my brother, and for five years I was at their mercy. I, too, have killed. I am very ashamed. The brainwashing has taken my ability to think. Thank you."

I have no idea who wrote the note, but it sits on my desk in a small frame. Every once in awhile, I read it and realize again *why* I am writing, and *for whom* I am writing.

There are many "Sarahs" around the country. This particular "Sarah" needed all the professional support she could get. I hope that such a unique team of skilled and caring people were available for her. I hope that she is well on her way to healing. Tragically, though, the Sarahs around the country far outnumber the people who are willing to make themselves available members of support teams.

What Is the Survivor's Job?

The survivor's job is the biggest one of all. It is to continue on in our journey to wholeness. We have a responsibility, both to ourselves and to our alters, to keep on in that journey. We dare not listen to those who would like for us to become non-existent. Our healing is far too important for our survival to let anyone intimidate us into retreating. We are on the front lines fighting for our survival. Many there be who are taking shots at us from the other side, *but now is not the time to retreat*!

If we choose to remain silent, then we will continue to live with the pain of heinous memories. We will continue to experience a messed-up life. We will continue to bear our wounds alone. If we choose to get ourselves into therapy, and stay there, even though it may become rough and wearisome at times, we will arrive at the end of our journey. Healing will never begin in the silence of hiding. At least we can be assured that healing will begin in therapy.

What about our alters? Do they have a right to learn about new choices they can make so they won't continue to be revictimized? Do they have a right to find out about each other so they won't feel so alone? I think so. If we choose not to get help for ourselves, we are also choosing not to get help for our alters. We are taking away their chance of being free from the cult. We are taking away their chance to feel safe, to be free from fear, from threats, and from further programming. We are ensuring that they will continue to be programmed and to experience reinforcements of that programming from the cult using pain and torture over and over again.

If we choose not to seek help, we are doing ourselves and our alters an injustice, for all of us will be on a never-ending merry-go-round of programming, control, and more abuse.

There's a saying that history always repeats itself. Does history really have to repeat itself in a survivor's life? If we choose to remain in our closets of fear and silence, we can be assured that history will repeat itself. The cycle of revictimization and control by the cult, by our parents, or by whomever, will never be broken. We will continue to be hurt emotionally and physically. We will not only be subjected to new abuses, but our memories of nightmares past will continue to haunt us, and we will continue to live in the aftermath of our trauma.

In the wake of those who want us to remain in our places of hiding and silence and have made it scary for us even to think about getting help, I can well understand the temptation to keep quiet. No survivor wants to be ridiculed. No survivor wants to be told that these kinds of abuses don't exist, and that therefore, either she is lying or her therapist is brainwashing her. It is frightening. I realize more and more why many survivors are choosing to remain silent or to go back into hiding.

Your silence will cause even greater pain for you and your alters. Silence is not safety. The pain of remaining unhealed will not go away. It will only worsen as time goes by.

I know. I've been there. *I am there!* And the healing process, however difficult and painful it has been and continues to be, is worth it in light of the progress I am making. By choosing to break my silence, I am breaking that on-going cycle of cult control and revictimization. I am making a choice that will ensure that history will not repeat itself in my life.

My fervent hope is that you will find the courage to make the same choice. The price you will pay for your freedom—freedom from more sexual abuse, freedom from self-mutilations, freedom from heinous nightmares, freedom from giving in to threats because of programming, and freedom for your alters—far out-weighs what it may cost you to obtain that freedom.

Let no one intimidate you. Let no one frighten you. Let no one deter you. Your job is to continue on in your journey to wholeness. I choose my words carefully when I say that we who are survivors truly have taken our own personal walks back to hell. And we have! But we have survived, and we now have the chance to be free. No matter what the obstacles we have yet to face, we will settle for nothing less than complete healing and freedom! Freedom is our inherent right.

In Martin Smith's paper from which I quoted in the previous chapter, I want to share his closing remark with you.

"Dr. Ganaway seems to want to shove ritual abuse back into the closet, slam and lock the door, and throw away the key. Perhaps, in light of our society's desire to stay in denial about abuse of *any kind*, we should keep the door open a little while longer."[2]

Thanks, Marty!

16

The Final Word—By Baby, et al.

Since my alters are the reason I've survived to write this book, and they are the real heroes, I thought it would be fitting to give them the chance to have the final word. The following remarks are by alters who came out to speak. They are all aware of this book and know that their expressions will be read by many people. Their remarks were told to Dr. Lady who wrote them down for me.

Amor

"I just want people to know I'm here, and that my name means love. I've been hiding for a long time, because I don't trust anybody."

Master Controller

"My name is M.C. I want to keep Lauren safe. I'm going to make sure that no one inside does anything to hurt her. I'm in charge of most everyone! I'm the Master. That means I'm big time! I keep my eyes on everybody. Sometimes Baby gets scared. Then I take over and keep her safe.

"I have good eyes, and I don't need those glasses Lauren wears. I watch out for the bad guys 'cuz I see good.

"I used to be in charge of the bad ones inside, but now I make sure everyone stays on the good side. I'm doing a very good job. I'm the star of the book!"

Bob

"My name is Bob! My name is a loud name. You have to say it loud. There was a movie we watched about a Bob who went to see someone like Dr. Lady and New Lady. That's why I picked the name Bob.

"I have new job now. I don't work for the bad guys no more. I'm doing good job. I was supposed to make Lauren dead, but I help keep Lauren safe now. It's important, the most important job there is. I go everywhere Lauren goes. I watch out for her."

David

"I keep Lauren safe when she's driving. When she goes by places that make her sad, I help her drive by them. I'm a good driver. My job used to be to drive to places that Lauren didn't want to go to, but now we only go to good places. I know the way to Dr. Lady's office and even to New Lady's office which is far away.

"If anyone would like to learn how to drive, tell them to contact David. That's me! Remember not to drive too fast, and watch out for the police cars. That's what I do!"

Little Girl

"I'm still crying. 'Cuz there are lots of things to cry about."

Baby

"Me name Baby. Me four. Me love Lauren, but she no hear me. Me try make her feel better when she cry, but me no know how. It never work. But me never gonna leave her. Me always gonna be here for her. Me make it so she no have 'member all that yucky stuff. Me let her hold Me-Baby, too. Sometime she cry when she hold Me-Baby. But sometime she happy.

"Others like Lauren who have little kids in them like

me, they don't have no mommies. They all alone like me was. All little kids need mommies so they can get hugs and peanut bars and crayons draw pictures with. Me lucky! Bye-bye."

Epilogue

"I Whispered"

I whispered . . . when I tried to walk to the police station to get help. I was about five years old. I was wearing only my nightie and slippers. A neighbor spotted me and carried me back home.

I whispered . . . when I packed my nightie in a suitcase, walked across the street, knocked on a neighbor's door, and asked if I could live at her house.

I whispered . . . when I refused to share anything that happened to me in the sharing time. I was in the second or third grade.

I whispered . . . when I began to deliberately burn my fingers and the palms of my hands on the toaster and slam my fingers in drawers. I never told anyone what I had done. I just had to take my feelings out on someone, and the only one I could really hurt was myself. I was about nine years old.

I whispered . . . when I drowned the altars and church pews with my tears, Sunday after Sunday, week after week, and month after month.

I whispered . . . when I told my Sunday School teacher that I didn't want to live at home any longer.

I whispered . . . when I told my pastor that I was afraid to live at home any longer.

I whispered . . . when I told my counselors at summer camp year after year that I didn't think I would live if I had to remain at home.

I whispered . . . when I talked with my band teacher about my home life. I even remember that it became so late after talking to him one afternoon that he gave me a ride home.

I whispered . . . when I hid out in the assistant pastor's apartment that adjoined the church. It was after a Sunday evening service. I was sobbing. I told him that I was too terrified to go home with my mother. Then she knocked on the door . . . and I went home.

I whispered . . . when a policewoman came to the house. I was too frightened to talk to her in front of my mother. So my mother did all the talking. I came off as the disobedient child.

I whispered . . . when I began to sleep with a knife under my pillow. If my mother awakened me in the middle of the night with her ranting and raving, I'd be able to protect myself. I was so fearful of what she might do to me when she lost her temper. I didn't want her to scare me any more.

I whispered . . . when I asked my Spanish teacher if she would talk to me out in the hall. She got me excused from having to take a test in another class, because life was becoming so unbearable at home that I couldn't concentrate on my studies.

Then I screamed . . . but it was only heard as a whisper. I ran away, never to come back. I was fifteen years old.

I screamed . . . but it was only heard as a whisper. I went to the police. They told me to go back home. I'd be sixteen years old in six months. They said that when I was sixteen I could choose who I wanted to live with. But I thought I'd probably be dead by then.

I screamed . . . but it was only heard as a whisper. I took the city bus to juvenile hall. My high school principal gave me the money for the bus ride. I walked in, went up to the window, and asked if I could stay there. They said yes, but I only got to stay for two days. My mother called my father and asked him to come and get me.

I screamed . . . but it was only heard as a whisper. I banged my head against the concrete blocks of the wall in the college dormitory.

I screamed . . . but it was only heard as a whisper. I said I had been sexually abused. Then I got scared and said that I had made it up.

I screamed . . . I wrote a book about my traumatic life. Most people listened, but there were those who wanted to shut me up. They called me "dysfunctional," a "fraud," a "liar," and a "Munchausen." Finally, they said that survivors really believed their stories, but they weren't true—that the therapists were the ones who were implanting these stories into their clients' minds.

I'm still screaming—for myself and for other survivors. We wonder, Can people hear us? How loud will our screams have to be before all peoples will believe us? We have wondered, If we killed ourselves, would people **then** hear our screams? But then . . . it would be too late.

Many survivors have joined me. One voice can be silenced. Many voices cannot.

**Let us listen to the whispers,
so we don't have to hear the screams.**

Appendix

The following is an extract from a brochure entitled *RITUAL ABUSE: Report of the Ritual Abuse Task Force of the Los Angeles County Commission for Women*. It was published on March 15, 1991, and is used by permission.

RITUAL ABUSE AND THE USE OF MIND CONTROL

Mind control is the cornerstone of ritual abuse, the key element in the subjugation and silencing of its victims. Victims of ritual abuse are subjected to a rigorously applied system of mind control designed to rob them of their sense of free will and to impose upon them the will of the cult and its leaders. Most often these ritually abusive cults are motivated by a satanic belief system. The mind control is achieved through an elaborate system of brainwashing, programming, indoctrination, hypnosis, and the use of various mind-altering drugs. The purpose of the mind control is to compel ritual abuse victims to keep the secret of their abuse, to conform to the beliefs and behaviors of the cult, and to become functioning members who serve the cult by carrying out the directives of its leaders without being detected within society at large.

The information available about how ritually abusive cults indoctrinate young children comes primarily from child and adult survivors who have been able to remember how the cult achieved mind control over them and

311

others in the cult. Therapists who have worked extensively with ritual abuse victims have gleaned a significant, although still incomplete, degree of understanding of the process by which the mind control is achieved. A key element of the victim's recovery from ritual abuse consists of understanding, unraveling, and undoing the mind control which usually persists for a long time, even in victims who no longer participate in the cult. Undoing these controls is critical, for victims may remain unable to disclose their abuse, or vulnerable to cult manipulation if the systematic programming is not dismantled. As more ritual abuse victims are helped to free themselves from cult mind control, the body of information about this important aspect of ritual abuse continues to grow.

Satanic cults focus their initial efforts to achieve mind control most frequently and strenuously with children under the age of six. Like developmental psychologists, satanists understand that people are most susceptible to having their character, beliefs, and behavior molded during this early period of development. This review of the mind control techniques utilized by satanic cults will focus primarily on the techniques used on very young children, both those in ritually abusive families, and those in extrafamilial settings, such as day-care and preschools. Children who are abused in intrafamilial settings are subjected to ongoing mind control that is often sustained in extreme forms throughout their childhood and adolescence.

There is a growing body of research into the indoctrination techniques which are used by a wide range of destructive cults. It is helpful to consider how satanic cults make use of these and other techniques to control their victims.

In *Cults, Quacks and Non-Professional Psychotherapists*, West and Singer have described elements of cult indoctrination as follows:

1. Isolation of the recruit and manipulation of his environment.
2. Control over channels of communication and information.
3. Debilitation through inadequate diet and fatigue.
4. Degradation or diminution of the self.
5. Induction of uncertainty, fear, and confusion, with joy and certainty through surrender to the group as a goal.
6. Alternation of harshness and leniency in a context of discipline.
7. Peer pressure generating guilt and requiring open confessions.
8. Insistence by seemingly all-powerful hosts that the recruit's survival—physical or spiritual—depends on identifying with the group.
9. Assignment of monotonous or repetitive tasks such as chanting or copying written materials.
10. Acts of symbolic betrayal or renunciation of self, family, and previously held values, designed to increase the psychological distance between the recruit and his previous way of life.

Satanic cults use many of the same techniques, but apply them in unique ways to indoctrinate and control very young children. To begin with, they impose a variety of *PHYSICAL, EMOTIONAL,* and *COGNITIVE CONDITIONS* which are conducive to indoctrination.

PHYSICAL CONDITIONS

1. HUNGER AND THIRST

    Ritually abused children are often deprived of food and water for extended periods of time, and are told they will be left to die of hunger and thirst. Their deprivation and fear of dying make them willing to comply with virtually any behavior or belief necessary to be given food or water again. The cult member who finally does feed the child is perceived as an ally and benefactor. The child feels deeply grateful and is thus susceptible to bonding with that cult member, thereby increasing the child's vulnerability to identifying with the cult and its beliefs and practices.

2. PAIN

Ritually abused children are physically tormented and sexually abused in very painful ways. The pain can cause them to dissociate and, like prisoners of war subjected to torture, they become willing to do whatever is demanded of them in order to make the pain stop. For a young child who is ritually abused in an out-of-home care setting, even a brief encounter with intense pain profoundly impacts that child's susceptibility to cult mind control. For those children raised in cults, the use of pain and the threat of pain continues for as long as they are submitted to the cult, causing an ongoing and deepening degree of subservience to the cult.

3. DRUGS

Both child and adult victims of ritual abuse have described being abused with mind-altering drugs. Some drugs are injected or administered in suppositories. Others are hidden in food or drink, or simply swallowed under duress.

The drug effects include hypnotic and paralytic effects, causing victims to experience mental and emotional states ranging from confusion and drowsiness, to passivity and helplessness. Memory distortions occur as well. Victims tend to recall very real and painful experiences only with difficulty as though they were unreal or even just dreams. Additionally, in such drug-induced states, young children are even more pliable than they would otherwise be, and more open to the belief system into which the cult is attempting to indoctrinate them. Cult leaders capitalize on drug-induced reality distortions to create the illusion that they have absolute power to which the child must submit.

4. EXHAUSTION

Ritually abused children are often deprived of rest and sleep. In the extrafamilial settings in which ritual abuse occurs, children are frequently deprived of needed nap and rest periods. In ritually abusive family settings, children may be deprived of sleep for extended periods of time. The influence of repeated drugging further deepens their sense of exhaustion. People in a state of exhaustion are more open to mind control because fatigue saps their normal coping capacities. This effect is especially pronounced in young children.

5. ISOLATION

Ritually abused children are put into closets, holes, cages, coffins, and other confined, usually dark, spaces. The children are often isolated there and told they will be left to die. The sensory deprivation that may result can cause some degree of disorientation. The isolation causes the child to feel desperate and overwhelmed with fear and dread. An abusive adult who subsequently releases the child from confinement is perceived by the child as a rescuer, often causing the young child to bond to that cult member. The child's bonding with one or more cult members increases the degree of the child's identification with the values and beliefs of the cult. In other words, both the isolation and the rescue make the child more susceptible to indoctrination into the destructive beliefs and practices of the cult.

6. SEXUAL ABUSE

Ritually abused children are subjected to brutal sexual abuse which involves severe pain and may involve sexual arousal with which the children are neither physically nor emotionally prepared to cope. Sometimes the sexual abuse is performed with symbolic instruments (e.g., penetration with a crucifix or wand) which reinforces the satanic belief system of the cult. The pain, especially if in combination with arousal, is extremely disorienting and overwhelming, again making the child willing to comply with the demands of the cult members in order to make the feelings stop. The sexual arousal can contribute to the formation of distorted bonds with the abusers, leading to identification with the abusive cult.

7. BRIGHT LIGHTS

Adult and child victims of ritual abuse describe having harsh, intensely bright lights shined in their eyes immediately before and during indoctrination. The lights appear to disorient them and to induce a state of trance which lowers the victim's resistance and heightens the susceptibility to indoctrination.

EMOTIONAL CONDITIONS

1. TERROR

Ritually abused children have been terrorized and are profoundly afraid of their abusers. They have endured physical torture and painful sexual assaults. They have witnessed the terror, torture, and murder of other children and adults in group settings, experiences which greatly intensify the child's own overwhelming fears. Their terror is heightened by what they perceive as the omnipotence and omniscience of their abusers, including what they believe are their abusers' abilities to control them through the use of demons and evil spirits.

Ritually abused children have also been threatened repeatedly with death to themselves and their families should they disclose. This state of terror causes the child to be willing to do or believe anything to appease the abusers, thereby reducing the degree of threat the child feels from them.

2. GUILT AND SHAME

Ritually abused children have been forced to engage in humiliating and degrading activities such as handling, smearing, and ingesting urine, feces, blood, and human flesh. They have been photographed pornographically and, sometimes, been made to view these pictures. They have been forced to participate in the abuse, torture, and killing of animals, and the murder of children and adults.

They are then made to feel responsible for their actions as though these actions were freely chosen by them. They are threatened with exposure as perpetrators, and fear being rejected completely by their families or even being arrested and jailed. Their feelings of guilt and shame contribute to a perception that through their actions, they have already shown their loyalty to the cult and its beliefs. They are made to feel that the abusive group itself is their only refuge of acceptance. By turning to the abusive group for a sense of acceptance and protection, these children are open to even further indoctrination.

3. EMOTIONAL ISOLATION AND DESPAIR

   Children who are ritually abused are made to feel cut off and rejected by their families and the rest of the world. They are often told that their "real parents" have died or have abandoned them, and that the people with whom they live are pretenders. Sometimes they are told that the cult members are their "real parents" who will someday "rescue" them from their homes. These ritually abused children often come to feel emotionally estranged from their families. The deep loneliness which results opens them to bonding with abusive cult members, identifying with them, and thus becoming open to indoctrination into the cult's system of beliefs and practices.

   In addition, children who are ritually abused are profoundly sad. They experience tragedy and horror, as well as isolation, at an intensity which would induce an overwhelming sadness in a mature adult. They may come to feel utterly hopeless, and in their despair they are likely to feel that cult abuse and cult membership are all that they deserve and all that they can imagine for their future. The cult convinces them that there is no place to turn for help, and thus no way out of the cult.

4. RAGE

   Ritual abuse provokes children to feel enormous rage, because the violation which they experience is so great. This rage within the child contributes to the cult's efforts to indoctrinate that child into a belief system in which violence and rage are valued and encouraged. A child who has been repeatedly violated by the cult over time, and not permitted to express any emotion about his/her abuse, may be eager to vent his/her rage by striking out and victimizing others. The assaultive behavior which ensues is encouraged and rewarded by adult cult members, and is used to make the child feel s/he already is just like the abusive adults who have provoked the rage.

COGNITIVE CONDITIONS

1. LACK OF INFORMATION

Young children who are being ritually abused lack sufficient information and experience to know that much of what their abusers tell them is untrue. They lack the cognitive development to perceive the contradictions in some of the lies they are told. They are likely to accept the misinformation offered by the cult members as part of the mind control process.

2. CONFUSION

Ritually abused children are confused by the infliction of pain, the extreme sexual arousal caused by sexual abuse, the incessant directives to do things they know are wrong, the extensive lying and deception by cult members, and the perceived loss of control over their own behavior and the behavior of those around them. Children in such situations long for explanations from adults to reduce their confusion about what is happening to them. The result again is an increased vulnerability to indoctrination as they open themselves to any explanations offered by the adults in the cult.

THE ROLE OF TRANCE STATES

These conditions—physical, emotional, and cognitive—exacerbate the impact of the child's ritual abuse, especially in combination with the used trance states. It is important to look at the role of trance states in achieving mind control over the ritually abused child. When children are in a state of trance, they are more open to indoctrination and other techniques for attaining control over their minds and behavior. For example, a child who hears an adult state repeatedly, "Satan has the power," is much more likely to incorporate that as a deeply held belief if the child is in a state of trance, than if the child is in a normal waking state.

There are many means by which trance states can be achieved with children during the course of ritual abuse. The rituals themselves contain many trance inducing elements, among them, chanting, isolation, sensory deprivation, pain, and other forms of extreme physical discomfort. Trance states are also induced in ritual abuse victims by using hypnosis and hypnotic drugs.

Traumatic experiences which occur while the victim is in a trance state can be used to indoctrinate victims. These experiences have a profound and long-lasting impact on the beliefs, feelings, and even the behavior of victims, despite the fact that these experiences cannot always be remembered consciously. Only later in life, usually with the help of a highly skilled therapist, are some ritual abuse victims able to painstakingly reconstruct what happened to them while they were in various states of trance or dissociation.

The fact that certain events are not easily remembered does not mean that they do not have a significant impact on the life of the individual. Until the memories are surfaced and worked through in a safe environment, the survivor of such abuse is still controlled to some extent by these past experiences. Typically, the survivor will react most strongly to past indoctrination when triggered by an event which is a reminder of it. For example, if the survivor was abused in childhood by a cult that conducted abusive rituals on every full moon, s/he may feel compelled as an adult to seek out a cult and participate in rituals whenever the moon is full. Or s/he may be triggered to perform a physically or sexually assaultive act on the full moon without seeking out a cult. Alternatively s/he may act out in some other compulsive way to cope with the anxiety associated with the dissociated memory of this traumatic event.

Survivors experience triggering of certain beliefs into which they were indoctrinated, or certain behaviors that they are programmed to enact. They are usually unaware of what it is that is triggering them. With help, a victim can bring the triggering events to conscious awareness, and then can gradually become empowered to free him/herself from these compulsions.

Behaviors can be triggered spontaneously by cues that by chance happen to remind the individual of past indoctrination or programming. Cues may be implanted by the cult during indoctrination which can also be employed deliberately by cult members to elicit particular behaviors from a victim. For example, a survivor who was ritually abused and indoctrinated in early childhood can often be called back into the cult years after the indoctrination occurred when approached by a cult member who knows what trigger words or signs to use to access that individual's programming and gain the desired response.

The abusive system of mind control described has distinct *EMOTIONAL CONSEQUENCES*, as well as a major impact upon the *COGNITIVE* and *RELIGIOUS BELIEFS* under which the victims function.

EMOTIONAL CONSEQUENCES of ritual abuse and mind control for both adult and child survivors include the following.

1. TERROR

Ritually abused children are overwhelmed with profound fear. They are hypervigilant, feeling that they are constantly being watched. They are anxious and agitated, sometimes mistakenly perceived as "hyperactive."

2. GUILT AND FEAR OF DISCOVERY

Ritually abused children experience profound fear both of punishment and loss of love from family and friends. They have been made to feel that their participation in heinous acts was freely chosen and that they are responsible for their actions. They are especially fearful of being found responsible by their families or by the authorities (e.g., police) and of being punished for their participation in the violence, sexual contacts, pornography, and murders.

3. LONELINESS

Children abused ritually outside of their families feel painfully cut off from their families and deeply lonely. They feel that the acts they have committed, and the vows they have been forced to make to the cult and to Satan, separate them from their families irrevocably. This kind of emotional estrangement from their parents is often accompanied by profound despair.

4. IDENTIFICATION WITH THE GROUP
   AND A SENSE OF PERSONAL BADNESS

Ritually abused children tend to feel identified with the evil performed by the cult. This feeling of being "one of the bad people" often leads to compulsions to behave in physically and sexually assaultive ways.

5. RAGE OVER VICTIMIZATION

Enraged child victims are encouraged to act out their anger by assaulting others and are then told that this is evidence that they are truly becoming members of the abusive group. Thus, even their own rage is turned against ritually abused children, thereby heightening their sense of hopelessness and entrapment.

6. LOSS OF SENSE OF SELF

Ritual abuse victims feel a loss of boundaries between the self and the group. Often, they come to be so identified with the group that they feel like an extension of it. This loss of the sense of self contributes to feelings of personal badness and of rage.

7. ABSENCE OF FREE WILL

As a result of techniques like magic surgery, the perception that controlling evil spirits are present, that cult members know everything that the child thinks or does, and the use of impossible double binds (e.g., stab or be stabbed), the victim comes to feel that there is no choice but to comply, and yet is still burdened by guilt and shame.

COGNITIVE BELIEFS imparted by ritual abuse and mind control, seen in both adult and child survivors, include the following.

1. THERE IS NO ESCAPE

"The cult members are everywhere. The spirits, monsters, demons, devils, etc. that the cult controls, surround me, too. They know if I violate any of the rules of the cult, and they will punish me. I can never leave."

2. THE CULT COMPLETELY CONTROLS ME

"I am controlled by the cult and by the demon which the cult has placed in me to both control and monitor my behavior. I have no freedom and must follow the orders of the cult leaders in all things. I must be ready to assault others and neither trust nor make any close associations with anyone outside the cult."

3.   I AM INCAPABLE OF PROTECTING MYSELF

"I am inadequate. I have no control and no power. I am paralyzed."

4.   THE CULT IS MY ONLY TRUE FAMILY

(In extrafamilial cases)—"My family is dangerous to me and only the cult members accept me. I will eventually live with them forever because they are my true family."

5.   MEMORIES ARE DANGEROUS

"I must hurt myself if I begin to remember. I must cut myself, beat myself, or kill myself if I remember what happened. Terrible things will happen to me and my family if I remember."

6.   DISCLOSURES ARE DANGEROUS

"The cult will know if I tell anyone. If I do tell, I or my family will be hurt by them, or I will be compelled to hurt myself."

RELIGIOUS BELIEFS imparted by ritual abuse and mind control, seen in both adult and child survivors, include the following.

1.   SATAN IS STRONGER THAN GOD

"Satan has all the power. He is stronger than God. God has not been able to do anything to protect me from what has happened."

2. GOD DOES NOT LOVE ME

"I am despised and rejected by God. I am guilty of crimes that God could never forgive. I am evil and beyond hope for redemption or restoration."

3. GOD WANTS TO PUNISH ME

"I am profoundly afraid of God who must want to destroy me."

4. MY LIFE IS CONTROLLED BY SATAN

"I belong to Satan irrevocably. His power lives inside me and has taken over my life. I am possessed by an evil spirit or demon that controls my life."

5. MY LIFE IS DEDICATED TO SATAN

"I have taken vows to serve Satan throughout my life. I will serve him by willingly committing acts of evil and destruction. In turn, he will protect me from harm and allow me to gratify all of my desires."

Notes

Preface—Into the Fire
1. Richard Wurmbrand, *In God's Underground* (IN: Living Sacrifice Books, 1968), p. 58.

Chapter 1—Branded
1. *PrimeTime Live*, ABC, January 23, 1992. "Free From Silence." Fifteen-year-old Lucy Harrison has autism. Through the miracle of a new technique which allows a single finger on a child's hand to be isolated by a light counterweight, the heretofore unspeakable, non-understandable, and often thought retarded autistic child speaks via computer keys. This sentence was one of Lucy's first communications ever.
2. Republican National Convention, Dallas, Texas. August 19, 1992.
3. *People Weekly*, "The Darkest Secret," June 10, 1991, p. 90.
4. *Larry King Live*, CNN, June 23, 1992. "Our Priest's Victims Confront Past Abuse."
5. Richard Kluft, M.D., "An Update on MPD," *Hospital & Community Psychiatry*, April, 1987, Vol. 38, No. 4, p. 372.

Chapter 2—Hiding Inside the Mind
1. Linda T. Sanford, *Strong at the Broken Places: Overcoming the Trauma of Childhood Abuse* (NY: Random House, 1990), p. 26.
2. *The Oprah Winfrey Show*, ABC, May 21, 1990, "Truddi Chase: A Story of Multiple Personalities."
3. Ibid.
4. Ibid.
5. Ibid.
6. Ibid.
7. Richard Wurmbrand, *In God's Underground* (IN: Living Sacrifice Books, 1968), p. 65.
8. From Margaret Atwood, *Two-Headed Poems* (Simon & Schuster), reprinted in *Torture By Governments* (NY: Amnesty International, U.S.A., 1984), p. 50.

9. Robert Jay Lifton, *The Nazi Doctors* (NY: Basic Books, 1986).
10. Roland C. Summit, M.D., "The Specific Vulnerability of Children," from *Understanding and Managing Child Sexual Abuse*. Edited by Kim Oates, M.D. (Sydney, Australia: Harcourt, Brace, Jovanovich, 1990), p. 64.
11. Virginia Klein, Ph.D., *Sonya Live*, CNN, February 13, 1992.

Chapter 3 — The Birthing of Baby
1. R. J. Lifton, *Home from the War: Vietnam Veterans: Neither Victims nor Executioners* (NY: Simon & Schuster, 1973), p. 287.

Chapter 7 — Mind Control
1. Richard Wurmbrand, *In God's Underground* (IN: Living Sacrifice Books, 1968), p. 246.
2. Ibid., p. 245.
3. Ibid., p. 246.
4. Richard Wurmbrand, *Tortured For Christ* (IN: Living Sacrifice Books, 1967), p. 40.
5. Richard Wurmbrand, *In God's Underground* (IN: Living Sacrifice Books, 1968), p. 248.
6. Ibid., p. 257.
7. Ibid., p. 270.
8. Ibid.
9. Ibid., p. 271.
10. Ibid.
11. Ibid.
12. Ibid.
13. Richard Wurmbrand, *Tortured For Christ* (IN: Living Sacrifice Books, 1967), pp. 5,6. "Christians in Norway negotiated with the communist authorities for Wurmbrand's release. The communist government had begun 'selling' their political prisoners. The 'going price' for a prisoner was $1,900. Their price for Wurmbrand was $10,000. As the communist police handed him his passport, he was warned to not speak against them . . . 'otherwise you will be silenced for good. We can hire a gangster who'll do it for $1,000 — or we can bring you back, as we've done with other traitors'. In 1969, Wurmbrand testified in Washington

before the Senate's Internal Security subcommittee and stripped to the waist to show eighteen deep torture wounds covering his body."

14. *The Voice Of The Martyrs* (OK: Christian Missions to the Communist World, Inc., December, 1991), p. 2.

15. *Ritual Abuse, Definitions, Glossary, The Use Of Mind Control,* Report of the Ritual Abuse Task Force, Los Angeles County Commission for Women (CA: Los Angeles County Commission for Women, 1991), p. 15.

16. *PrimeTime Live*, ABC, "Virtual Reality."

17. Howard Rheingold, *Virtual Reality* (NY: Summit Books, 1991), p. 44.

18. Ibid., p. 45.

19. *Hate On Trial*, PBS, February 5, 1991.

Chapter 8 — Cult Alters

1. *Unsolved Mysteries*, NBC, "Diabolical Minds," March 25, 1992.

Chapter 10 — Winning the War

1. Claude Lanzmann, *SHOAH* (NY: Pantheon Books, 1985), p. 59.

2. *The Living Bible* (IL: Tyndale House Publishers, 1971), Ecclesiastes 4:12.

Chapter 11 — The Macabre

1. One of the alleged perpetrators had phoned one of the girls and said that he had a human skull to show her. After first arming herself with a concealed knife, she and two of her friends went to his house. After viewing the skull, they enticed the perpetrator to go down into the basement where the actual murder took place. The girls then snatched the skull and ran.

2. *The Book Of Shadows* contains the Satanist's writings of formulas, chants, prayers, etc. that he uses in rituals. The formulas often vary from ritual to ritual. Teenagers often use something as generic as a spiral-bound notebook to save their writings.

3. Bob and Gretchen Passantino, *When The Devil Dares Your Kids* (MI: Servant Publications, 1991), p. 58.

Chapter 12—The Devil's Workshop

1. *The Voice Of The Martyrs* (OK: Christian Missions to the Communist World, Inc., December, 1991), p. 6.
2. *Children, The Youngest Victims*, Amnesty Newsletter, *FOCUS* (NY: Amnesty International Newsletter), March, 1989, p. 6.
3. Ibid., September, 1990, p. 6.
4. *Guatemala, Extrajudicial Executions and Human Rights Abuses Against Street Children* (NY: Amnesty International, July, 1990), p. 23.
5. *Children, the Youngest Victims*, Amnesty Newsletter, *FOCUS* (NY: Amnesty International Newsletter), October, 1989, p. 6.
6. Ibid.
7. *The Oprah Winfrey Show*, ABC, "Mothers and Fathers Who Kill," January 15, 1992.
8. *Larry King Live*, CNN, March 30, 1992.
9. *60 Minutes*, CBS, May 31, 1992.
10. *The Los Angeles Times*, October 19-20, 1988.
11. Ibid., October 19, 1988.
12. Ibid.
13. Ibid.
14. Ibid., October 20, 1988.
15. Ibid.
16. Ibid.
17. Ibid.
18. Ibid.
19. Ibid.
20. *Satanism Unmasked* (OK: Infinity Video, 1988).
21. A copy of Tommy Sullivan's letter which was included in the advertisement packet of Jerry Johnston's book, *The Edge Of Evil* (TX: WORD Publishers, 1989).
22. "Satan's Children," TV Interview with Connie Chung, 1986.
23. Source anonymous.
24. A "Sabbat" is a gathering of witches to commemorate a special date.
25. "Satan's Children," TV Interview with Connie Chung, 1986.
26. Ibid.

27. Ibid.
28. Source anonymous.
29. *Larry King Live*, CNN, April 12, 1989.

Chapter 13—Fact or Fiction?

1. It is on record that many Nazi guards and murderers at the Jewish Holocaust concentration camps repeatedly taunted the prisoners with this most ominous of warnings.
2. In a speech to attorneys and judges in Orlando, Florida (September 8, 1989).
3. Jean-Jacques Gautier, "The Case for an Effective and Realistic Procedure," *Torture: How to Make the International Convention Effective* (International Committee of Jurists—Geneva, Switzerland, 1980), p. 37.
4. *Watching Detectives*, Arts & Entertainment Channel (December 27, 1989).
5. Claude Lanzmann, *SHOAH* (NY: Pantheon Books, 1985), p. 70.
6. "Listen to the Children," *Time* magazine, May 4, 1992, p. 20.
7. Arthur Lyons, *Satan Wants You* (NY: The Mysterious Press, 1988), p. 152.
8. Kenneth Wooden, *The Children of Jonestown* (NY: McGraw-Hill Book Company, 1981), p. 4.
9. In a telephone conversation with Dr. Michael Durfee (July 28, 1992).
10. Myra Riddell, "Letters to the Editor," *The Los Angeles Times*, May 6, 1991.
11. Jan Hollingsworth, *Unspeakable Acts* (NY: Congdon and Weed, 1986), p. 146.
12. Ibid., p. 148.
13. Ibid., pp. 147,148.
14. Ibid., p. 590.
15. Ibid.
16. Ibid., p. 591.
17. *Ritual Abuse, Definitions, Glossary, The Use Of Mind Control*, report of the Ritual Abuse Task Force, Los Angeles County Commission for Women (CA: Los Angeles County Commission for Women, 1991), p. 18.

18. Arthur Lyons, *Satan Wants You* (NY: The Mysterious Press, 1988), p. 152.
19. Heide Vanderbilt, "INCEST," *LEAR'S* magazine (NY: LEAR Publishing, Inc., February, 1992).
20. Patricia Toth, in an unpublished letter in *UPDATE Newsletter*, Vol. 4, No. 3, March, 1991, (American Prosecutor's Research Institute; National Center for Prosecution of Child Abuse), p. 2.
21. Dr. David Young, "Study finds children rarely make false allegations of sexual abuse," *The Bakersfield Californian*, November 12, 1985, p. A5.
22. Heide Vanderbilt, "INCEST," *LEAR'S* magazine (NY: LEAR Publishing, Inc., February, 1992).
23. Ibid.
24. Ibid.
25. Ibid.
26. Ibid.
27. Aline Kidd, "A Presumption of Guilt," *San Francisco Examiner*, September 28, 1986, p. A7.
28. Arthur Lyons, *Satan Wants You* (NY: The Mysterious Press, 1988), p. 150.
29. Ibid.
30. Dr. Lee Coleman, "Ritual Killings Have Satanic Overtones," *Christianity Today*, September 2, 1988, p. 53.
31. Kenneth V. Lanning, "Satanic, Occult, Ritualistic Crime: A Law Enforcement Perspective," *Satanism in America* (CA: Gaia Press, 1989), Appendix Two, p. B8.
32. Jan Hollingsworth, *Unspeakable Acts* (NY: Congdon and Weed, 1986), p. 166.
33. Ibid., back cover copy.
34. Ibid., p. 461.
35. Gary R. Collins, Ph.D., Editor, "Satanic Ritual Abuse," *Christian Counseling Newsletter*, Vol. VI, No. 6, June, 1992.
36. Ralph Underwager and Hollida Wakefield, "Cur Allii, Prae Aliis?" *Issues in Child Abuse Accusations* (Vol. 3, No. 3:190, Summer, 1991) quoted from Bob and Gretchen Passantino, "The Hard Facts About Ritual Abuse," *Christian Research Journal*, WINTER 1992 (CA: Christian Research Institute).

37. John Rabun, "Ritual Killings Have Satanic Overtones," *Christianity Today*, September 2, 1988, p. 53.
38. *Ritual Abuse, Definitions, Glossary, The Use Of Mind Control*, report of the Ritual Abuse Task Force, Los Angeles County Commission for Women (CA: Los Angeles County Commission for Women, 1991), Introduction.
39. Gary R. Collins, Ph.D., Editor, "Satanic Ritual Abuse," *Christian Counseling Newsletter*, Vol. VI, No. 6, June, 1992.
40. Andrew Gindes, "1000 years for molesters," *The Bakersfield Californian*, July 7, 1984, p. 1.
41. Roland C. Summit, M.D., "Too Terrible To Hear, Barriers To Perception Of Child Abuse," p. 9. (Adapted from a paper written in support of testimony before the U.S. Attorney General's Commission On Pornography—Miami, Florida, November 20, 1985).
42. Claude Lanzmann, *SHOAH* (NY: Pantheon Books, 1985), pp. 71,72.
43. This is a commonly used quote. It has been attributed to the German philosopher, Arthur Schopenhauer. As of yet, I have been unable to verify its source.

Chapter 14—The High Cost of Survival
1. F. Scott Fitzgerald, *Bartlett's Familiar Quotations* (MA: Little, Brown and Company, 1980), p. 835.
2. In a telephone conversation with Dr. Neomi Mattis (August 9, 1992).
3. Shawn Carlson and Gerald Larue, *Satanism in America* (CA: Gaia Press, 1989), p. 30.
4. Gretchen Passantino on "The Bible Answer Man" (KKLA radio, April 23, 1992.)
5. Jon Trotton, *Larry King Live*, CNN, August 20, 1991.
6. Lauren Stratford, *Satan's Underground* (LA: Pelican Publishing, 1991), "Afterword."
7. Anonymous, *Five Thousand Quotations For All Occasions*, edited by Lewis C. Henry (NY: Garden City Books, 1952), p. 153.
8. Amaro Gomez Boix, "The Persistence of Darkness," Charles J. Brown and Armando M. Lago, *The Politics of Psychiatry In Revolutionary Cuba* (New Brunswick: Transaction Publishers, 1991), p. 139.

9. *20/20*, ABC, August 14, 1992.

10. Jeffrey S. Victor, "Satanic Cult 'Survivor' Stories," *Skeptical Inquirer*, Vol. 15, No. 3 / Spring 1991 (NY: The Committee for the Scientific Investigation of Claims of the Paranormal), p. 276.

11. Ibid., p. 277.

12. This is one paragraph of a letter that was sent, along with an FMS Foundation Newsletter, to The American Family Foundation.

13. Martin R. Smith, M.Ed., an unpublished paper, "A Reply To Ganaway: The Problem of Using Screen Memories As an Explanatory Device in Accounts of Ritual Abuse," p. 1.

14. Richard Wurmbrand, *Marx & Satan* (IL: Crossway Books, 1986), p. vii.

Chapter 15 — Will We Survive?

1. Gerald Coffee, Captain, U.S. Navy (Ret.), *Beyond Survival* (NY: The Berkley Publishing Group, 1990), p. 103.

2. Martin R. Smith, M.Ed., an unpublished paper, "A Reply To Ganaway: The Problem of Using Screen Memories As an Explanatory Device in Accounts of Ritual Abuse," p. 3.

Recommended Reading

Satanism and Ritual Abuse in General:

Carl A. Raschke, *Painted Black* (CA: Harper Publishing, 1990).

Ritual Abuse, Definitions, Glossary, The Use Of Mind Control. Report Of The Ritual Abuse Task Force, Los Angeles County Commission For Women. (Order from: Los Angeles County Commission For Women, 383 Hall of Administration, 500 West Temple Street, Los Angeles, CA 90012. The thirty-one-page booklet, including shipping and handling, is five dollars.)

Help Books:

Judith Lewis Herman, M.D., *Trauma And Recovery* (NY: Basic Books, 1992).

Nancy W., *On the Path, Affirmations For Adults Recovering From Childhood Sexual Abuse* (CA: Harper Publishing, San Francisco, 1991).

Rachel Downing, M.S.W., L.C.S.W., *Can I Look Now! Recovery From Multiple Personality Disorder* (Order from: Educational Recovery Communications, 1498M Reisterstown Road, #333, Baltimore, Maryland 21208. The thirty-three-page booklet, including shipping and handling, is $5.50.)

A New Beginning, Daily Devotions for Women Survivors of Sexual Abuse (TN: Thomas Nelson Publishers, 1992). From a spiritual perspective.

Daniel Ryder, CCDC, LSW, *Breaking The Circle of Satanic Ritual Abuse* (MN: CompCare, 1992).

Ellen Bass and Laura Davis, *The Courage to Heal, A Guide for Women Survivors of Child Sexual Abuse* (NY: HarperPerennial, Revised 1992).

Laura Davis, *Allies in Healing, When the Person You Love Was Sexually Abused as a Child* (NY: HarperPerennial, 1991).

Help Magazines and Newsletters:

Beyond Survival magazine. (Subscribe to: Beyond Survival

Network, 1278 Glenneyre St., #3, Laguna Beach, CA 92651. The subscription rate for the bi-monthly magazine is fifteen dollars per year.)

Many Voices newsletter. (Subscribe to: Many Voices, P.O. Box 2639, Cincinnati, Ohio 45201-2639. The subscription rate for the bi-monthly newsletter is thirty dollars per year.)

Survivorship newsletter. (Subscribe to: Survivorship, 3181 . Mission Street, #139, San Francisco, CA 94110. The subscription rate for the monthly publication is thirty dollars per year for survivors and students and forty-five dollars per year for professionals.)